ENGLAND INVADED

EDWARD FOORD & GORDON HOME

AMBERLEY

First published in 1913
This edition published 2014

Amberley Publishing
The Hill, Stroud, Gloucestershire, GL5 4EP
www.amberley-books.com

Copyright © Edward Foord and Gordon Home, 1913

ISBN 978 1 4456 4372 4 (print)
ISBN 978 1 4456 4404 2 (ebook)

British Library Cataloguing in Publication Data.
A catalogue record for this book is available from the British Library.

Typesetting by Amberley Publishing.
Printed in Great Britain.

Contents

Preface

Since the year 1794, when England seethed with excitement through fear of a French Republican invasion, no book has been produced dealing with the invasions of England. The historical and archeological work of the century that has passed has shed so much light on dark and shadowy periods of English history that the materials available for a new work on the subject have become increasingly extensive, and the authors have endeavoured to take full advantage of all this new material. They have, either together or separately, visited all the important, and many of the minor, battle sites and campaign areas mentioned in the text, and, as a result of close study, they have in certain instances arrived at conclusions at variance with those generally accepted.

By careful topographical work, aided by every shred of historical evidence available, the authors venture to hope that they may have thrown a little new light upon the great campaign in which the Roman general Paulinus crushed the British struggle for independence under Boudicca. They have also devoted much time and thought to the elucidation of the problem of the identity of the heroes of the Romano-British contests with the oncoming Teutons, and to the areas of their chief military operations. After much consideration and study of the available authorities, they have arrived at the conclusion, which they have not hesitated to express, that Arthur, or Artorius, is a well-established historical figure. One of the authors has, through his family's territorial connection with

Statue of Suetonius Paulinus at the Roman Baths in Bath. (*Courtesy of Ad Meskers*)

the Eastern Border, had exceptional opportunities for becoming familiar with the topography of the wild and intricate region in which both are inclined to place the fields of at least four, and perhaps six, of Arthur's twelve famous victories.

The field of Senlac has been examined by the authors in the company of Sir Augustus Webster, Bart., the present owner of Battle Abbey, himself a practical soldier. The result of their investigations has been to convince them that the line of the Norman advance lay considerably to the east of where it is generally placed, and that the great hulk of Harold's army was massed about the site of the abbey itself. His right wing, being almost unassailable owing to the protection given to it by the marshy ground in its front, was probably very weakly held. Relying on the contemporary evidence of the Bayeux tapestry, and considering the circumstances of Harold's march, the authors arc inclined to discount any effective entrenchments palisading.

In regard to the strategy and tactics of Flodden, a close study of contemporary documents and authorities tends to emphasize certain features which are often overlooked or ignored. First, the Scottish army evidently changed its position twice to counteract Surrey's puzzling flanking movement. Second, it can have had no proper service of scouts, and was too cumbrous to manoeuvre readily, circumstances which left it at the mercy of its numerically inferior antagonist. Third, it was never able to form a complete line of battle owing to the slowness of the right wing in coming into action. Fourth, so far as appears from the letters of the English leaders, there was no slackness on the part of the Scottish Lord Chamberlain who commanded the left wing.

Much has been written on the relative strengths of the English and Spanish fleets in 1588. The authors' opinions may be summarized as follows: (1) The Spaniards had an undoubted superiority in tonnage, but in strength of ships actually built for war the English had the advantage. (2) The English ships, being manned by a majority of sailors, were infinitely better handled; and the galleons of the Royal Navy were faster sailers than those of the Spanish. (3) There is no real reason to think that the Spaniards were outmatched in number and power of guns, but the English gunnery, though bad, was better and more rapid than that of their antagonists. (4) The Spanish tactics, as compared with that of the English, was antiquated, being based on the formation of line abreast and a close order, which hampered the manoeuvring of individual ships and impeded the use of broadsides. The exigencies of space have compelled the authors to pass briefly over the later period of attempted invasions, and to concentrate attention upon those attempts which actually succeeded so far as to effect a landing upon English soil. An exception has, however; been made in regard to Napoleon's project of 1804–05, which has been briefly discussed. It was the last attempt of an ancient enemy, France having been actively organizing invasions of England in 1744 and again in 1759. The latter project was ably planned by Choiseul and Belleisle, and was at least as feasible as Napoleon's far more celebrated design; but it shared its fate of hopeless failure owing to Britain's supremacy on the sea.

To Mr Julian Corbett the authors are indebted for his kindness in reading the proofs of the chapters on the Armada period. The observations on Napoleon's project of invasion are based entirely upon the works of Mr. Corbett and Colonel Desbriere.

In writing on a subject of such permanently vital interest to the British nation as the question of invasion, it may be thought desirable that the authors should express the conclusions to which they have been led in the course of their researches. They, however, prefer to merely direct the attention of their readers to the fact that no successful invasion of England has taken place since 1066 without the active sympathy and assistance of a considerable section of the population. Prior to that date, Britain and England were not in any real sense of the word single united communities.

The salient fact is that so long as England remained strong at sea, and her strength was intelligently and vigorously directed, she was able to beat off every serious attempt against her. It is unnecessary to insist here on the universally accepted axiom that British national and imperial existence rests on the maintenance of a supreme navy.

The maps have all been drawn by the authors for the express purpose of illustrating their deductions, and among the objects illustrated are several which have never before, it is believed, been depicted in any published work.

EDWARD FOORD
GORDON HOME
September 1913

I

Caesar's Invasions

In the year 57 BC Gaius Julius Caesar, Roman politician, statesman, and legislator, and already, though he had only girt on the sword at forty-three years of age, a famous soldier, was campaigning in northern Gaul. The year before, a mere carpet warrior, as his enemies would have men believe, he had come up the Rhone with six legions of sturdy swarthy Italian yeomen, and summarily put an end to the great Helvetic migration, a migration perhaps little less dangerous than that of the Cimbri and 'Teutones', which his kinsman Marius had annihilated at Aqure Sextiae and Vercellae. Then, grimly resolute, with reluctant officers, with the scented young nobles who had followed him for a little plunder and mild excitement foreboding disaster, with even the stout legionaries – all save the men of the immortal Xth – hanging back and half afraid, he had turned on the Germans who were overrunning Gaul, and hurled them in rout and ruin across the Rhine. And – significant fact! – he wintered not in the sunny Roman Province – that Provence which still proclaims to the world from a hundred sites that Imperial Rome swayed her sceptre there for twenty generations – not in the Italian Gallia along the Po, but there, where he was, in the very homeland of the Celts, which five hundred years before had sent forth the hordes that had wasted Italy and burned Rome. The Gauls, disunited, faction-ridden, fickle, and suspicious of each other, but proud, brave, and patriotic, began to take alarm.

Whether Caesar had intended from the first to subjugate Gaul, or whether his horizon became enlarged as his successes multiplied, are

Statue of Caesar at the Roman Baths in Bath. (*Courtesy of Ad Meskers*)

questions that cannot be discussed here. But he certainly seems to have shown his hand in 58 BC 'Celtic' and 'Aquitanian' Gaul remained passive, but in the north, where the 'Belgae' had had little to do with Roman envoys and traders, much less with Roman generals and legions, a confederacy was quickly formed to oppose Caesar. It was headed nominally by Galba, King of the Suessiones, whose predecessor, Divitiacus, had ruled an ephemeral dominion extending over a large region of northern Gaul and parts of Britain. So writes Caesar in the second book, 'De Bello Gallico'; and thus, in a single terse sentence of his perfect, unadorned Latin, Britannia is swept by a roving searchlight of historical allusion.

Early next year Caesar came up from Central Gaul, now with a formidable force of eight legions, with cavalry from Gaul and elsewhere, with Numidian light troops, with archers from the East and slingers from the Baleares, with engineers and siege artillery, to deal with the Belgians. The great ill-cemented confederacy was shattered with slight difficulty, but the fighting Nervii and other tribes, which would not be daunted by a single defeat, proved foes worthy of Caesar's steel, and were only subdued after a desperate battle. In 57 BC all the coast tribes from the Loire to the Rhine united against Caesar, and this time there is distinct reference to regular intercourse between Gaul and Britain. This confederacy was crushed, after hard and harassing fighting, by a great naval victory off the southern coast of Brittany. It had been supported by British troops, and perhaps by British ships. At any rate, it must have been plain to the great proconsul that Britain was a factor that could not be ignored in dealing with the Gallic problem.

On Caesar's staff at this time was a Gallic noble named Commius, whom he had made king of the Atrebates in Belgium. The most important fact about him for our present purpose is that he had connections with Britain. The Belgre had indeed far overflowed the limits of their Gallic territory; it is possible that the entire south-east of Britain from the Wash to the Somersetshire Avon, and thence to Southampton Water, was occupied by Belgic or Belgicized tribes. In a region roughly corresponding to Wiltshire, Hampshire, and Somerset, there was a confederacy which preserved the racial appellation of Belgre. In Berks. and Surrey dwelt the Atrebates, evidently cognate with the Atrebates of Belgica; while the name of the great and warlike Catuvellauni of the south-east Midlands clearly points to a connection with the Catalauni of the Marne. It is at least possible that the other tribes of the south-east – the Cantii of Kent, the Regni of Sussex, the wealthy Trinobantes of Essex and Suffolk, and even the Iceni of Norfolk – were of Belgic origin.

So much Caesar may easily have learned from Commius, or from hostages and prisoners. That there was a close ethnic affinity between the tribes on either side of the Channel a man of his intellectual powers would not be slow to infer. Whether he was fully acquainted with the economic condition of the island is another matter. Pytheas he may have, Polybius he must have, read, but possibly the scepticism of the Achcean may have prejudiced him against the Massiliot.

But be this as it may, when Caesar began to collect intelligence concerning Britain from Gallic merchants, he was presented with information largely untrustworthy, and some of which its furnishers must have known to be false. The statement that some of the British tribes practised polyandry may or may not be true – the traders had no obvious motive for deceiving Caesar on such a point; but they may themselves have depended upon hearsay evidence. But otherwise they appear to have done their best to misinform the proconsul, with the obvious intention of inducing him, to abandon any idea of an invasion. Their motive was clearly trade jealousy. The whole British trade, which appears to have been considerable, was in their hands; they feared – naturally enough – Italian competition. Then, too, they may have been influenced by political motives. Britain was, as things went, an admirable place of refuge for Gallic organisers of revolt and for defeated leaders.

So, as far as one can see, Caesar's Gallic informants told him as little as possible. On the one hand, they seem to have done their best to overrate the savage ferocity of the people; on the other, they depreciated the wealth of the island. As they could hardly assert that systematic cultivation of cereals was unknown in the island, they explained that this was the case only in the south-east; elsewhere the people lived on milk and flesh, and, having no knowledge of weaving, dressed in skins. It is difficult to know how far Caesar was deceived. To some extent he certainly was, for he repeats the false statements which were made to him. It may perhaps seem curious that he did not verify them while in Britain, but, of course, he had military business in plenty to occupy him. His statement about the iron bar currency is the strangest of all, since it is certain that gold coins, struck in imitation of Philip of Macedonia's gold staters, had been in circulation for not less than a century. It is just possible that he means that iron bars took the place of a copper coinage. It seems incredible that he can have marched for more than a hundred miles into Britain without meeting with some of the gold pieces of which so many survive, even if he had not seen them in Gaul. In that part of Britain with which he was personally acquainted he notes that the population was dense, and dwellings, or groups of dwellings, thickly dotted over the country-side. But it is clear that in many respects his information was very imperfect.

Upon Caesar's credibility as an historian volumes have been written. To the impartial observer the absolute frankness with which he admits the commission of deeds which shock, or are supposed to shock, the not over-sensitive consciences of twentieth-century Europeans, is evidence in his favour. In curt unadorned phrases, without a trace of emotion, he tells of the enslaving of human beings by scores of thousands, or of the pursuit by cavalry of crowds of women and children. The fact, of course, is that such occurrences were common in war as it was waged in those days. Caesar herein was neither better nor worse than hundreds of Roman or Greek generals. He was better than many, for he never massacred his own captive countrymen. It cannot be said that he was worse than Skobelev, who at the taking of Geok-Tepe in 1880 sent his cavalry in pursuit of a flying horde that was largely composed of women and children, just as Caesar did at the destruction of the Usipetes and Teucteri in 55 BC All this is simply to lead up to the point that, while Caesar may, as is suggested by a good many critics, have had unworthy motives for his expedition – such as greed of slaves and plunder, or a desire to dazzle the Roman populace – he gives a perfectly sound, statesmanlike reason for his action. He says that he had found that there were usually British contingents in the ranks of the hostile Gauls, and that he thought it advisable to cow the islanders. That some of his officers expected, like professional soldiers of every age, to enrich themselves is certain; it is at least probable that Caesar hoped that the expedition might prove a paying investment. But that he regarded it only as a plundering raid there is no reason to think. Neither is there any solid evidence to show that his position as a Roman party leader ever affected his military operations. That when he left Rome to take up his command he had a general idea of using his army to attain supreme power is possible, even probable. But once in Gaul the natural genius of the man as soldier and statesman was devoted to consolidating his country's position there. His action as regards Ariovistus shows that self-interest was already subordinated to statesmanship which must benefit Rome, and could only serve his own ends incidentally.

In 55 BC Caesar was very active in Belgic Gaul. He had swept the Teutonic hordes which had invaded Gaul in the winter back into Germania with frightful slaughter, not without treachery on his part; he had bridged the Rhine, and displayed the Eagles in a long raid on its eastern bank. This bad occupied him until late in the summer. Then, as he says, it occurred to him that the short remainder of the campaigning season might be utilised for an expedition to Britain for the purpose of collecting useful information – in short, for what in modern military parlance would be termed a reconnaissance in force. It does not appear that he had anything further in mind. Later on he tells us that he had no intention of making a long stay, and he took only a few days' provisions. More over, the time was too short for collecting anything like the number of ships required for the transportation of several legions.

Nevertheless, the concentration of the Roman Army of Gallia on the coast opposite Dover was an event which could not but alarm the Britons, and, while Caesar was completing his arrangements, some of their tribes sent over envoys. Presumably, the idea was that by making a nominal submission the invasion might be averted. Caesar, however, quietly observed that he would visit them at home in a few days, and sent them back with, as his personal emissary, Commius the Atrebatian. Commius had instructions to use his influence to bring about a general submission, but his British companions made him prisoner immediately upon landing. Caesar meanwhile was collecting Gallic merchant-ships for the transit, and had sent a trusted officer, Gaius Volusenus, with a galley, to reconnoitre for landing places. The haste and incompleteness of his preparations were so far of slight account, since, though the Britons were determined on resistance, there was no time to form a confederacy. Caswallon (Cassivellaunus), king of the Catuvellauni, the most powerful chieftain of Britain, was endeavouring to coerce the Trinobantes; the attack would be met by the local tribal levies only.

Having gone so far, it may be advisable to say a few words on the subject of the invading army and the forces which were likely to oppose it. The Roman Army of Gaul, though it had perhaps hardly reached the pitch of excellence which it attained at the outbreak of the Civil War, was, nevertheless, in 55 BC, one of the finest that the world has ever seen. There were eight legions of Italian troops, and of these the two newest had seen three years' hard service. Two had served four campaigns, and the remaining four were the pith of the army. Their numbers were VII., VIII., IX., and X. All of them had served four years under Caesar, had learnt to idolize him and to follow him with perfect confidence, and all were composed of war-hardened veterans of many years' experience – men to whom the hardships of war were but matter for jests, and a battle a mere incident of everyday life. Knowing them as we do, thanks to the man whom they served so well, we may fairly doubt whether any soldiers of any age ever surpassed them. The Xth has come down through the ages associated with, perhaps, the noblest eulogy ever paid by any leader to his soldiers. A great Roman army, not yet knowing itself or its leader, was trembling at the thought of meeting the dreaded warriors of Germany. Its fears came to Caesar, and Caesar made his immortal reply: 'So be it! Since none else will follow, I will go forward with the Xth Legion alone. It will not forsake me!' And the legion sent to thank its leader for the honour of being allowed to die with him. Never again did Caesar's soldiers hang back, but the Xth always remained 'Caesar's Own.' But Caesar was not Napoleon; he never nursed or favoured it as Napoleon did the Old Guard. When it forgot its discipline, Caesar punished it like any other corps; it shared equally in all the trials of the Army of Gallia. At its head Caesar took his stand on the field of Pharsalus, and to this day, when an exalted standard of devotion is sought, it is enough to cite that of Caesar's Xth Legion.

The Xth was undoubtedly the finest of the legions, but the three other old corps were not greatly inferior; and the younger divisions were steadily improving, proud of themselves and of their leader.

The legion of Caesar's day was a division of six thousand infantry at full strength, exclusive of officers. It was divided into ten battalions (cohortes), and each cohort into six companies (*centuriae*), each of one hundred men, under a centurion (*centurio*) generally, so far as is known, promoted from the ranks. Into the complicated question of the ranking and promotion of these officers, there is no need to enter here; it is sufficient to say that the senior centurions were entitled to sit in councils of war, and that the senior of all (*primi pili centurio* or *primipilus*) often appears as playing a very distinguished part. Attached to each legion were six officers called tribunes, frequently young gentlemen learning the art of war. Often, as might be expected, they were rather a nuisance than otherwise; but there were exceptions, notably C. Volusenus, who has just been mentioned. Probably the trouble was to induce them to take their military position seriously.

Caesar's higher executive officers were his ten lieutenant-generals (*legati*), of whom we frequently meet several in command of one, two, or more legions. The best was Titus Labienus, strangely enough the only one who sided against his general in the Civil War. He was a greedy, cruel, and unprincipled man, but beyond doubt a great general; Caesar repeatedly gives him unstinted praise. Of the others, probably the most promising was the young P. Licinius Crassus, who was to perish on his father's ill-starred expedition against the Parthians; but several were men of real distinction. Among them may be mentioned M. Antonius, afterwards the rival of Augustus; Decimus Junius Brutus, the hero of the naval victory over the Veneti; C. Fabius Maximus; Q. Tullius Cicero, brother of the more famous Marcus, but himself a soldier of great merit; and C. Trebonius. Caesar's chief administrative officer was his *qutestor* (quartermaster-general), M. Licinius Crassus.

The legionary soldier's equipment was perhaps unsurpassed in those ages for lightness and completeness. His clothes consisted of a sleeveless woollen shirt, drawers reaching to just below the knee, and over them a tunic. On his feet he wore half-boots with light uppers, and heavy soles studded with nails. His defensive arms consisted of a corselet of long overlapping strips of steel, a helmet with a low crest, and a semi-cylindrical shield some 4 feet long, made of wood covered with ox-hide, with a rim and central boss of iron, combining the minimum of weight with the maximum of protection. For purposes of offence the soldier bore two of the famous *pila*, and a short, sharp-pointed, double edged sword. The *pilum* was a long, heavy javelin, which could also be used as a pike. It consisted of a thick wooden shaft some 4 feet long, with a slender iron rod, terminating in a mall lance head, projecting for about 3 feet more. It appears to have had a range, when in practised hands, of some 50 yards. Rank after rank delivered volleys of these heavy missiles, and when the well-drilled swordsmen charged, they usually found the enemy severely shaken. Against mounted troops bearing the bow the legion, intended for close fighting, was, of course, at a great disadvantage, but for many centuries it was the lord of Mediterranean battlefields.

The defects of the legion had not escaped the notice of Roman military organizers, and it was already accompanied by auxiliary cohorts of light troops. In Caesar's army they were not very numerous as compared with the legionaries – perhaps about as one to six. Northern Africa supplied excellent skirmishers – its light cavalry was world-renowned, but Caesar does not appear to have had any of it in Gaul. Crete supplied him with archers, and Balearic slingers served with him as with Hannibal. Later the proportion of auxiliaries is found steadily on the increase. Under the Empire there were at least as many auxiliaries as legionaries. Caesar, however, depended mainly on his legions. For cavalry he relied chiefly on friendly Gallic tribes, though it is probable that he had a small body of Italian or Italian-Gallic horse. From 52 BC onward he had a brigade of German cavalry in his pay.

The engineering department of the Roman army has never been equalled. There was a corps of engineers, but entrenching was part of the private soldier's training. No body of troops ever halted for the night without surrounding themselves with a rampart and ditch. The result of constant experience of spade-work was that Roman troops Caesar's invasions frequently accomplished feats of engineering that seem almost miraculous. The work that in modern armies falls upon the engineers was in that of Rome chiefly done by the infantry privates. Caesar in his campaigns made good use of the siege artillery of the period, and his march was generally accompanied by a train of *balistae* (gigantic crossbows), *catapultae*, and *scorpiones*.

Every legion had a baggage train, of course, and probably every privates' mess had at least one slave for menial service; but the legionary bore a great part of his baggage himself, and it is a marvel how he contrived to march – as we know he did – anything from fifteen to twenty-five miles a day under his burdens. Besides arms, armour, and cloak, he carried grain or flour to last for a fortnight, a spade, a saw, a basket, several pales wherewith to crown the camp rampart, as well as his share of the mess service and other matters.

The standard of the legion was now always the famous Eagle, which had been introduced or generally established by Marius. The Eagle-bearer (*Aquilifer*) was always a soldier chosen for good conduct and gallantry. He wore the skin of a wild beast over his helmet as the sign of his honourable position. With one of these gallant men we shall soon make acquaintance.

Against this magnificent military machine the Britons had little but a mass of disorderly and ill-armed levies, formidable in numbers, individual courage and physical strength, but without cohesion. Most of them fought on foot, and few can have possessed body-armour; they were protected only by helmet and shield, perhaps not always the former. They were armed with badly tempered iron swords and spears, and in battle made free use of missiles of all kinds – chiefly, it would seem, darts and stones. Of cavalry there were few; the British horses were too small for riding. The bulk of the wealthier warriors fought from timber cars. This chariotry was evidently a formidable force, and gave the Romans serious trouble. The small active horses took the cars along at a great rate, and the picked warriors who manned them – strong, active, and brave, as well as skilled with their weapons – were capable of being extremely dangerous. The cars certainly were not armed with scythes on their axles; their effectiveness lay chiefly in their mobility and the skill with which they were manoeuvred, to which Caesar bears emphatic testimony. In the nobles who went into battle on them the pomp and circumstance of British war was seen at its best With their brightly-dyed garments, their tall helmets surmounted by bronze ornaments or waving plumes, their body armour and shields bright with enamel and gilding, and displaying all the wonderful intricacies of Celtic spiral metalwork, their beautifully wrought scabbards and sword-hilts, their golden bracelets and collars, the British chiefs must have been splendid figures.

Volusenus returned after a cruise of five days. He had not ventured to land, but brought information of value as to landing places. Some ninety-eight vessels were now collected in the country of the Morini, most of them probably at the modern Boulogne, and on eighty of them Caesar embarked his two best legions, the VIIth and the Xth, with no doubt, some light troops – perhaps ten thousand men in all. On board the other eighteen, which lay in a neighbouring harbour, were to go about five hundred cavalry. The order reached them late, and there was further delay in carrying it out.

Meanwhile, probably on the evening of August 25, the main body of the transports, escorted by some warships, set sail, and early next morning was off Dover. The war galleys were in front, the heavy transports slowly coming up from the rear. Volusenus had, no doubt, pointed out Dover Harbour as the most usual place for landing, but the Britons were in force to oppose the disembarkation. The beach was lined with chariots, the slopes of Castle Hill and the Western Heights were swarming with foot-levies; and in a place where, as Caesar says, darts could be rained upon the beach from the cliffs a landing would be extremely dangerous. From Volusenus he knew that only six or seven miles northward there was the open shelving beach of Deal. At noon the whole fleet had assembled, and Caesar gave the order to weigh and move northward.

The Britons at once followed suit. Horse, foot, and chariots faced to their left, climbed over Castle Hill, and streamed down its farther slope. The infantry were soon left behind; the charioteers and horsemen, however, outpaced the heavily-laden Roman ships, and galloped down to the shore in time to oppose the landing. The ships, heavy-draft Gallic merchantmen, grounded some way out, and the troops, smitten by showers of missiles, and seeing the gallant show on the beach, hesitated to jump with arms and armour into several feet of water. Caesar ordered the war galleys, manned by the archers and stingers, to row forward and engage the Britons. This was done, but the only effect was to make them withdraw a little way; they still stood threatening to charge. A lead was necessary, and it was given by the standard-bearer of the Xth, who sprang into the surges and led the way, bearing the Eagle of Rome against the enemy. 'Forward, comrades!' he shouted, 'unless you would betray the Eagle! I will do my duty to Rome and Caesar!' With a cheer every man on his ship followed. All down the line men sprang recklessly overboard, and singly and in groups began to wade up the shingly beach; and all along the shore, in gallant response, the Britons drove their chariots forward to the attack. There was a furious struggle among the breakers, and for some time the men of Kent held the strand; but when the steady Roman veterans began to close up into regular bodies, with boats full of archers covering their flanks, the Britons gave way. The Romans completed their landing, and laid out and fortified a camp.

Next day the Britons sent envoys to Caesar. They brought with them Commius, whom they now released, and offered submission.

Caesar was, no doubt, highly pleased. He exacted hostages. Some were brought during the next two days; others were to follow.

On the morning of the 30th, however, a northeaster came roaring down Dover Strait. Caesar's cavalry transports, on their way at last, were swept back and scattered into various harbours; the main fleet was seriously damaged. Twelve vessels were destroyed; many others so shattered as to need extensive repairs. The troops, knowing that they had only a few days' food in hand, were depressed, as Caesar himself admits. If we needed any proof that nothing but a reconnaissance had been intended we have it here; it is evident that the force had not even the usual fortnight's grain.

Caesar set the men to work on the necessary repairs; but the Britons were encouraged by the disaster to renew hostilities. Their chariotry and horsemen caught the VIIth Legion while it was foraging, and would have undoubtedly defeated it had not Caesar come up just in time with two cohorts of the Xth. Several days of heavy rain followed, but the spirits of the Kentishmen were high. On the first fine day they moved up against the camp, and when Caesar's legions formed line outside they attacked them furiously. They were of course driven back, and fled in disorder, and Commius, with thirty mounted retainers and officers, was able to pursue and cut up some of the stragglers.

The weather was now fine; Caesar had no intention of being again stormbound. He could now be sure of a quiet embarkation; but while he was making his preparations, Kentish envoys again appeared. He ordered them to send twice as many hostages as before, but this time to Gaul, as he was returning that night. The passage was effected without trouble; but once they saw their enemies clear of their coast, the men of Kent troubled no more about hostages. Two clans alone sent their quota. Probably the Britons argued that Caesar's departure was a confession of defeat, and as a number of modern writers have endeavoured to maintain the same, we cannot blame them. Victories have been claimed in modern times on no better grounds than that a reconnaissance has been driven in. In sober military terms the situation was simply this: Caesar had made a reconnaissance in force in Britain. Owing to various accidents and mistakes, he had been obliged to make a longer stay than he had intended. He had obtained some knowledge of the kind of resistance that he was likely to experience, and his troops had held their own in such fighting as had taken place.

Caesar, on returning to the Continent, went on as usual to the 'Province' and Cisalpina, but left his legions on the coast, with orders to build as many ships as possible specially designed for disembarkation work, and also fitted with oars. He quietly tells us that during the winter the troops built no less than six hundred, as well as twenty-eight war galleys! The magnitude of the task and the speed with which it was accomplished are alike amazing, but the history of the Army of Gaul is full of such feats.

The place of concentration for the fleet was 'Portus ltius,' about thirty (Roman) miles from Britain. The latest and best authority on Caesar appears to think that this must be the modern Wissant, four miles east of Cape Gris Nez. In all some 800 warships and transports were assembled there by the beginning of July, 54 BC The expeditionary force consisted of five legions, 2,000 cavalry, chiefly Gauls, and some thousands of light troops – perhaps 30,000 men in all. Caesar took with him to Britain several Gallic chiefs as a measure of precaution. Labienus was left in charge of Portus Itius with three legions, some auxiliaries, and 2,000 cavalry.

Meanwhile, in Britain, Caswallon of the Catuvellauni was striving hard to form a defensive confederacy. But the Trinobantes hung back, and *moribus majorum* Caswallon tried to coerce them. He slew their king, but the only result was that the dead chief's son, Mandubracius, fled to Caesar for protection, thus furnishing him with a very pretty *casus belli*. Caswallon was left to face the Romans with the Trinobantes still hostile – almost at his door.

Caesar landed near Sandwich, this time unmolested. The vast size of his fleet precluded all idea on the part of the Kentishmen of opposing the landing. Caswallon was collecting his levies, and was still far behind. Caesar landed his force, fortified a strong camp, in which he stored his reserve supplies, and told off ten cohorts (i.e., probably two from each legion), and 300 cavalry as its garrison, under an officer named Quintus Atrius.

During the day information was brought in that the Kentish levies were entrenched in a defensive position about twelve (Roman) miles inland. Caesar, anxious to strike a heavy blow at the local resistance, marched off to attack them before dawn next day. The British position was probably on the Stour, near Thanington, where there are traces of ancient entrenchments.

In any case, whether the men of Kent were at the Little Stour, as has been thought, or the Great Stour by Canterbury, their position was stormed without difficulty. From Caesar's description it appears that their chariotry and cavalry were thrown forward, and harassed the Roman columns as they moved towards the main position. They were, however, pushed back or aside, and the VIIth Legion, forming the dense shield-covered column of attack, which the Romans aptly termed the tortoise (*testudo*), carried the entrenchments with slight loss. The defenders fell back into the woods. There was no pursuit.

Next day, just as Caesar was feeling his way forward with cavalry, a message of disaster came from Atrius. In the night there had been a heavy gale, and great damage had been inflicted on the fleet. Caesar's fighting eagerness, and consequent neglect to profit by last year's lesson, nearly led to a grave disaster. As it was, he was obliged to move back to the coast and keep the whole army hard at work for ten days hauling the fleet up the beach beyond high-water mark, and protecting it with embankments. Forty vessels were so shattered as to be incapable of repair. Many of the rest were seriously damaged. Labienus was ordered to send across a detachment of artificers chosen from his legions to assist in repairing them. Caesar's trust in his good fortune had carried him too far.

The result was that Caswallon was able to reach the front with his Midland levies, and rally the Kentishmen. Caesar, on his part, sent the exile Mandubracius to the Trinobantes to raise trouble in his adversary's rear; and, having as far as possible put his ships in safety and seen repairs well under way, again took the road inland. His objective, as he clearly indicates, was the nearest point of passage on the Lower Thames. Once across the river, he would be in the territory of the Catuvellauni, and able to communicate with the Trinobantes.

He was to have no easy task. Caswallon was a foeman worthy of Caesar's steel. He seems to have fully realized that the British foot-levies were useless against the legions except at a great advantage. He declined to defend the line of the Stour, but as soon as it was across the stream, the Roman column found itself engaged in a running fight, in which the heavily armed and burdened legionaries were at a disadvantage. The next day Caswallon set upon the Romans as they were laying out their camp, drove in the outposts, killing the tribune in command, burst through the intervals of the supporting cohorts, and drew off with little loss, after causing great confusion. This half success, however, led to a severe defeat. Probably the king could not restrain his eager and undisciplined foot-levies. On the morrow Caesar sent out all his cavalry and three legions under Trebonius to forage. The force was attacked by the British mounted arms, but the foot-levies got out of hand and charged the legions while they were still in close order. They were repulsed with much bloodshed, of course, and the Roman cavalry, closely supported by infantry, was able to cut them up badly before they could regain the woods.

Caswallon, unshaken, fell back on his guerrilla tactics. His chariotry and cavalry were intact. Caesar says that they were about four thousand, a moderate estimate which shows it to be near the truth. With them he faced his great antagonist, while the southern levies took refuge in the Weald, and those of the Catuvellauni went back to entrench the fords of the Thames. From the neighbourhood of Canterbury to that of London the Romans advanced slowly, probably along the line of the later Wading Street, while Caswallon moved parallel to them in the woods, hung about the line of march, and harassed it incessantly. The Gallic horsemen never dared to move far from the infantry columns. Caswallon was ever watchful. But it was not guerrilla warfare, however skilful and gallant, that could stay the march of Caesar's legions. The advance was slow and difficult, but still it continued steadily until the Thames was reached. Caswallon retreated across it, and the Romans followed.

Where the British leader was stationed it is hard to say. The course of the Thames, meandering among marshes, must have varied much from what it is today, and, having no embankments, it was probably much shallower. Caesar may have crossed near Brentford or Halliford; there are said to be the remains of a stockade in the bed of the river opposite the former place. At any rate, Caesar gives the impression that the ford was well known. Its northern end was guarded by entrenchments, and the passage itself was obstructed by stakes. The position was a formidable one, yet it was carried with unexpected ease. The Roman cavalry led the way into the Thames, the infantry followed, with the water at their necks, passed the stakes – how we do not know – carried the stockade, and drove the Britons off towards the north.

Caesar, having passed the Thames, halted for a time to receive hostages and supplies from the neighbouring Trinobantes. Caswallon fell back on his tribal stronghold (almost certainly Verulam), and sent orders to the four sub-kings of Kent to attack Caesar's base-camp, and so draw him back from the Thames. It was the last fine stroke of Caswallon's admirable strategy, but fate was against him. Atrius marched boldly out to attack the men of Kent, defeated and scattered them with great loss, capturing a prominent chief named Lugotorix. Caesar, having rested his men in the Trinobantian territory near London, advanced upon Verulam. He describes it as a great earthwork among woods and marshes. It was captured by a simultaneous attack on two fronts. The British loss was heavy, and included thousands of captives, besides vast quantities of supplies. Verulam had evidently been the place of refuge of a great part of the tribe.

Caswallon had done his best and had failed. Through Commius, who was with the Romans, he made overtures, and Caesar was not unready to accept them. Reports were coming in from Labienus of alarming unrest among the Gauls, which was soon to blaze out into a great national uprising. It was clearly time to go. Caesar was justified in supposing that he had done enough to convince the Britons that interference in Gallic affairs would, for the future, be dangerous. His terms of peace were, therefore, moderate enough. Caswallon was to keep the peace with Mandubracius, pay a yearly tribute to Rome, and, of course, give hostages for the observance of the conditions. They were accepted, and, with his hostages and captives, Caesar returned to the coast. Two trips were necessary owing to the large number of prisoners to be trans ported. Apart from them (and being only fit for rough field and house work, they would hardly fetch a high price) there appears to have been little spoil of value, much to the disappointment of many greedy officers. Cicero quaintly voices this discontent in his letters. We bear, however, that Caesar dedicated to Venus a cuirass ornamented with British pearls, so that possibly some were lucky. All this probably weighed little with Caesar beside the fact that he was not likely to have Britain on his rear during the Gallic disturbances. If Caswallon, a man, as far as we can see, of remarkable ability for war, had been able to intervene in the great struggle with Vercingetorix two years later, the consequences might have been very serious. As it was, we hear no more of British aid given to the Gauls, and Caesar was content. Whether the tribute was paid we do not know; possibly it was so long as Caesar was in Gaul. When the civil war broke out, it probably lapsed; but the general political results of the expedition appear from Caesar's point of view to have been satisfactory.

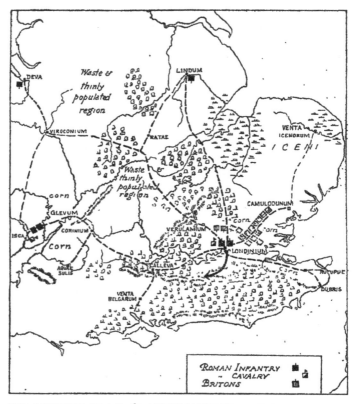

THE CAMPAIGN OF A.D. 60 AGAINST BOUDICCA. THE POSITION AT
THE TIME OF PAULINUS'S ARRIVAL IN LONDON.

The chief roads (mainly British trackways) are shown with broken lines. Each
infantry block roughly indicates 5,000 men. The whole country north of the
Thames was hostile to the Romans, perhaps much of that to the south also.
The Roman troops at Lindum (Lincoln) were only the defeated remnant of the
IXth Legion. It should be noted that of the settled and corn-growing districts,
one was occupied by the Britons, and there remained open for Paulinus's army,
and the crowd of refugees which accompanied it, the choice between Kent or
the Lower Severn Valley. The IInd Legion at Isca Silurum (Caerleon) had
orders to march on Londinium, and Paulinus would expect it to be well on its
way. The heavy black line stretching south-west from London indicates the
probable direction of the Roman retreat.

II

The Claudian Invasion and the Roman Conquest

Of the history of Britain during the century succeeding the Caesarian expeditions we have some fairly satisfactory glimpses. The terror of Caesar was sufficient, on the one hand, to prevent the British chiefs from interfering in Gallic affairs. It also appears to have deterred Caswallon from again attacking the philo-Roman Trinobantes, for numismatic evidence shows that they were independent at a much later epoch. But it does seem certain that it helped forward British unity, since we find a tendency to form groups or 'empires' that certainly included more than one tribe. One of these was founded by Commius the Atrebatian. He had taken sides with his countrymen against Caesar in the last great Gallic uprising, and, after some remarkable adventures, had escaped to his kinsmen in Britain. By then he appears to have been acknowledged as king; at any rate, coins have been found bearing his name in what is known to have been the territory of the Atrebates. He and his sons extended their rule over the Cantii, the Regni of Sussex, and over some at least of the small clans known as Belgre.

Meanwhile, north of the Thames, the Catuvellauni was recovering from the effects of Caesar's invasion. It is at least possible that the discovery of rich gold mines had something to do with their undoubtedly rapid rise in power. At any rate, Tasciovan, very probably the successor of Caswallon, coined most extensively in gold, silver, and bronze, and his widely-diffused coins show strong traces of Roman influence. His capital was certainly Verulam (St Albans), since on most of his coins the Latinized name of the place figures. The Cantii and Trinobantes, however, still appear to have been the most civilized peoples of Britain. Tasciovan perhaps initiated a policy of aggression upon the Commian kingdom, and his son, Cunobelin, extended his sway over the entire south-east and south. The Iceni (Norfolk) and the Damnonii (Somerset, Devon, Cornwall) appear to have kept their independence, but may have paid tribute; and the Silures of South Wales were probably in Cunobelin's sphere of influence. His capital seems to have been not his father's Verulam, but the Trinobantian Camulodunum (Colchester).

The result of Cunobelin's supremacy was that tribal wars ceased, and civilization and industry made great strides. Probably Cunobelin took care to pay polite attentions to Augustus and Tiberius – Strabo says as much – and though the former Emperor sheltered fugitive Commian and Trinobantian princes, there was no intervention in British affairs. Trade flourished. Strabo says that Britain exported gold, silver, and iron, as well as pelts, slaves, hounds, corn, and cattle. The last two items seem dubious, yet the sceptical Strabo is hardly likely to have noted them without good reason. Roman traders and travellers passed freely to and fro, and the southern regions became well known. It is at this period more than at any other that we must look for the rise of a commercial settlement at London. One of Cunobelin's sons, Adminiust rebelled against him in AD 39, and fled to the Emperor Caligula. The latter's military demonstration near Gessoriacum (Boulogne) has been noted (and probably misunderstood) by Suetonius. In AD 41 Caligula was assassinated, and succeeded by Claudius I, and in the same year Cunobelin died.

There is reason to believe that the flight of Adminius was only one of the family troubles that vexed the last years of the old 'Rex Brittonum.' His death was followed by intestine war; but after a short struggle, two sons, Togodubn and Caradoc (Caratacus), gained the ascendancy, and ruled jointly over their father's realm. They doubtless had much to do in reconquering rebellious vassals, and, to add to their difficulties, one of their dispossessed brothers (or half-brothers) fled to Claudius. Togodubn and Caradoc thereupon very unwisely demanded his surrender. The result was the Roman Conquest.

Claudius I was perhaps tempted into the invasion by his dislike of the cruel rites of Druidism, which, now that Gaul was Roman, had its main stronghold in British Mona. But Roman capitalists had for years been acquiring interests in the island; when the occupation was an accomplished fact, they settled down to bleed it in true usurers' fashion, with disastrous results. It is probable that the formation of something like a British Empire close to Gaul, where the old times were not forgotten, and where a great revolt did actually break out a generation later, seemed an alarming phenomenon. Doubtless also there were plenty of ambitious soldiers and politicians anxious to prove to the sensible and kindly, but weak, old Emperor that the honour of Rome could not brook the undiplomatically blunt requests of the British kings. Probably all these influences were brought to bear upon Claudius, and induced him to undertake a conquest which in the end contributed materially to the weakening of Roman power.

For the invasion Claudius concentrated four legions, with auxiliaries and cavalry, in Gaul. This meant 24,000 legionaries, supposing the cohorts to be at full strength, with, as is probable, as many auxiliaries. Taking the cavalry into consideration, and making a deduction of 20 per cent for absentees, we can hardly reckon the force at less than 40,000 effectives; it may have been even stronger. The commander was Aulus Plautius, a veteran who had grown grey in war, and who, to judge from his record, was singularly fitted for his post. Claudius himself was on the way from Rome to join his army with the Praetorian Guard.

For all practical purposes the Roman army was still the army of Marius and Caesar, but the proportion of auxiliaries and cavalry was much greater. Of the legions three came from the Army of the Rhine: II, 'Augusta'; XIV, 'Gemina Martia'; and XX, 'Valeria Victrix.' From the Army of Pannonia, or the Upper Danube, came Legio IX, 'Hispana.' The XIVth was to win the proud title of 'Conqueror of Britain' during its stay of twenty-five years. 'Valeria Victrix' remained for more than three centuries, and the IInd did not leave until 407.

The legions had now become so fixed in their frontier cantonments that to move them bodily to other regions was a delicate business. The new Army of Britain grumbled, and seemed about to mutiny. Its temper was not improved by the fact that the Imperial commissioner appointed to inquire into their grievances was the Emperor's treasurer, Narcissus, a Greek civilian! One can almost hear the Roman 'Tommies' asking, with much profanity, why their dignity should be thus insulted, and they expressed their contempt for the unmentionable civilian by a riotous demonstration. The old General, however, whom they respected, soon recalled them to their duty. The affair had important results, for the British kings were induced by the news to believe that the expedition would not sail, and so were unprepared when it suddenly appeared in Kent.

The landing-place this time was probably Rutupire (Richborough, near Sandwich), which for some centuries to come was to be the usual starting-point for the Continent. The men of Kent were too unprepared to attempt to oppose the landing, but they harassed the flanks of the army as it marched for the Thames along the old, old track that Caesar had traversed a century before. This time the British guerrilla tactics had slight effect; there was ample cavalry to feel ahead, and ample light infantry to guard the flanks. We hear no more of the stunning and disordering surges of chariotry among the Roman battalions – indeed, there is some reason to believe that, with the introduction and breeding of larger horses fit for riding, it was already in a state of decline.

Meanwhile Togodubn and Caradoc had crossed the Thames, and were prepared to oppose the Roman advance at the Medway, probably near Rochester. The position was a strong one, with the broad river and expanses of mud flat and marsh in its front. Plautius, however, forced the passage by a wide turning movement up the river under his able legatus, T. Flavius Vespasianus, while a large body of Batavian and North Gallic auxiliaries, accustomed to amphibious operations, with the greatest daring swam the river on the right. The Britons were thus forced to abandon the river-bank, but they fell back on the high ground towards Cobham and Shorne and stood firm. Next day a great battle was fought. The Britons made a fine resistance, and nearly captured the legatus Hosidius Geta; but were at last defeated, and retreated to the Thames. One could wish that we had some better authority than Dion Cassius, who wrote more than a hundred and fifty years later, and is so confused and rhetorical that we read him with deep distrust. We long for even the unmilitary and epigrammatic Tacitus, but his books relating to the early years of Claudius are lost.

Dion says, in brief, that the Britons crossed the Thames near where it enters the sea. They did so easily 'because they knew the firm ground ... and the easy passages, ... but the Romans following them came to grief at this spot.' We can hardly imagine the Thames as fordable anywhere below London, and the probable meaning of the passage is that the Britons traversed the marshes by well-known tracks, and then crossed the river in boats or on rafts.

Now comes the most curious part; and, if Dion could be relied upon, we have an invaluable reference to the earliest London Bridge. The Celts, he says, again swam the river, and other troops forced a bridge a little way upstream. We can hardly imagine a bridge existing below London, and if it stood anywhere, it would certainly be at the one place clearly marked out by Nature for the passage across the river of the road from the south-east to Verulam. London was such a remarkable road centre in Roman times that we cannot easily believe that it was not so long before, and the construction of a pile bridge was certainly not beyond the resources of a powerful ruler like Cunobelin, who had, without any doubt, skilled foreigners at his disposal, besides abundance of unskilled labour. Moreover, it explains satisfactorily the importance of London, which Tacitus describes as a great trading centre only eighteen years later.

Whatever his authorities, Dion's account of the operations, studied with the aid of the map, is logical and clear. The Britons are driven back from the Medway, and retreat to the estuary of the Thames across dangerous marshes – that is, we can hardly doubt that Vespasian's turning movement cut their line of retreat on London, and they were forced to fall back northward by Higham into Cliffe Marshes. The Roman pursuit was checked by the difficulties of the ground, but Plautius was between the Britons and London. He therefore marched for the bridge. The Britons, hurrying from Tilbury Marshes, reached London too late to destroy the bridge or occupy it with more than a fraction of their forces, if indeed at all. The bold action of the Batavians, who accomplished a more difficult feat than the swimming of the Medway, coupled with the seizure of the bridge, forced the Britons to abandon the defence of the Thames.

Togodubn had been slain in the course of the campaign, but Caradoc was alive and undismayed. He retreated towards Camulodunum, not upon his ancestral capital of Verulam. Clearly, Camulodunum was of greater importance. Meanwhile Claudius had landed with the Imperial Guards and was coming up. Dion says that the fighting had been so fierce that the reinforcements which he brought were very necessary. This may be a flight of rhetoric, but it is evident that the resistance was stubborn. Having effected a junction with his general, Claudius advanced on Camulodunum. Caradoc stood to fight somewhere on the road – perhaps at the Blackwater – and was defeated finally and utterly. Camulodunum was taken, the empire broke up or submitted, and the king, with his family and a remnant of his army, fled away across Britain into the country of the Silures (South Wales). Claudius himself only waited to enter Camulodunum and to declare it the capital of the Roman Province of Britannia, and then returned to Gaul.

The heart of the Catuvellaunian dominion was now occupied with little difficulty. The Iceni and Regni sent in their submission; but Caradoc with the Silures was preparing for a last desperate stand for freedom, if not for empire; and the Belgre and Durotriges made a gallant resistance to Vespasian, who marched against them with Legio II. Thirteen fierce engagements were necessary before the conquest was complete, and Vespasian on one occasion owed his life to his son Titus, the future destroyer of Jerusalem. But his work was very thoroughly done, and within six years Roman rule was firmly established as far as the Exe, The wild Damnonii beyond that river were left now and afterwards very much to themselves. No doubt they made submission, but the great western road never went beyond Isca Damnoniorum (Exeter). The tin trade of Cornwall seems to have languished during the Early and Middle Empire; but when in the third century the mines once more began to disgorge their treasures, the ingots were carried to the sea on the backs of pack-animals. Until the eighteenth century pack-trains with correspondingly narrow tracks were the rule in Devon and Cornwall. The famous bridge of Bideford was scarcely more than wide enough to admit of the passage of a loaded horse.

By AD 47, when Plautius went home to enjoy a well-merited triumph, the whole south and east of the island appeared to be passing with little apparent effort into the form of a Roman province. The frontier probably followed for the most part the lines of the Lower Severn, Avon, and Welland, but in the centre it bulged outwards around Ratre (Leicester). Here it would have been well for Rome to have halted. The territory already occupied was fairly settled, capable of great development, and the frontier was easily defensible. But a forward policy invariably brings trouble in its train. In the North Midlands the Coritani and Cornavii were restless, and behind them the great Brigantian tribe, which held the whole breadth of the North from Humber to Tyne, was ever raiding. Still greater was the danger in Wales, where the Silures of the south and the Ordovices of the north were the fiercest warriors of Britain, where was the Druids' sacred home of Mona, and where King Caradoc, the last warrior of Caswallon's famous line, had taken refuge.

Publius Ostorius Scapula, the new governor, had perhaps no alternative to the 'forward' policy; at any rate, he committed himself to it. He conquered the weak Coritani and Cornavii with slight difficulty, stationed Legio IX at Lindum (Lincoln) to keep guard over them, and established a colony of time-expired veterans as a garrison for Camulo dunum. Then he turned upon Caradoc. Legio II moved forward from Glevum (Gloucester) to Isca Silurum (Caerleon), while Scapula with the XIVth and XXth established himself with his base at Viroconium, the camp, afterwards the town, beside Wrekin, whose ruins have been laid bare in our own days. The men of Cambria were thrown on the defensive by the great force directed against them. Caradoc manoeuvred among the mountains, harassed the Roman line of march, cut off detachments, but was at last brought to bay in A. D. 50. All that could be suggested to counterbalance the superiority of the Romans in everything but mere numbers he did. He posted his army behind a roaring mountain torrent, with both flanks protected by craggy heights, and his centre covered by 'sangars' of piled stones. The wild warriors of Wales swore by their gods to conquer or die. Caradoc rode up and down the line, bade them save themselves and those they loved from slavery and death, told them (with justifiable stretching of truth) how his ancestors had repulsed the mightiest of the Caesars, and besought them to do their duty to the last. They did not fail him, but fortune was against them. The battle was furiously contested, but the entrenchments were stormed at last; and after bravely rallying in the face of the legions and renewing the fray, the Britons finally broke and fled. Caradoc's wife and daughter were taken captive in the camp, and the king, fleeing for aid to the Brigantes, was surrendered to the Romans by the Queen Cartimandua. The story of how he and his family were dragged in chains through Rome to make a holiday for its cosmopolitan populace, and released by the kindly Emperor, is well known. One could wish that the old ruler, whose character has suffered so much at the hands of detractors, had spared a brave man and two helpless women the cruel humiliation ot public exposure as well. But probably no Roman was capable of such generosity. Aurelian treated Zenobia as Claudius treated Caradoc, and from the has-reliefs on the column of Arcadius we see that the Christian Romans of the fourth century were capable of dragging female captives, pinioned like criminals, in triumphal procession.

Undismayed by the fate of their King, the Silures fought on desperately. Again and again they gained considerable guerrilla successes. Foraging detachments were attacked; two cohorts destroyed; Claudian Invasion and Roman Conquest a strong brigade of legionaries surrounded, severely defeated, and only saved from destruction by the arrival of reinforcements. Scapula died of vexation and fatigue, and the Silures just afterwards attacked and defeated a whole legion. Scapula's successor, Didius, was threatened by the Brigantes, who were growing angry at the ignominious part to which Cartimandua's policy condemned them, and the Cambrians, despite constant warfare, remained unsubdued.

In AD 59 C. Suetonius Paulinus, one of the best soldiers of the Empire, took command in Britain, and at once initiated a vigorous offensive. He determined to turn the flank of Wales, as it were, and strike a staggering blow by uprooting the Druid stronghold in Mona. Didius appears to have fortified Deva (Chester), and now Paulinus enlarged it, moving the XIVth and XXth Legions there from Viroconium, and making it his base for the advance. In AD 60 he arrived on Menai Strait with flat-bottomed boats for the transport of his infantry. The Ordovician warriors were massed on the shore of Mona to oppose the landing; frantic women, clothed in black and bearing blazing torches, with wild eyes and tossing hair, like the Furies, as the superstitious soldiers muttered, rushed about exhorting the men and screaming curses at the hated Romans. Behind the Druids were engaged in their dreadful rites, and the shrieks of the perishing victims rang over the Strait. For a while there was something like incipient panic among the Romans, but the fierce adjurations of their officers steadied them, and when they had effected a landing, burning with rage at their hesitation, there was small hope for the Britons. The fighting men were cut down in thousands, women and children involved in the hideous massacre. The Druids were slaughtered at their rites, or tossed upon their own flaming pyres. The sanctuaries were destroyed, the sacred groves cut down, and Paulinus might hope that he had dealt a decisive blow, when jaded messengers dashed into camp with the stunning tidings that all Roman Britain was in a flame of revolt.

The rebellion had been long brewing, and for it the Roman civil and military administration, above all the Roman capitalists, were to blame. To create farms for retired veterans the military chiefs had recklessly evicted native landowners. The military settlers insulted and oppressed their British neighbours. The discipline of the legions, relaxed by years of guerrilla warfare, was probably bad, and it would seem that Paulinus, a soldier before all, was not the man to trouble himself about the rights of civilians, especially if they were also barbarians. The Imperial procurator (i.e., practically financial agent), Decianus Catus, was calling for the repayment of various loans advanced by Claudius to chiefs; presumably Nero needed money for his expensive pleasures. The British chiefs were careless and ostentatious, and, now that they could not enrich themselves by plunder in war, were apt to borrow heavily – of course, from Roman capitalists. Many of them were hopelessly embarrassed, unable to pay the iniquitous interest, much less the principal; and the greedy usurers were only too ready to drag them further into the toils. Nero's famous minister, the Stoic

Seneca, was one of the worst offenders. Usury was a chief source of his vast income. Now, as if to add fuel to the smouldering fire, he suddenly called in his British loans, 40,000,000 sesterces (£360,000). *Cherchez la femme!* say the French when trouble threatens. No doubt the saying is not without truth, but a study of history, and especially of Roman history, leads rather to the conclusion that the greed of the speculator has been responsible for a great deal of the world's misery.

Just at this juncture died Prasutagus, King of the Iceni. He made the Emperor heir to his kingdom, and joint inheritor of his vast personal wealth, evidently in the hope that his widow Boudicca and her two daughters would thereby be assured of protection. Paulinus and Catus must share the blame for what followed. The country of the Iceni was treated like conquered territory. Military violence went hand in hand with civil spoliation. The widowed queen was actually whipped by the scoundrels who dishonoured the Roman name; her orphaned daughters were foully outraged. One can only hope that the vile deeds were committed by one or two especially degraded creatures; but neither their associates who looked on, nor those who sent them, can escape blame.

It was the last straw. The Iceni rose as one man at the call of their outraged Queen. Tall and stately of presence, with bright eyes and thick, flowing, red-gold hair, was the sorely wronged widow of Prasutagus, and as, splendid in the barbaric magnificence of a British queen, she harangued her liegemen, told of violence and lashes, and insults unmentionable, pointed to the shame-bowed forms of her violated children, the rage of the Iceni rose to fever heat. Out from the bounds of their country poured the wild barbaric host, and ill fared it with the Roman who strayed across its path. News of the rising came all too late. Quintus Petilius Cerealis at Lindum called in all that he could of the IXth Legion and marched southward, but the Iceni had a long start. On they rushed across Suffolk towards doomed Camulodunum, the Trinobantes rallying to them with fierce unanimity. 'Colonia Victrix' had no walls; only the temple of Divus Claudius and some neighbouring buildings formed a sort of citadel. Catus sent what soldiers he could only two hundred – to help the colonists in the defence; but time was lacking wherein to raise entrenchments, and little had been done when the Britons were at hand, and swept through the city in a whirlwind of vengeance and destruction. Some of the defenders held out for two days in the temple, then it, too, was taken. There were hideous scenes. The outrage-maddened princesses were little likely to restrain their furious tribesmen. The innocent perished with the guilty, without distinction of age or sex; women were stripped, scourged, horribly mutilated, and left to die a lingering death of agony impaled on stakes. Such was the harvest of the seed sown by military oppression and capital-owning greed.

Now followed a great but obscure campaign. Tacitus is a little less vague than usual, but gives not a hint as to chronology. The main point is that London was already the most important place in the island. This is clearly indicated, but everything else is exceedingly difficult to follow. So far as can be ascertained, the sequence of events was this: Boudicca, having destroyed Camulodunum, faced round to meet Cerealis, who was approaching from Lindum. His force was attacked by the raging horde of Britons and practically annihilated. Some 3,000 legionaries and many auxiliaries perished; only the remains of the cavalry, with Cerealis, cut their way out and escaped.

Paulinus meanwhile was hastening to the scene of operations. He left, perforce, a strong garrison in Deva, and marched for London with the XIVth Legion, some picked cohorts of the XXth, some auxiliaries, and cavalry. He sent off orders to the IInd and IXth Legions to join him. A glance at the map of Roman Britain will show that London was the natural place of concentration.

We may assume that Cerealis's action in marching from Lindum had, at any rate, drawn the Britons away from the vital point. Paulinus reached London before Boudicca. Then the blow fell. No troops were there. The IXth Legion, we know, had been destroyed. Pcenius Postumus, the temporary commander of the IInd, paralysed by the responsibility, perhaps thought fit to transmit the order to his absent superior, and at any rate stood fast on the Lower Severn. London was not fortified – it must have been crowded with fugitives – and Paulinus's entire strength, according to Tacitus, was but 10,000 men. There is really no reason to believe, as has been suggested, that he had outpaced his army and had only his escort with him. The position is quite clear. He had ordered a concentration at London, and it had failed. Instead of 20,000 men or more, he had only 10,000 wherewith to defend an open town crowded with refugees. He decided that London must be abandoned. Of its population, swollen, probably, by much of that of Verulam, those who had most to fear – the Continental residents followed the march. Some, doubtless, escaped on shipboard, but many, probably those of British birth, remained.

Conjecture has been busy with the direction of Paulinus's march. The old view was that he moved on Camulodunum; the more modern one, followed by most recent writers, is that he retreated on Deva to rally its garrison. Neither, however, commends itself to the authors. Let us study the position. Paulinus at London had 1o,ooo combatants in hand but was burdened with a mass of non-combatants at least equal in number. At and about Deva were perhaps half a legion and auxiliaries – say, 5,000 men. At Lindum, practically blockaded, were the remains of the IXth. About Isca Silurum and on the Lower Severn was the IInd Legion with its auxiliaries. At Viroconium and other places in the west, and in some of the Kentish towns (i.e., Rutupice), there were certainly garrisons. The British host was somewhere north-east of London.

The question of supplies must be considered. It was probably near harvest-time, as the Welsh campaign and the subsequent operations would have consumed most of the summer. The richest districts of Britain were Essex, Kent, and the Lower Severn Valley; but Essex was in the hands of the Britons, and Paulinus could draw no supplies from it.

Wherever Paulinus went he had to feed his army and its hapless incubus of refugees. The London–Deva road traversed the thinly-peopled and thickly wooded Midlands; the way to Colchester was barred by the Britons.

The object of Paulinus was to complete his frustrated combination. At Deva, two hundred miles away, were perhaps 5,000 men; at Lindum, a hundred and thirty miles to the north-east, perhaps an equal force, dispirited by defeat. If he took the road to Deva, or that to Lindum, he would have the Britons upon him. Is it conceivable that this able general, with supply difficulties aggravated by his mass of non-combatants, would deliberately plunge into the midst of the enemy, in order to join one of his two smaller detachments, when in the Lower Severn Valley lay a whole legion and its auxiliaries. If his orders were being obeyed, it should be already on the march; but if it had not yet concentrated, its nearest detachments were only a hundred miles away. A study of the map will show that, if London were abandoned, Corinium (Cirencester) would be the natural point of concentration for Paulinus's army, the IInd Legion, and the garrisons of Deva and Viroconium. The troops round Lindum and the garrisons in Kent must, for the moment, be left to themselves. We are justified in thinking that Paulinus would .move in the direction of his largest outlying corps – the IInd Legion. Considerations of supply would also take him westward. Food might be found in Kent, but not reinforcements. The conclusion is that, for every reason, the direction of the retreat would be westward. Paulinus no doubt crossed the Thames, presumably by the bridge at London, which would, of course, afterwards be destroyed, and retreated towards Calleva (Silchester).

It is probable that Verulam was taken and sacked by the Britons after Paulinus had passed through it. Tacitus only says that it fell at about the same time as London. The British host then moved on to London, which shared the fate of Camulodunum and Verulam. The massacre here was probably the worst, for it would, naturally, apart from its commercial importance, be full of fugitives.

From the ruins of London the Britons moved on after Paulinus, who was marching slowly, troubled, so Dion says, with want of supplies, and encumbered so with the refugees from London. Another massacre would have taken place but for the fact that before the pursuers could get at the victims they must reckon with the ten thousand desperate veterans who formed the rearguard. But the danger grew greater. The Roman army was too small to adequately guard the unhappy throng of fugitives that impeded its march; the IInd Legion did not come, and Paulinus turned to bay. He chose a strong position in a defile, with woods behind and on both flanks. His legionaries were deployed across the entrance; the light troops apparently along the front and in the woods; the cavalry behind. This narrow valley may reasonably be looked for among the hills between the south-west of London and Silchester, and as the most open, and therefore safest, route would have probably been by Banstead, Epsom Downs, Headley, Ranmore, and Guildford, the scene of Boudicca's defeat may be somewhere along that line. The retreating Romans would, in this case, have quite likely debauched into the gorge of the Mole by the valley that runs into it from Headley. Continuing their westward march, the way up to the top of the downs would be almost facing them as they crossed the shallow river where Burford Bridge now stands. It is conceivable that the idea of turning to bay at this point would occur to Paulinus as his force marched up the dry and rapidly narrowing valley, whose sides are sufficiently steep to concentrate the attack on one front.

The generalship of the British chiefs appears to have been contemptible. They staked everything on a wild frontal attack. Worse still, their movements were encumbered by hordes of followers and a vast train of waggons, which was parked confusedly in the rear. For the last time Boudicca drove along the line and bade her warriors strike a crushing blow. Paulinus, on his side, addressed his men in brief soldierly words, which Dion amplifies into an harangue covering pages.

The Britons, as they came on, were smitten by storms of missiles from the light troops, which made havoc in their dense masses, but the headlong charge, nevertheless, seems to have driven in the skirmishers and reached the legionaries. But they were received with volley on volley of pila; rush after rush recoiled from the steady line; and then, when the fury of their charge began to slacken, Paulinus ordered the advance. The legionaries pressed forward shoulder to shoulder, like a wall of iron; the auxiliaries charged manfully on the wings of their heavily-armed comrades. As the line left the file the cavalry swept round the flanks and fell upon the Britons, and though bodies and individuals doubtless fought bravely to the end, panic seized the host as a whole, and it fled wildly to the rear. The fatal waggon park dammed back the flying horde, and the Romans closed upon it and slaughtered their fill. The massacres of the Britons were avenged by the butchery, it is said, of 80,000 men, women, and children. Like many of the semi-barbarous peoples of the past, and the Abyssinians of today, their armies were encumbered by a numerous following of womenfolk. Boudicca poisoned herself in her despair.

With the victory of Paulinus the last united opposition to Rome ceased. The reconquest of the south gave much trouble, and Paulinus himself was soon recalled, rightly enough, for his harshness and lack of political wisdom were clearly not less than his warlike skill. Civilian governors set to work to heal, so far as possible, the wounds of Britain, and for eight years the new policy of conciliation and reorganization was steadily carried out. After 71 the conquest of the Brigantes in the North was taken seriously in hand by Petilius Cerealis, now governor of the province. The brave Silures of South Wales submitted in 78, and the northern tribes were by 80 sufficiently cowed to enable that brilliant but overrated figure, Gmeus Julius Agricola, the father-in-law of Tacitus, to make his famous invasions of Caledonia. But in 86 they again broke out into revolt, and for thirty years gave continual trouble. About 119 they set upon Legio IX, the ever luckless 'Hispana' – where is unfortunately not known – and annihilated it; never more does it appear in the Imperial muster-rolls. The subjection of the North seemed as far distant as ever.

So in 120 the Emperor Hadrian himself arrived in Britain to study the problem, bringing with him, to replace the lost troops, Legio VI. ('Victrix'), whose headquarters were to be at Eboracum (York) for nearly three hundred years. He decided to draw a connected line of defence across the island from Tynemouth to Solway, which might serve at once as a bulwark against the North, and a base of operations against the Brigantes. The idea had been Agricola's, thus showing that some at least of his relative's overstrained eulogy is not misplaced. The line of forts which he had established was now reinstated, new ones built, and all connected by a solid rampart of turf, fronted by a deep ditch. While this was being carried out, and Hadrian was busy in the south, the field army, assisted by detachments from the Army of the Rhine, set to work to tame the Brigantes, and for a time succeeded. Hadrian's policy, as is known, was to withdraw behind definite and easily defensible frontiers, and concentrate the energies of the government upon internal development rather than aggression. The trouble in Britain was that a true frontier was hard to find. Hadrian's chosen line corresponded roughly with the Brigantian border, but it cut athwart the British tribes. To move on to the Forth was merely to add a large tract of very wild and sparsely peopled territory to the province, with the restless Brigantes still unsubdued far in the rear. As the conditions then were, Hadrian's policy was sound; but it may be said, in short, that the original error of occupying the island was not to be redeemed by anything short of its complete conquest, and for this task, enormously difficult and entirely unremunerative, the Roman Empire, on the verge of decline in population and resources, had not the means.

Hadrian's Wall is now crowned, except at one point, by the reconstruction in stone by Severus I ninety years later; hence it was often supposed that the first wall was a stone structure. This idea may now be regarded as thoroughly disproved; the later wall stands upon and hides the foundations of the former, but near Birdoswald Severus's engineers diverged a little from Hadrian's line, and the earlier emperor's construction may still be seen. The turf wall, replaced by stone, ran for seventy-three miles from Gabrosentum (Bowness) to Segedunum (Wallsend). In front of it, where it did not crown precipitous cliffs, was a ditch about 36 feet broad, and perhaps 30 feet deep. At each milestone there was a redoubt (castellum), and at more or less regular intervals along the whole line were fifteen large forts. Roughly parallel to the wall ran a military road, and a little way south of it a wide but shallow ditch between mounds, commonly called the 'Vallum,' the reason for which is a puzzle. It is best here to adopt Professor Oman's very reasonable theory that it was the civil boundary of the province.

The wall and its forts were constructed by detachments from the legions, but it was garrisoned by the auxiliary cohorts, while the heavy infantry lay in reserve at the old military centres. Twenty-one infantry cohorts and six also of cavalry made up the original garrison, and some of them kept their stations for centuries. Nearly three hundred years later there were at least eleven, and probably more, of these regiments still on the wall. Behind, the legions occupied their camps for generation after generation, as if nothing could disturb them. For two hundred and eighty-two years after Hadrian's visit, Legio VI lay at York. The XXth 'Valeria Victrix' made its home at Deva (Chester) for more than three centuries; while Secunda Augusta, which had landed with Plautius in 43, did not leave Britain until 407, after a sojourn of three hundred and sixty-four years!

III

The Roman Province and the Earlier Teutonic Invasions

After Hadrian, in what Florus jokingly termed the great Emperor's 'walking about Britain,' had reorganized the island, and established the famous military frontier, Britain settled down to a more or less eventful existence as a Roman province. The unfortunate results of the enterprise, into which Claudius had perhaps been led partly against his will, soon began to be apparent, even if to all thinking men they were not plain as early as the reign of Hadrian. The military boundary chosen by Trajan's successor corresponded roughly with the northern border of the Brigantes, but it was not the frontier of Britain, which extended from Clyde to Forth. Therefore, in 140/141, the governor, Lollius Urbicus, the lieutenant of Antoninus Pius, moved the frontier forward to this line, and covered it by another rampart, strengthened by ten forts, only a few miles apart. It was the old, old story – a forward policy can never halt.

The Roman terminus stood between Forth and Clyde for a few years only. The wild Caledonians – 'Picts,' as perhaps the Roman troops were already calling them – saw their independence threatened now as formerly by Agricola. About 155 the irrepressible Brigantes again broke out into rebellion. They were only subdued after a fierce struggle, during which the garrison of the northernmost wall must have been largely recalled. The result was the gradual abandonment of the recently occupied territory. The Caledonians raided through the ill-occupied wall, inflicted at least one severe defeat on a Roman force, and, as excavations appear to show, stormed some of the forts. By about

190 the frontier was again at Hadrian's Wall, with advanced stations at Habitancium (Risingham) and Bremenium (High Rochester), respectively twelve and twenty miles from Corstopitum (Corbridge), just south of the Wall, Castra Exploratorum (Netherby), and one or two other places. So, after every effort, the 'British Enterprise' ended in an unsatisfactory compromise. The Roman frontier was neither ethnic nor natural, and the wretched Britons between Roman and Pict were literally between hammer and anvil. In 196–197 the governor, Decimus Clodius Albinus, took almost the entire army to Gaul to contest the Empire with Severus I. He was defeated and slain at Lugdunum (Lyons), and the troops returned to Britain; but they must have suffered very heavily, besides being thoroughly discontented with the Emperor, who had slain their own commander. This weakness and disorganization gave the wild Caledonians too good an opportunity to be missed. They appear to have occupied the territory north of the Wall, and even to have crossed the fortified line itself.

So in 208 Severus himself arrived with powerful reinforcements. In 209 he advanced, and for two years pushed slowly and doggedly forward. His solution of the problem was the heroic one of subduing the whole island. The losses of the army in the two campaigns were relatively enormous – fifty thousand men, it is said. The stern old Emperor was generally ill; he suffered fearfully from gout, but he never faltered. On over the desolation of wild Caledonia, slowly, painfully, but with a grim determination more terrible than the fiercest onslaught, with Severus in his litter at its head, the devoted army wrought its way, and at last drew near to the 'extreme end of the Isle of Britain' (Herodian). Severus had won his last victory, for the barbarians were cowed by the steady advance. They sued for peace, and the grim old conqueror returned to Eboracum to die. His worthless son Caracalla retroceded the conquered territory to the Picts, receiving in exchange a more or less nominal homage; but there is every reason to believe that the barbarians were daunted, and gave little trouble for many years. Severus left behind him, as a perpetual monument to his greatness, the gigantic reconstruction in stone of Hadrian's Wall, whereof the remains survive to this day.

After his departure, Britain entered upon a period of prosperity hitherto unknown. It was saved by its insular position from taking more than a passive part in the wild chaos of civil and foreign war that overwhelmed the Roman Empire in the third century, and is described by a contemporary writer as being in a very flourishing condition. The Picts were held completely in check by the fortified lines of the Wall. Perhaps, also, they were involved in warfare among themselves. At any rate, not until the end of the century did Britain again know the fear of foreign invasion. This time it was not from the North, but from overseas. The little cloud, no bigger than a man's hand, had arisen in Germany, which was to grow until it overshadowed all the heavens, and ended by forming a new nation on what had been Celtic soil.

For long generations Germania had been seething with disorder, for reasons which cannot here be considered. Tribe was pressing on tribe; the whole mass of wild barbarism was being forced against the Rhine and the Danube, behind which lay the Roman Empire, sorely weakened by invasions, plague, famine, economic decay, and misgovernment. The North German tribes – Franks, Saxons, Angles, Jutes, Frisians – finding raids over the Rhine difficult, dangerous, and more and more unremunerative, began to take to the sea. Their craft as yet – perhaps to the end – were small open vessels, incapable of rough sea-work, and obliged to hug the shore as far as possible. The raiding flotillas ran down what are now the coasts of Denmark, North-West Germany, and Holland, and turned to right or left on Britain or Gaul, according to information or inclination. Others, more daring, or encouraged by spells of fine weather, ran across from Frisia to the coasts of Essex, Suffolk, and Norfolk, and landed for hasty raids on those rich agricultural districts. These appear at first to have been met merely by detachments of troops; the Roman naval force in the Channel was small. But when the famous organizer and statesman, Diocletian, took up the task of saving the Empire in 284, he abandoned timid defensive strategy. His colleague, Maximianus, to whom he entrusted the West, organized a great fleet in the Channel, and placed in command a distinguished naval officer, Marcus Aurelius Carausius, with the title of 'Count of the Saxon Shore.' He cleared the sea of the pirates, but, presently accused of misappropriation of booty, set up in Britain as independent ruler. He even endeavoured to conquer Gaul, but only succeeded in permanently holding Gessoriacum (Boulogne).

His naval power, however, rendered his position in vulnerable, and Diocletian and Maximianus stooped to acknowledge him as their colleague. He was assassinated in 293, but his murderer and successor, Allectus, held the province for three years longer. He was not the equal of Carausius, and allowed Constantius Chlorus, Caesar of the West, to build ships unmolested in Gaul until he was able to cross the Channel and overthrow Allectus (296).

Constantius and his more famous son, Constantine the Great, resided for long periods in Britain, and, partly to this circumstance, partly to the renewed peace brought about by the protection of the fleet of the Saxon Shore, the province enjoyed another lease of prosperity. Indeed, there is some reason to believe that the period 296–350 was the most prosperous that Roman Britain ever knew. Building was going on vigorously. When Constantius II rebuilt Augustodunum in Gaul he levied artisans for the work in Britain, a circumstance which points to a condition of great prosperity. The western mines were being actively worked; Damnonia (Devon and Cornwall) was evidently being drawn much more closely into the Roman sphere of civilization. Something of the same kind seems to have been taking place north of the Wall, though here the Imperial influence was of a much fainter character.

Something must be said of the towns. They were not numerous or specially important. It must be remembered that Britain as a province was comparatively poor and unsettled as compared with Spain or Asia Minor. Its relative prosperity at this period was thrown into relief by the fact that Gaul had long been suffering from barbarian invasions; it is not improbable that there had been immigration from the Continent. To return to the towns: Camulodunum seems never to have recovered from its destruction by Boudicca. When it was rebuilt, its walls enclosed an area less than that of several other places. Glevum, and probably Lindum, were *colonia*; Verulam had been a *municipuum* since the commencement of the Roman epoch. Eboracum was undoubtedly the principal place north of the Trent; Corinium, Viroconium, Calleva, Isca Silurum, and other places, had con siderable local importance. Aqure Sulis was much frequented as a health resort; but the most important city of the province from the time of Carausius onwards was undoubtedly London, which about 340 received the title of Augusta, with, in all probability, exceptional privileges. Its name was far too ancient to be ousted by a mere honorary appellation, but Londinium Augusta was certainly the largest and most important, if not the finest, of Romano-British towns. Its walls enclosed an area of some 380 acres. The average of population per acre in modern London is about sixty, but in Berlin it is one hundred. Sanitation was ill-understood in those days, and in a commercial centre like London the crowding was probably often dense. The normal population may have been about 50,000. The area of Verulam was about 203 acres; its population, perhaps, 20,000. Such importance as it still retained may have been largely due to the fact that it was a pleasant place of resort from busy and overcrowded London. Viroconium, with an area of 170 acres, and Calleva with 102, can hardly be credited with more than 10,000 and 5,000 inhabitants respectively. Population does not flock into places of no special commercial importance. Glevum, Lindum, Eboracum, and Corinium were all perhaps, as large as Verulamium. Many of the ports on the south coast must have attained considerable size. But Britain, unlike Gaul, was not a province of great cities. Apart from resorts of merchants, such as London, the real centres of social life seem to have been the numerous villas.

Nor, apart from prosperity at certain periods, can Britain ever have been a paying province. The number of troops permanently maintained there must have approached 40,000; while Severus was in the island there were probably 100,000; in 400 the Notitia shows over 50,000. Besides the expense of the army, there was that of the vast and ever increasing bureaucracy, and of the maintenance of roads and military works.

When the chief towns were walled we do not know. There is some reason to think that the fortification of London was begun by Severus I, but it is probable that most of the wall dates from a later period. The opinion of the authors, based upon careful examination of the quality of the work, is that it was constructed in great haste. The wall of Verulam is especially strong and massive, but whether it is so early as it is claimed to be is some what doubtful. Inscriptions are plentiful on the Wall of Severus, but not on those of the towns; and since the practice of commemorative inscriptions tended to die out in the fourth century, we are, perhaps, justified in supposing that the fortification of the towns was undertaken comparatively late. Everything is doubtful at present. We only know that the 'departure of the Eagles' left most of the British towns walled. Since at Silchester the wall crosses the ends of streets diagonally, the inference is that it was built at a late date to enclose only the closely inhabited area.

About 343 the Picts, hitherto more or less quiescent, again took to the warpath. Apparently the defences of the North had been somewhat neglected; the Wall of Severus was pierced, Corstopitum burned. The Emperor Constans came in haste from Gaul in the winter to face the danger, drove back the raiders, and appears to have received some sort of homage from them, for Julius Firmicus speaks of the Emperor as having 'extended the Empire.' His coercion was at any rate severe enough to impose peace for seventeen years. But in 360 troubles again broke out. The Picts renewed their raids, and for the first time we hear of a new enemy to Britain – the Scots. They were destined to give their name to the northern part of Britain in the far future, but for the present they were probably neither more nor less than adventurers from Ireland. The name may signify a 'broken' or landless man, though the Scots as a whole appear to have had their home in north-east Ireland. Perhaps they were a confederation of broken clans and war-bands. They crossed to Caledonia, and established a settlement in the modern Argyll. At the same time some of the Picts had effected a small settlement in Ireland and in Galloway. The two peoples were thus in close communication, and a united attack from them was what might have been expected.

About 360, then, Picts and Scots began to direct raids upon the north and west of Roman Britain. After a while they were joined by the Attacotti, who seem to have been a confederation of the Britons beyond the Roman Wall – i.e., between Tyne and Forth. For a time these raids produced only slight effect, and in 360 Britain was exporting quantities of grain to Gaul for the relief of suffering provincials there. But by 364 the invaders were growing more daring. There is reason to think that other Irish tribes were assisting them, and now the 'Saxons' – that is Angles, Frisians, Jutes, as well as Saxons – appear once more on the scene. Ammianus Marcellinus says that they were 'in conspiracy'

– that is, were acting in unison – and this is very probable. In 367 they made a combined attack and broke up the defence by two almost simultaneous victories. The Roman Army of the North was defeated; its commander, Fullofaudes, was slain, and the force broken up and dispersed; while Nectarides, Count of the Saxon Shore, was defeated and slain by the Saxons. The results were very serious. Probably here and there detachments of troops held out behind the walls of the larger towns and fortresses; but the invaders seem to have overrun a great part of the country north of the Thames. Ammianus says that they dispersed over the country in small marauding bands.

The Emperor Valentinian I. sent to cope with this most dangerous irruption a gallant Spanish officer, Theodosius, entrusting to him large reinforcements of Teutonic mercenaries and two regiments of the Imperial Guard. Theodosius's first care was to clear the Midlands, a task involving much rapid marching and hard fighting, but successfully carried out. He wisely did not threaten disbanded troops with military punishment, and thus was able to rally the Army of Britain on the corps which accompanied him, and to completely reorganize it. In 369 he cleared the north, and, so Claudian tells us, pursued the enemy oversea to their refuges – presumably the Irish coast and the Hebrides. Whatever exaggeration may be behind the poet's eulogy, there is no doubt that Theodosius gained great and, for the time, decisive successes. Although the theory of a new 'province of Valeiitia' between the Walls of Hadrian and Antoninus is due to a misunderstanding of the words of Ammianus, there is some reason to think that Theodosius did in a sense advance the border. He abolished the 'Arcani,' a sort of frontier intelligence corps composed of border Britons, and this may imply supersession of them by advanced detachments of regulars. Secondly, we find Attacotti soon after serving in considerable numbers in the Roman army, a circumstance which seems to imply complete defeat, if not political subjection. Thirdly, while Ammianus says that Theodosius restored all the frontier forts, excavation appears to indicate that the line of the Wall with its mile-castles was not repaired. The evidence is not quite conclusive, for the remains of the last occupation lying nearest to the surface would be the first to perish. The frontier was guarded in force till forty years later. This has been contested by Mommsen, who suggested that the roll of the Army of Britain in the Notitia Dignitatum was copied from an earlier list in order to hide the chasm caused by the destruction of corps in the Picto-Scottish wars. Professor Oman has satisfactorily rebutted this theory. He points out that, though there is a remarkable survival of old regiments, yet intermingled with them are many with unquestionable fourth-century titles such as 'The Thundering Moors,' 'The Senior Lions,' and 'The Bears of Valentinian.' Claudian distinctly states that to meet Alaric, Stilicho withdrew troops from the North of Britain. Coins of Maximus (383–388) have been found on the Wall, proving an occupation until almost the end of the fourth century; and lacking, as there is, information of any great disaster, it cannot be asserted that the Roman hold on Britain was not effective until the last. The case of the Attacotti is suggestive, and there is evidence (some of it certainly late) that the British tribes between the walls were practically adjuncts of the province and co-operating in its defence.

The arrangements of Theodosius sufficed to ensure the safety of the province for some fourteen years. That much damage had been inflicted is certain, and perhaps Britain never entirely recovered from the effects of the invasions of 364–368. It has been suggested that Deva, Viroconium, and other towns in the west, had been destroyed by the Scots; but this seems very doubtful. A fact to be noted is that there was already a considerable Teutonic element in the island in the shape of many numeri formed out of prisoners taken in the chronic wars on the Rhine. In 371 the Emperor Valentinian sent over to Britain a whole Alemannic sub-tribe.

In 383 the Army of Britain revolted against Gratianus, the successor of Valentinian I, and proclaimed as Emperor an able Spanish general, Magnus Clemens Maximus, who held high command in the island, but had been passed over by Gratian's ministers for promotion. The Picts and Scots seized the opportunity to renew their raids, but were repelled by Maximus, who then, however, crossed to Gaul to expel Gratian. The troops joined him, Gratian was murdered by one of his officers, and Maximus became supreme over Gaul and Spain. Gratian's brother, Valentinian II, retained Italy for a while, but in 387 Maximus expelled him. He hoped, perhaps, to repeat the deeds of Constantine I, who had conquered the whole empire from the West, but fate decreed otherwise. In 388 Theodosius I, Emperor of the East, son of Count Theodosius, came up against him, and he was defeated at Aquileia, captured, and executed.

Gildas says that, to defend himself against Theodosius, Maximus stripped Britain of her warriors, and so paved the way for the ruin that was to come. This, however, is very doubtful, and Gildas cannot be relied upon except for his own times. But Claudian may be believed when he says that Britain suffered from Pictish and Scottish raids, though he no doubt paints his picture in the darkest colours. The 'Historia Brittonum' says that about 385–390 the Scots were in possession of North Wales, but that they were driven out by an army led by Cunedda and his eight sons from the land of the Otadini – i.e., the Lothians (Manau Gododin). If this statement – and it is very precise – may be taken as historical fact, it can only mean that the Otadini now formed part of the province, and that an auxiliary force led by one of their chiefs was employed to clear North Wales of the Scots. Cunedda was clearly a Romanized Briton; his father Æternus and his grandfather Paternus bear just the quaint names that were common among Romans in the fourth century. It is possible that Cunedda's campaign was initiated by Maximus. 'Maxim Gwledig' (Maximus Imperator) bulks largely in British legend, and it is permissible to suppose that there was some solid reason for the respect paid to his memory. The theory that Wales, and possibly Damnonia, were defended by their own local levies accounts satisfactorily for the fact that in the Notitia we find no regular troops stationed in those regions. It also explains the early formation of monarchical states among them, which is a feature of the next century. Finally, if a large part of the warriors of the Otadini went to Wales, we might expect to find the defence of the north weakened, and, if Claudian may be trusted, this is what did happen.

When Theodosius the Great died in 395 the Roman Empire was already sorely pressed, but for more than ten years ruin was staved off by the great Vandal Stilicho, guardian of the weak young Emperor Honorius, and Commander-in-Chief in the West. Amongst other things, he reorganized the defences of Britain. The General in the North was called the 'Duke of the Britains' (Dux Britanniarum). From

Brancaster, in Norfolk, to Southampton Water extended the district of the Count of the Saxon Shore (Comes Littorzs Saxonici). Both were under the supreme command of the Count of the Britains (Comes Britanniarum), who controlled a reserve force which could be used at need to strengthen either north or east. The VIth Legion was still at York; the IInd was now at Rutupire; and there were besides thirty-seven auxiliary regiments of infantry and sixteen of cavalry – nearly 60,000 men in all. There were also two naval squadrons – one stationed on the 'Saxon Shore,' the other off the Lancashire coast.

One most important fact must be kept steadily in mind: the Army of Britain, though it contained some foreign corps and a large number of soldiers of foreign extraction, was in the main British in composition and feeling. For centuries the troops of each Roman province had been very largely recruited locally, either by conscripts or the children of the soldiers themselves, often trained to camp-life and war from their youth up. A so-called Moorish cohort would perhaps not contain a single Moor, and so on throughout the army. A regiment stationed in Britain kept its name, but was made up with British recruits.

In 402 King Alaric and the Visigoths set out to invade Italy, and Stilicho was forced to weaken the Army of Britain for the defence of Ravenna and Rome. Among the troops withdrawn was the VIth Legion – its long residence at York at last at an end –and none of them ever came back; for though Stilicho hurled invasion after invasion out of Italy, on 1 January 406, a horde of Teutons poured over the frozen Rhine and began to waste Gaul. Like an army whose line has been pierced, the provinces found the Germans interposed between them, and Britain was cut off from Italy.

Thereupon the Army of Britain appears to have decided that Honorius and Stilicho were useless as defenders of the Empire, and resolved to save it themselves – by mutinying! They selected a certain Marcus as emperor, and almost immediately murdered him. A second, named Gratianus, had the same fate; but the third, Constantine, was made of sterner stuff, and wore the purple for over three years – perhaps because he was wise enough to leave Britain. He decided to imitate the example of 'Maxim Gwledig,' and crossed to Gaul in 407. This is the event so often, and wrongly, caped the 'departure of the legions.'

Constantine had been chosen Emperor in order to carry out the task with which Stilicho had failed to successfully grapple. Is it to be supposed that he would have dared to leave Britain defenceless, even had he so desired? The idea is absurd. He no doubt took to Gaul a considerable force, which must have been mainly British, and his chief general, Gerontius (Geraint), was a Briton. But to suppose that, as Gildas wails, the province was left defenceless, and that the inhabitants were so effeminate and cowardly as to be incapable of bearing arms, cannot be allowed. It is certain that the Britons were among the best fighting peoples of the Empire, and when Constantine crossed to Gaul in 407 he undoubtedly left his base properly garrisoned. It is not even certain that the IInd Legion left Britain.

Constantine laid hands on a great part of Gaul and Spain – so far as they were not held by barbarians – and marched down to the Rhone to oust Honorius, who had just murdered his guardian and principal stay, the great Stilicho. Gerontius, however, revolted from him, and in 411 he was besieged in Arelate (Arles), captured, and executed. Meanwhile; what of Britain? In 409 came the first mutterings of the coming storm. The Saxons and their allies made raids both on Britain and Gaul. Thereupon the provincials disowned Constantine, who was clearly no more of a success than Stilicho, expelled his officials, elected others of their own choosing, raised new levies of troops, and repulsed the raiders. This is vouched for by the chronicler Zosimus. The ministers of Honorius, beset by many troubles, had already sent word to the British communities that they must defend themselves, and the provincials probably regarded their action as one of adherence to the legitimate Emperor as against usurpers of the type of Constantine. Certainly there was no conscious withdrawal from the Empire.

The course of events can only be dimly conjectured. In the east the Romanized cities probably took the lead. In the west and north matters went differently. These regions were less civilized, and the political unit was the tribe and not the city. In North Wales Cunedda was practically king, and small monarchialtates soon sprang up elsewhere. In the north, about 450, St Patrick tells us of a military state (Strathclyde), ruled by a chief whom he calls Coroticus, who possessed both a paid army and a fleet, and had not only beaten off the Scots, but had made retaliating raids on Ireland. Both Cunedda and Coroticus are called Gwledig (overlord) in the Welsh genealogies, and Cunedda at least appears to have held the post of Dux Britanniarum (General of the Northern Frontier). Apparently after his death a new state named Reged arose on the Wall; it was founded by Coel – the 'Old King Cole' of an irreverent nursery rhyme. Speaking roughly, we may say that in South Wales and Damnonia tribal kingdoms, in North Wales and the north-west military states, were the rule; while the cities apparently kept up Roman traditions, and by means of their walls maintained independence.

It will be seen that in many ways the outlook was bad for Britain. The interests of the military chiefs of the tribal dynasts and of the Romanized cities were certain to diverge, and hostilities be· tween them were almost inevitable. Probably even the cities did not always find co-operation easy. It is possible that there were already numbers of Teutons in the country; there may have been Teutonic settlements on the coast of Lothian as early as 400. The fleet of the Saxon Shore had apparently disappeared, presumably during the troubled period 407–411. Finally, the country lacked the unifying bond of a common religion. It is practically certain that though the Christian Church in Britain was a vigorous organization, its adherents were in a minority. The church at Calleva is so small as to make it certain that the Christian population was only some hundreds in number, the total of inhabitants being, perhaps, 5,000. The fragments of a local god were found by the explorers around its pedestal – i.e., the statue was standing there when disaster overtook the place. When St Germanus visited Britain in 429 he baptized thousands of converts. Probably in Britain, as elsewhere in the failing Empire, the adhesion of the upper classes to Christianity was nominal or non-existent, as it was to be for some generations; and the majority among the masses was frankly pagan.

Thus divided, distracted, with a defensive system disorganized by repeated withdrawals or shifting of troops, and with little prospect of co-operation between its cities and tribal cantons, Britain had to face attacks from three sides. On the north were the restless Picts, on the west the Scots, on the east the Teutons.

To construct anything like a connected narrative out of the few authorities who shed light on this period is almost, if not quite, impossible.

The whole epoch has been called the 'lost period,' but it would not be by any means unfair to describe it as neglected. The authorities are scanty, obscure, and hopelessly confused; but it is possible, by careful study, to construct a not improbable skeleton of facts.

From 409 to 429 we have no clear indication of the course of events in Britain. It seems, however, to have been somewhat as follows:

Internally the process of reorganization with city states, tribal principalities, and military monarchies went on, probably with much jarring and intense strife, of which there are indications in Gildas, and the queer mosaic of fairy tales, legends, genealogies, and scraps of lost chronicles called the 'Historia Brittonum.' The most remarkable fact is that the Picts and Teutons were in communication, and acted at times in conjunction. Various statements in the Life of St Germanus, and in the 'Historia Brittonum' lead one to infer that the earliest settlements of the English in Britain were neither in the south nor the east, but on the Firth of Forth. According to Northumbrian genealogies in the 'Historia Brittonum,' Soemil, the predecessor of Aella of Deira, in the fifth generation, was the first to separate Deira from Bernicia. This must mean that he founded a Teutonic principality in the north-east Bernicia is, apparently, a corruption of Brigahtia (Bryneich, or Berneich, in the 'Historia').

If, as early as 420 (Soemil can hardly be placed much later), the Angles were able to effect permanent settlements in north-east Britain, they were probably raiding there years before. That their raids, more or less in conjunction with the Picts, penetrated a considerable distance south is also probable, though the establishment of the kingdoms of Strathclyde and Reged in this quarter tended to check them. It was probably during the intense struggles, which resulted in the founding of these states, that the English effected their lodgments. The men of Strathclyde and Reged soon began a series of fierce attacks upon them, and for a century and a half they were confined to narrow, and perhaps disconnected, slips of coast; but once established, they were never really dislodged. The Britons, who had the Picts and Scots also on their hands, and were further distracted by dynastic broils, never made the united attack which might have driven the English, to use Napoleon's famous phrase, 'into the sea.'

In the west the Britons were probably more occupied with the Scots and Irish than with Picts, though it is highly probable that German pirate squadrons occasionally harassed the south-west. In Lancashire and western Yorkshire was the kingdom of Theyrnllwg, and to the east another called Elmet, whose capital was Loidis (Leeds). Both these states may have represented sub-tribes of the Brigantes. In the western Midlands was the kingdom of Powys, and in the south-west Damnonia. In Wales there were at least three states, probably corresponding to the old tribal cantons of the Ordovices, Silures, and Demetce. Gwynedd, under the dynasty of Cunedda, appears to have been generally regarded as the chief state, and the suzerainty of its kings was sometimes effective. There are indications that Cunedda, at least, ruled both Gwynedd and Theyrnllwg, but, as usual in Celtic dynasties, his successors divided his heritage.

On the whole, it seems, as is natural, that while the British states were in course of formation, the Picts and Scots were able to raid the province with com parative success for some years. About 425 Dathi, Ard-righ (suzerain king) of Ireland, is said, in the Irish annals, to have been slain oversea; and this may have occurred on a raid against the Britons. In 429 Germanus, Bishop of Auxerre, who had formerly been 'Dux' of Atemorica, and Lupus, Bishop of Troyes, came to Britain to combat the Pelagian heresy which had sprung up in the island. It is curious that a Church which had so far failed to Christianize the province could produce a heresiarch like Pelagius; but the phenomenon is not by any means unparalleled.

Germanus was one of those fine men about whom all that was best of society rallied in those terrible days. One biography of him, written by a Gallic priest, survives; another, probably composed in Britain, is lost, but was known to one of the compilers of the 'Historia Brittonum.'

Germanus and Lupus met their Pelagian opponents in synod at Verulam. We are told that they worshipped at the tomb of St Alban; and as this lay outside the walls, it may be considered as certain that the south-east had not been visited by raiders. The sanctity of the spot explains the choice of it as the meeting place. We might rather have expected London, but it is noteworthy that St Paul's is said to have been built on the site, not of a former church, but of a temple of Apollo; and it is possible that London, a great resort of merchants, was rather a stronghold of eclecticism, if not paganism, than of Christianity.

The Gallic bishops had other and more mundane work to do before they departed. Some part of the island, probably the north-east, was being wasted by a joint invasion of Picts and 'Saxons.' There must have been men in the British levies opposing them who had heard of Germanus as a soldier – officers and men of the old Imperial cohorts – and a message was sent begging the Gallic bishops to join the camp. The point upon which the biographer dwells is naturally the conversion and baptism on the eve of battle of thousands of the pagan peasant soldiers, but we may suspect that the old warrior Germanus was busily engaged as well in drilling and organizing his motley troops. His generalship appears to have been very good; he drew the enemy into a battle on his own chosen ground. The British army was stationed in a valley, the centre in battle array at its head, the wings carefully concealed, thrown forward along both sides. To inspirit the new levies, Germanus gave as the word for the day 'Alleluia.'

The 'Saxons' and Picts, presumably in the dense column formation common to barbarians, pushed boldly up the valley against the British centre, but when they came to close quarters Germanus let loose the ambushed wings. With wild shouts of 'Alleluia! Alleluia!' the Britons poured down to the attack, and a complete rout ensued, the barbarians breaking up and throwing away their arms in panic stricken flight. A river lay athwart their line of retreat, and the passage of this proved as fatal as the battle. The result appears to have been to secure the north for a time at least. When next we get a glimpse of these regions we find a strong British state taking the offensive against the Picts, and gaining territory from them; this may very well have been due to the victory of Germanus. The battlefield cannot be identified, but it is as well to warn visitors to Maes Garmon, near Mold, that this site is an extremely unlikely one. Picts are not likely to have raided in this direction, and the English did not appear there for at least a century and a half.

It is to be inferred from the 'Vita S. Germani' that in the south-east at least Britain was still under Roman civil government. We hear nothing of kings or even chiefs. Roman official titles are mentioned, and we are told that the magnates were richly attired. It is impossible to make anything of the strange statement in the 'Anglo-Saxon Chronicle' that in 418 the Romans in Britain burned their treasures and fled to Gaul. The Chronicle is far too late to be of any authority for this period. Its chronology cannot in any case be depended upon; but it is just possible that there really was during this period a migration of some sort, perhaps of non-British officials and their families. It must not be forgotten that Britain not only extended northward to the Forth, but also, perhaps, already had a colony in Gaul – the modern Brittany. The 'Historia Brittonum' makes the quite credible statement (though some of the details look rather absurd) that this settlement was initiated by Magnus Maximus, but, at any rate, we know from Sidonius Apollinaris that in 469 it was a very large one. Possibly, the statement above may refer to some incident connected with Brittany.

Finally, it is very necessary even today to warn readers against the foolish idea that Romans and Britons were at this date distinct peoples. A Roman meant during the Imperial period anyone under the Roman Government possessing civil rights – that is, almost all the free population. A Roman might be by birth a Briton, a Gaul, an Italian, a Greek, an Illyrian, a Jew; and a Briton or a Greek was neither more nor less a Roman than an Italian. The average Roman legion rarely contained Italians, much less inhabitants of the city of Rome; but, nevertheless, the soldiers were Roman. So with the civil administration: a Roman Ministry might contain members of every race under the Roman rule. Once, again, we must repeat that men were Roman by virtue of their political status, and not by reason of their national origin. The Britons were Romans – Romano-Hellenic, that is, in manner and customs, Latin in speech. The Roman government never definitely abandoned Britain. In the troubles of the fifth century the province was left, like many other regions, under local autonomy until such time as the central government could again exercise control, and for various reasons this never occurred. The country almost insensibly drifted apart from the labouring Roman world, but a hundred years later its people still called themselves 'Cives,' and were proud that they were Romans.

After the events of 429, it appears that the course of history somewhat changed. The 'Alleluia' victory apparently checked serious foreign invasions, but there is no reason to doubt that, as the 'Historia' says, Britain was in alarm. The Roman world was in wild disorder, which must have affected Britain; but when, in 447, Germanus once more came to combat Pelagianism, we do not hear of foreign war. Yet a Gallic chronicle says that Britain was conquered by the Saxons in 441, and Gildas states that in 446 some British provincials sent a miserable letter, called 'The groans of the Britons,' to the great general Aetius, who then upheld the Roman name in Gaul. The latter statement we can neither accept nor deny. Possibly it is only one of Gildas's rhetorical flights; possibly, if the incident occurred, it referred only to a single community. The Gallic chronicler may have been misinformed, or his chronology may be wrong. In any case, his statement must be rejected. Perhaps there was a raid in 441, the consequences of which were exaggerated by those who were responsible for the report made of it in Gaul. It seems impossible that, if the English conquest had already begun in 447, we should hear nothing of it in connection with the second visit of Germanus.

The only conclusion to which it is possible to come is that after the 'Alleluia' victory Britain, though more or less harassed by sporadic raids, was for some years comparatively free from barbarian attacks.

BRITAIN FROM ABOUT 500–570.

Showing the probable effects of the Romano-British rally under Ambrosius Aurelianus
and his successors. No towns are indicated within the English areas, as it is
probable that all had been deserted or destroyed.

IV

The English Conquest

Although the English invasion of Britain is by far the most important of all those which have affected the island, it is impossible to focus any very clearly defined picture of the happenings during the long period of nearly two centuries that followed the so-called departure of the Romans. The picture is blurred, but certain strong outlines are conspicuous, and in this chapter an attempt has been made to concentrate attention on these salient features.

The incident which led to the English invaders obtaining a secure foothold in south-east Britain was probably connected with internal troubles rather than foreign invasions. The Celtic chieftains of the south-west were less occupied than their northern contemporaries in repelling foreign invaders. They must have cast longing eyes upon the wealthy Romanized cities, and cherished hopes of bringing them, or some of them, under their sway. Vortigern, one of these rulers, probably prince of the Silures, seems to have partially succeeded in doing so, and about AD 450 appears as supreme over the south as far as Dover Straits. Whether his suzerainty extended north of the Thames must be considered very doubtful. The 'Historia Brittonum' describes the situation as follows:

After the above-said war, the assassination of their ulers, and the victory of Maximus, who slew Gratian, *and the termination of the Roman power in Britain, they were in alarm forty years.* Vortigern then reigned in Britain, and in his time the people had cause of dread, not only from the inroads of the Picts and Scots, *but also from the Romans, and their apprehensions of Ambrosius.*

The passage is a very confused one, and what appear to be the significant sentences are italicized. The opening statement is a kind of summing-up of the confused sections which precede it. It has been seriously misunderstood by several authors, but its meaning is fairly obvious. The chronology of the 'Historia' is its most hopeless feature, but here it presents no great difficulty. Forty years after the end of the Roman power, Vortigern reigned in Britain. As we have seen, direct Roman rule ended in 410–411. We therefore arrive at the year 450–451. Bede says that Hengist entered Britain in the reign of Marcianus and Valentinian III, i.e., after 450; but he is out in his reckoning, and so makes the date AD 449 Gildas makes it after 446. Probably it was after 447, for in that year St Germanus again came to Britain, and no foreign troubles are mentioned. On the other hand, the 'Historia' says that Vortigern died while St Germanus was in the island – i.e., in 447. This would place the invasion of Kent in 445 or 446, and if it really did occur then, it agrees somewhat better with the famous letter to Aetius recorded by Gildas. But we dare not trust Gildas for anything before 470, and the 'Life of St Germanus' used by the compilers of the 'Historia' was evidently a very fanciful work. On the whole the chronology of the English invasions is very uncertain. The one definite indication is that Vortigern's reception of Hengist took place forty years after the end of Roman power in Britain.

Vortigern was also in fear of Ambrosius. This is a most interesting statement. The Ambrosius here mentioned may very well have been the father of the greater figure soon to be noticed. The name is a Latin one, and Ambrosius was almost certainly the leader of the Romanized inhabitants as distinct from the Kymry of the West. His family seems to have been a notable one, for we can hardly doubt that they are the forbears of the Ambrosius Aurelianus celebrated by Gildas. Where Ambrosius had his stronghold is not known; quite possibly he was in league with London, Verulam, and other Roman towns, and was perhaps the chief of their forces.

Finally, Vortigern was afraid of the Romans. This is probably exactly the state of affairs if he reigned from about 440 to 450; for the great general Aetius was very active in Gaul during this period, and may have sent assistance to the Romanizing party in Britain. Quite possibly in the letters mentioned by Gildas the 'barbarians' were the Kymry, and the second visit of St Germanus may have been as much political as religious.

However this may be – and everything during this period is largely conjecture – there is no reason to doubt that Vortigern, whose suzerainty was evidently a most uneasy one, did, as the 'Historia' says, employ German mercenaries under Hengist and Hors, or Horsa. Very likely he had other bands in his pay, but the fame of this one has outshone that of the rest.

Hengist is practically beyond doubt an authentic historical figure. He is probably to be identified with the Hengist in the famous poem of Beowulf, who made a truce with the Frisian slayers of his lord Hmef. The custom was for the followers to die with their lord or avenge him. The fact that Hengist did neither would be quite enough to cause his disgrace, and the 'Historia Brittonum' distinctly says that he was an exile. It also appears to bear out the 'Historia's' character of him as a cunning and low-minded, if able, man.

The followers of Hengist only manned three ships, and possibly they were in a distressed condition when Vortigern took them under his protection. As the small band can hardly have been of much account by itself, we must suppose either that the king employed Hengist to raise a mercenary force, or that when the breach between employers and employed occurred, the latter were joined by swarms of adventurers. The 'Historia' says that, owing to Hengist's persuasions, Vortigern employed in all fifty-nine ships' crews. The romantic feature of the affair, according to the 'Historia,' is that Vortigern fell violently in love with Hengist's daughter, who accompanied him, and married her. It was not quite an honour for the Jutish maiden Hrothwyn (Rowena), if indeed that was her name, for Vortigern's amours were numerous and indiscriminate. She merely became one of his harem. But if the incident be true, it is another application of the French proverb, *Cherchez la femme.* The marriage was certainly the beginning of woes for Britain.

Vortigern apparently defeated and slew Ambrosius with the help of his German mercenaries, but then his troubles began. The Isle of Ruim

(Thanet) had been assigned as the land-recompense of the mercenaries, but they declared that it was too small. Bede says that it supported six hundred families in his day, and as fifty-nine ships' crews would mean hardly less than fifteen hundred warriors, the latter were, from their own point of view, perfectly right. In any case, they were accustomed to living by their swords, and presumably believed that Vortigern, allied to them by marriage, would give way to pressure exercised by the old and still practised methods of slaughter and pillage.

At any rate, in 455, if we may trust the 'Anglo Saxon Chronicle,' the bands of Hengist broke out of Thanet and began to move westward, ravaging as they went. Probably at first they did not attack the walled towns; they may merely have intended an armed protest. Where Vortigern was or what he did we cannot say; his sons Vortimer and Categirn led the opposition to the invaders. A battle was fought at a place not specified, and Hengist was driven back into Thanet. Presumably reinforced from the Continent, he again emerged from his fastness, and encountered Vortimer in two battles, both claimed as British victories, but clearly indecisive. One was on the Durgwentid River (perhaps either the Stour or Darenth), the other at Rithergabail or Episford, generally supposed to be Aylesford on the Medway. Horsa and Categirn were both slain. It was apparently an English reverse, for the fourth battle was fought by a Roman monument on the shore of the Channel. The invaders were defeated and driven on board their ships; but Vortimer, unfortunately for the Britons, died soon afterwards, perhaps of wounds received in the battle. The story goes that he desired his followers to bury him at the spot where Hengist had landed – presumably therefore at Ebbsfleet – so that in death he might keep watch over the country that he had for the moment saved. He was not obeyed. Geoffrey of Monmouth, who may perhaps have had some written authority for his statement, says that he was buried at London.

Vortigern now reappears on the scene, and opens negotiations with the invaders. The 'Historia' says that Hengist arranged a conference and banquet of six hundred unarmed notables, three hundred from each side. He, however, ordered his own followers to hide knives in their shoes, and when the feast was in full progress every Jute drew his dagger upon his helpless British comrade. Vortigern alone was spared, and, probably in fear of his life, concluded peace on very disadvantageous terms. There is no reason to discredit the story, except the quite inadequate one that the ancestors of Englishmen could not be guilty of such treachery.

This catastrophe appears to have ended Vortigern's sovereignty in the south, and he fled to his own Welsh realm. There is a wild legend that Germanus called down fire from heaven upon him, but Germanus had died in Gaul some years before. The motive of the legend is obvious: no fate was too terrible for the hated dynast who had betrayed Britain, and the temptation to bring in Germanus must have been irresistible. Vortigern's genealogy appears to have been well known, and his descendants were ruling in south-east Wales ten generations later.

Hengist does not ever appear to have lost Thanet, and in the disorder after Vortigern's death he was again able to invade Kent. In 457 he won a victory at Crayford, and the Britons retreated to the walls of London; yet in 465, and again in 473, the invaders are apparently still fighting in Kent. As the Jutish kingdom never extended far beyond the bounds of the modern county, there is every reason to believe that the conquest of Kent was a very slow and difficult process.

Meanwhile, however, the successes of Hengist attracted the notice of his kinsfolk in Germany, and expeditions, not for purposes of plunder, but for permanent conquest, were being formed. The supposition must be put aside that England was founded as a number of separate states by independent bands of invaders. That the Britons made a stern resistance is beyond doubt, and to have been successful the invaders must have been acting in large and more or less organized bodies. Moreover, the invasions were national ones. Kent, indeed, possibly Sussex, may have been independent creations by chiefs of bodies of mixed mercenaries, but the whole English people (Angel-cynn) sooner or later took part in the settlement. It was a great national migration, and undoubtedly one of the most remarkable in history. The emigrants could not march by land, like the Goths and Franks, in great masses, which could bear down resistance by sheer weight of numbers and courage. They had to transfer themselves over hundreds of miles of sea in more or less frail open craft, at the mercy of every gale; yet in the course of a century the name of Angle had vanished from the Continent, and become peculiar to Britain. Possibly a remnant of the people remained behind; to this day a district of Schleswig bears the name of Angeln.

Bede says that the invaders came from three nations of Germany, the Angles, Saxons, and Jutes. This appears to be so far true in that these three peoples took part in the migration; but while practically the entire English nation came, they were accompanied by only a few Saxons and a portion of the Jutes. It is very probable, also, that fragments of nearly all the Teutonic tribes on the Continent were in the invading hosts. The kingdom of Kent is said to have been Jutish; certainly its social structure differed remarkably from that of the other English states, but Hengist himself seems to have been an Angle. Bede says that the Kentish Code was written in the English language. The confused grammatical structure of the present English tongue certainly points to a mingling of races, and on the whole we may infer that the invasion was conducted not only by the Angles, but by many kindred tribes, and that these latter in course of time gradually came to regard themselves as English also. Early mediaeval writers use the terms 'Angle' and 'Saxon' indiscriminately.

The invaders were no mere barbarians. Their deeds were often barbarous enough, no doubt; but it must be said that the picture drawn by Bede of kings like Aethelberht and Eadwine and their followers shows them in a very favourable light. Perhaps Bede idealizes; possibly in the course of a century the invaders had softened somewhat; but as that century had been passed for the most part in warfare, the latter conclusion is unlikely. At any rate, the English brought with them a highly organized social system, and judging merely from recorded facts, they were, as a nation, possessed of many of the elements of civilization.

Neither were the invaders a mere disorderly throng of ill-armed and unarmoured marauders. The evidence of archaology is all to the effect that they were acquainted with, and used, defensive armour. Probably only the upper classes wore it, but as elaborate and costly coats of mail have been found in graves in Schleswig and Denmark dating from this period, this deduction cannot be made without qualification. Mail and weapons, which latter have been found in thousands, would hardly be buried, and therefore lost, unless they could be easily replaced. The chiefs undoubtedly rode to battle; the deposits are full of horse-trappings. On the whole, we may imagine the armies which conquered Britain as being more or less like those of the Homeric Greeks. The nucleus consisted of the king and his retinue, with a larger or smaller following of nobles and their retainers equipped with mailshirt, helmet, and shield, and armed with sword and spear. Though they rode to war, they probably, with few exceptions, fought on foot. Whether their peasantry were regarded as fighting men is doubtful. Professor Chadwick thinks that they were not. In that case the conquest of England was effected by armies consisting of chiefs with larger or smaller bands of well-armed followers combined into armies under kings or generals. Perhaps only when they had gained a firm foothold in the country did the English bring over their peasant retainers and serfs to till the land, while the fighting men protected them or carried out further conquests. The frequent gaps in the war-bands may have been filled up partly by levies from the peasantry, partly by adventurers from all sides. Success must have brought many of the latter to the English standards.

Having said so much, we will proceed to give, as far as is possible, a sketch of the conquest; but the reader must be warned that it is largely conjecture. The skeleton narrative which follows has been constructed with care, after study and comparison of the earliest authorities – Gildas, Nennius, and Bede, and the few other early mediceval chroniclers who notice Britain – but probably there is hardly a statement which is not open to criticism.

At first the invaders appear to have come rather as bands of raiders than as conquering armies, but Gildas implies that some of them, at least, dashed right across the island to the Irish Sea. His lurid descriptions of the destruction of towns may be taken for what they are worth; it is to be noted that he does not name one of them. He appears to say that the shrine of St Alban had been destroyed, but as it almost certainly lay outside Verulam, it need not be assumed that the town shared its fate. As a fact, judging from what occurred on the Continent, walled towns were able to defy large hosts of barbarians.

No doubt the raids were destructive enough, and Gildas, despite his exasperating style, probably does not overstate the misery in those districts which were wasted by the marauders. But it is certainly rash to deduce from his narrative that the whole of Eastern Britain up to the central watershed, including all the important Roman towns, was conquered and ruined within a few years after 450. The archaeological evidence is of the scantiest The sites of the greater Roman towns are almost all built upon. Calleva and Venta Silurum were small places and of no special importance. The site of Verulam has scarcely been touched.

It is needless to say that all maps of Britain at this period are purely conjectural. There is no real clue as to the lines of advance of the invaders. The probability is that they made their way inland along the rivers. After a time the bands are found coalescing into armies; for this must be the meaning of Bede's statement that Aella, whose coming is placed by the 'Anglo-Saxon Chronicle' in 477, was the first 'Bretwalda.' The chronology is, of course, worthless, but that Aella really did command the English host for a time is highly probable. His main sphere of action is said by the Chronicle to have been Sussex; but probably, commanding as he did an army whose base was the sea, he had other fields of operations. His chief exploit is said to have been the storm of Anderida (Pevensey) in 491, according to the Chronicle, but probably earlier. He, with his son Cissa, 'beset Anderida, and slew all that were therein, nor was there afterwards one Briton left.'

The Britons, according to Gildas, were for a while unable to make any effective resistance to the attacks of their enemies, who were being steadily reinforced from overseas; but after a weary time of ravage and defeat, a Roman (Romanized Briton) named Am brosius Aurelianus, perhaps a son of the Ambrosius who had opposed Vortigern, took the lead. The plan of accepting the suzerainty of Kymric dynasts for the sake of peace and unity had led to disaster, and men were ready to rally to one who stood for Roman traditions. Ambrosius succeeded in organising an effective resistance, and the result seems to have been that he was acknowledged as king in the south at least. The 'Historia Brittonum' states that Vortigern's son Pascentius was subject to him, and in the Welsh traditions he appears as 'Emrys Gwledig.'

Nevertheless, the success was only partial. It appears certain that the Teutons were firmly established on the eastern coast as well as in Kent and Sussex. Ambrosius fought against them incessantly with varying fortune all through his reign, but if he confined them to the territory which they had already won, and checked their raids inland, it was as much as he could do. The invaders' base was the sea, and they could attack when and where they pleased; we do not hear, nor is it probable, that Ambrosius succeeded in organizing a navy, and no other means could have definitely checked the advance. On the other hand, Ambrosius probably had to some extent the advantage which unity of command gives, while his opponents' operations would often be disunited and erratic. In the midst of the struggle Ambrosius died.

His gallant efforts appear to have produced important results. Not only was he able to pass on his power to his descendants, as Gildas witnesses, but a more or less united resistance was kept up against the invaders. In the place of Ambrosius the cities and kings appear to have chosen as Commander-in-Chief, or *Dux Bellorum*, a certain Artorius, famed in legend as 'King Arthur.' He may or may not have been the immediate successor of Aurelianus; perhaps here again Geoffrey of Monmouth had some authority for interposing a third figure between the two, though 'Uther' looks suspiciously like a variation of Arthur. Artorius may have been a relation of Ambrosius.

At any rate, his leadership was signalized by a long succession of victories. The 'Historia Brittonum' gives the rather suspicious round number of twelve, but as it is obtained by there having been four battles in the same locality, there is no obvious reason for doubting it.

The first battle was at the mouth of the river Gleni; the second, third, fourth, and fifth on the river Dubglas, in the region Linuis; the sixth on the river Bassas; the seventh in Celidon Wood. The eighth was at Gwinnion Castle, and in this fight it is especially noted that Arthur's standard was an image or picture of the Virgin. The ninth battle was at the City-of-the-Legion, the tenth on the Ribruit or Tribruit, and the eleventh on a mountain called Agned. The twelfth was at Mount Badon, and in it Arthur is credited with the slaughter, single-handed, of nine hundred and sixty Saxons!

Of these twelve engagements the field of the seventh is practically certain. Coit Celidon must be the Caledonian Forest (on the upper Forth). This fixes some of the battles at least as fought in the north; and this is rendered more probable, because one recension of the 'Historia' says that the Virgin of Gwinnion was afterwards deposited at Wedale, near Melrose. The Gleni may be the Glen in Northumberland. The Dubglas must clearly have been a most important strategic point if four battles were fought there.

If the first batch of battles occurred in the north, it is fair to assume that they were fought against the Angles, and this practically fixes them in the northeast. There is good reason for believing that the Angles had very early established themselves in this quarter. Now, it is worthy of note that there is today a streamlet called the Dunglass at the entrance of Cockbumspath, the pass through the eastern corner of the Lammermuirs, south-east of Dunbar, which played an important part in the Great Civil War over eleven centuries later. Cockburnspath is just the place at which one might expect battles between rival forces moving from north to south and vice versa. The hills around are still covered with the remains of fortifications, many apparently of great antiquity. It may be that the course of the war in this neighbourhood was as follows: The English moving south from their settlements on the Firth of Forth were met and defeated by Arthur, perhaps on the Glen, and retreated to Cockburnspath. After a succession of engagements, they were driven thence, again defeated on the Bassas (locality unknown), and finally pursued into the Caledonian Forest.

The seat of war then appears to shift southward. Gwinnion may have been fought to drive off some of the invaders who had got into the rear of the Britons while the latter were fighting at the Forth. Urbs Legionis is probably in this instance York. The Ribruit and Agned cannot be identified; Mons Badonis or Badonicus is supposed to have been Bath, but there is no reason for this identification; it probably arose out of the similarity between Badon and the English appellation of Aquae Sulis. Wadon Hill, near Avebury, and Badbury (Baden-burh) Rings in Dorset have both been identified with this mysterious site. It seems from Gildas that it was a fortress. Probably it was besieged by the invaders, and relieved by Arthur in a battle which stayed the English advance for many years.

The date of these events is doubtful. Gildas, in a sentence which is the despair of all Latinists, seems to say that the battle of Mons Badonicus was fought forty-four years and one month before he wrote his book. We know that he wrote some years before the death of King Mrelgwn of Gwynedd (AD 547). This fixes the date of the battle at about 500. The 'Annales Cambriae' put it in 516, but the 'Annales' are as late as the 'Anglo-Saxon Chronicle.' Mr E. B. Nicholson has suggested that the forty-four years are to be reckoned from the appearance of Ambrosius to 516. It is quite possible that the great leader did commence his campaigns about 472, but Gildas hardly gives us the impression of a man capable of very accurate chronology. But if he were born on the day of the battle, as he says, it would be a simple matter. On the whole, we may reasonably say that the battle was fought about the year 500, and its effect was to stay the advance of the English in the south for at least forty-four years.

One would willingly hear more of the men whose efforts for a while stayed the flowing English tide; but practically all that is known is here set down. The 'Annales Cambriae' state that twenty-one years after Mons Badonicus Arthur and Medrant fell in a battle at Camlan. Arthur is repeatedly mentioned in the bardic poems of Wales, but we cannot tell to what extent these works may have been altered in later ages.

Whatever the fate of Arthur, and whatever the extent and nature of his influence in Britain, his victories staved off ruin for half a century, but no longer. The curse of Britain was that there were too many dynasts for ever warring among themselves. The picture that Gildas has painted may be highly coloured, but there is no reason to doubt that when the danger appeared to be over, the old tribal quarrels began again. Strathclyde and Reged were divided among the different branches of the Houses of Coroticus and Coel. About 540 the energetic but unscrupulous and dissolute Mrelgwn, King of Gwynedd, succeeded in getting rid of his related competitors. He may also have asserted a primacy in the south and west, for Gildas calls him 'Insularis Draco' (Island Dragon), though it is true that this may simply refer to the fact that the seat of the Cunedda dynasty was at Aberffraw in Mona. Gildas overwhelms him with turgid invective and garbled quotations from Scripture – in fact, his so-called history is, on the face of it, nothing but a sermon directed at Mrelgwn. He also denounces two other Welsh dynasts – Vortipore of the Demetce, and Cuneglass of Powys, and two princes with Latin names – Constantinus of Damnonia and Aurelius Caninus. The first name of the latter suggests that he may have been one of those degenerate grandsons of Ambrosius Aurelianus of whom Gildas speaks.

It is in the interval between Mons Badonicus and 577 that the Saxon Chronicle places the conquest of Wessex. To discuss this matter in detail would be to occupy far more space than is here available, but it may be said, in short, that there is every reason to believe that the Chronicle's chronology is wrong; that it is highly improbable that the West Saxons ever came up Southampton Water, the shores of which were occupied by Jutes at an early date; finally, that Cerdic is a very doubtful figure. The West Saxons were also, and commonly, called Gewissce, 'the Confederates.' Cerdic is a Celtic name; it is, indeed, the same as Coroticus, or Caradoc, and this fact, coupled with the curious name of the kingdom, suggests that Cerdic may have been a Celtic prince, who founded a kingdom with the aid of English mercenaries or allies, and became so identified with them that his origin was forgotten. The latest opinion is that Wessex did not start from Hampshire at all. Some of the battles mentioned – i.e., that with Natanleod – may be authentic, but they were the work of Jutes. Any delimitation of the territory occupied by the invaders at the time must necessarily be a very vague one; but it is probable that when Gildas wrote they fell into three sections. South of the Thames – largely south of the Weald – a long English-Jutish strip of territory stretched from Southampton Water to Thanet, never reaching far inland except in Kent, which was solidly occupied, and, perhaps, always the wealthiest of the new States.

North of the Thames indications are even vaguer. Professor Oman is of opinion that all the Romano-British cities in Eastern Britain perished very early, mainly on the authority of Gildas, who appears to give 'a picture of a Celtic Britain which does not extend anywhere towards the east coast'.

To attempt to make any definite geographical deductions from a writer so vague as Gildas is rash; as a fact, we know that his five dynasts are only some of several, and the territory of one of them who bears the most suggestive name of all is not specified. Aurelius Caninus may just as well have been king of London and Verulam as of Glevum, Corinium, and Aquce Sulis. Opinion is steadily trending in the direction of a belief in the continuous existence of London through the 'lost' centuries. This is too great a question to discuss here, but on practical military grounds it may be pointed out that London, strongly fortified, apparently populous, and situated astride of a great river, was eminently fitted to be the curb of a barbarian invasion. There is also to be considered the curious fact that the country round London was called Middlesex, as if it at one time formed a sort of buffer between East and West Saxons. The name certainly seems to show that London and its territory became English late.

The English north of the Thames possibly lay north and east of a line drawn from Leicester to the mouth of the Thames. If so, their abode corresponded roughly to the later 'Danelaw.' They probably formed, like the Vikings, a confused mingling of petty kingdoms, earldoms and the camps of war bands. What was going on north of the Humber is not known, but certainly the Bernician Angles in Lothian were fighting hard with the British kingdoms of Strathclyde and Reged. Not until 547 did

English moorland, Yorkshire.

they take Bamborough. The beginnings of Deira were probably still later; it is not at all certain that the English had as yet any footing in Yorkshire. Had a second Ambrosius Aurelianus or Artorius arisen to coerce the warring British states into unity, the English settlements might have been conquered, as were those of the Danes by Alfred and Eadward I.

This was not to be. About 540 the Anglian settlements were fast increasing in strength. The whole 'Angel-cynn,' in fact, were streaming over to Britain every year as fast as their ships could take them. Probably they were forced on by the disorder in Europe, and the pressure caused by the migrating Slavs and the raiding Avars with their kindred tribes. At any rate, about 550 we find the English once more on the move, and this time the Britons had no Ambrosius or Arthur to save them.

About 547 King Ida of Bernicia took Dinguardi, soon to be Bebbanburh, and began to push southward in the teeth of a desperate resistance from the Britons of Reged under King Dutigern. The struggle was celebrated in the songs of the great bards, Talhcern, Aneurin, Taliesin, and Llywarch. Ida left twelve sons, several of whom reigned after him. The most celebrated was the fierce raider Theudric – 'Flamddwyn,' the 'Burner,' as the Britons called him. After much fighting, he was completely defeated by Urien of Reged, and forced to take refuge on Lindisfarne. But Urien was murdered by his own jealous kinsfolk in the hour of victory, and Theudric, reinforced by new Anglian war bands, was able to take the offensive again. The murder of Urien seems to have broken the British power. His son Owen was slain by the 'Burner,' and Theudric ranged up and down the country, wasting it mercilessly, and finally establishing English Bernicia so strongly that it was never again in peril (circa AD 570).

Meanwhile, in the south, too, about 571, the English had begun a fresh advance under Ceawlin, the first authentic king of the Gewissce or West Saxons. He probably commanded a large confederate army collected from all the English states between Humber and Thames. A great battle was fought at Bedford. The English were completely victorious, and conquered the whole of the south-east Midlands as far as the Thames. The towns captured are given their English names by the 'Anglo-Saxon Chronicle,' which is only to be expected; by the ninth century their Roman appellations had vanished. The effect of the victory would naturally be to leave London isolated. Possibly it maintained its independence for some time, but by 596 it was certainly included in Essex or Kent. Perhaps it had been in alliance with Kent for some time, for Ceawlin had hostilities with the young King Aethelberht, and the possession of London may have been the *casus belli*.

The battle of Bedford firmly established the kingdom of the Gewissce, and Ceawlin probably extended his sway southward to the Weald and the New Forest. Perhaps it was now that Calleva was finally abandoned. The confines of the Britons were narrowed, and the last seats of the old Roman civilization (if it had not by now entirely disappeared) were about to fall into the hands of the English.

In 577 Ceawlin went westward, perhaps from Calleva, with the whole host of the Gewissce. At Deorham, probably Derham, north of Bath, he met a confederate British army under three kings – Conmail, Farinmail, and Condidan. The last name may perhaps be read (Aurelius) Candidianus. The English victory was complete; the three kings were slain; Glevum, Corinium, and Aqure Sulis, together with the whole valley of the lower Severn, fell into the hands of the conquerors.

Ceawlin's later fortune was not equal to that of his earlier days. He was defeated in an attempt to penetrate Wales, and his motley host then revolted and deposed him. The Gewissan state became subject to Aethelberht of Kent, who now succeeded to Ceawlin's position of 'Bretwalda.' Nevertheless, Ceawlin had done his work; the battle of Deorham was the most decisive struggle in the war which won Britain for the English.

North of the Humber, after the death of Aethelric, the last of Ida's sons, Aethelfrith, the son of Aethelric, became king of Bernicia about 593. He made himself supreme also over Deira, and in 603 gained a most complete and decisive victory over a confederation of Strathclydian and Regedian Britons, Scots, and Irish from Ulster, under Aedan, King of the Scots of Dalriada. The result was the destruction of Reged, which survived only in a few scattered fragments, and the consolidation of English power in the north. Then, in 613, the Northumbrian king advanced upon Deva; a glance at the map will show his admirable strategy. Bede's half-sorrowful praise of him (he was a heathen) was evidently well deserved.

Before Deva there gathered for battle Cadwan, King of Gwynedd, the most powerful of the Kymric princes; Brochmail, King of Theyrnllwg; and Selim, perhaps Prince of Powys. Near Deva lay the great monastery of Bangor Iscoed, with its 2,100 monks; and, after spending three days in prayer and fasting, 1,200 of the latter accompanied the Britons to the field. They stood apart, and a detachment of warriors under Brochmail guarded them. Aethelfrith watched the gestures and movements of the strange company, and the sound of their chants and prayers floated across to him. 'They bear not arms,' he said to his chiefs, 'but our enemies they be, for their imprecations assail us. Slay them first'. The grim order was obeyed. Brochmail and his followers were put to flight; the monks, were butchered ruthlessly, and then, having disposed of supernatural enmity, the English turned to fight their secular adversaries. The battle was long and desperately contested, and Bede says that Aethelfrith's army suffered severely; but it ended in another great English victory. Two British kings were slain; Cadwan and Brochmail fled with only a remnant of their army.

Aethelfrith did not live to complete the conquest of the north; he died in civil strife four years later. But the battles of Deorham and Deva ensured the complete conquest of Britain. The British states were hopelessly parted from one another, and could never again combine for resistance, even had they the will to do so. They were, in 620, as their foes had been in 520, cut into disconnected masses. Worse still, they occupied wild and barren territories, and the dynastic conditions did not make for internal peace. Nor did they ever again produce a really great leader. After Deorham and Deva there was never any real hope of recovering the lost ground, and to Ceawlin and Aethelfrith this result was almost entirely due.

Inadequate and nebulous as this narrative of the events of a period of such vital importance to the English nation may appear, yet out of it there stand forth certain clearly-defined epochs and figures. The invaders at first only plundered, until an apparently chance incident opened the way to permanent settlement. For a time the tide of conquest and occupation was checked by the series of brilliant victories gained by Ambrosius and Arthur, but the civil broils of the Britons prevented any permanent success over the continually multiplying enemy; and with the advent of two really great leaders on the side of the invaders, the older inhabitants found themselves hopelessly penned up in the barren regions of the west. Thenceforth Britain was Britain no longer, but Angle-land – England.

V

The Viking Ravages

From 596, the year of the coming of St Augustine, to 793, England was practically untroubled by foreign invasion, except in so far as the raids of the still independent Kymry come under that heading. The period was by no means peaceful; the three great kingdoms – Northumbria, Mercia, and Wessex – were frequently at strife, and once or twice the Welsh interfered with effect in their wars. Wessex was nearly always torn with intense war. After 758 the condition of Northumbria was one of chronic anarchy.

In 793 Mercia, under the great Offa, the friend of Charles the Great, was the suzerain state of England, supreme over all the English and Welsh kingdoms south of the Humber. Northumbria was ruled by Æthelred, son of Æthelwald (known as 'Moll'), a savage tyrant who, however, appears to have been capable of keeping order, if only by force, in his anarchic realm. He was in alliance with Offa, whose daughter Elflaed he married, and also with Charles the Great; and his position seemed fairly secure when, in 793, a squadron of pirate-ships sacked Lindisfarne. Next year the descent was repeated, and Bede's monastery at Jarrow was sacked. The pirate squadron was, however, shattered by a storm, and its leader taken and put to death.

The raiders were Scandinavians – 'Vikings (the 'I' in Vikings in short),' as they have come to be called, from the fact that their settlements, though scattered all over the Baltic region, lay thickest in the 'viks' (fjords), and especially along the shores of the great 'Vik', the Skager – Rak and Christiania Fjord. All these communities were ready, on slight pretext, to take to warfare and plunder, and leaders were never wanting. Politics, mere half-savage love of adventure, all played their part in driving them seaward; and once the Vikings had tasted plunder, desire of more soon led them far afield.

The Scandinavians were as yet heathens, and were to continue so for long centuries. They were not altogether barbarians, despite the savagery which appears so terribly in their deeds. Their social condition was well developed, and they were not without a tincture of civilized culture and art. In metal-work their achievements were notable.

They had long been renowned as boat-builders. Tacitus especially notes their proficiency in that science. It does not appear, however, that they took any part in the Teutonic attacks on the Roman Empire, but in 515 a Danish chief named Hygelac raided the coast of Frankland. He was defeated and slain by Theudebert I.

It was, perhaps, the conquest of the Saxons by Charles the Great which alarmed the Danes into attacking Christendom. Before 793 scarcely anything is heard of hostility from them. But Denmark, bordering on Saxony, naturally became the refuge of the Saxon chiefs, and was gradually drawn into the conflict. About 800 King Godfrid took up a position of open hostility to the new 'Roman' Emperor of the West. In 808 Charles apparently meditated an invasion of Denmark, and in 810 a Danish fleet of two hundred sail ravaged Frisia. Two years later Godfrid prepared to invade the Frankish Empire, but was assassinated. His successor sued for terms, and Charles the Great died in peace.

Nevertheless, the impulse had been given, and from 793 onward Viking ravages began to afflict Europe. For many years they were confined mainly to Ireland, which was wasted almost from sea to sea, the result being, of course, that its brilliant art and literature were steadily destroyed. The wasters of Ireland appear to have been chiefly Norwegians; Denmark was involved in civil war. Frankland, no doubt, appeared too powerful to annoy with impunity. England also seemed strong. The raids of 793–794 were directed on anarchic Northumbria.

However, in 834 the Danish civil wars were at an end. The Danish king was the savage Horik, 'Fel Christianitatis' – the Gall of

Christianity. In Frankland the kindly but weak Emperor Ludwig 'the Pious' was engaged in civil war with his sons. In England the Mercian supremacy had come to an end, and had been succeeded by that of Ecgberht of Wessex. The opportunity appeared to have come, and the Danes, backed by adventurers from all Scandinavia, began a series of terrible ravages in Western Europe. First, as with the English attacks on Britain, there were isolated plundering descents; then larger and better organized expeditions; finally, great hosts migrating for purposes of settlement.

Such terms as 'great' must here be taken in a relative sense. Scandinavia is today the most thinly-peopled region of Europe; a thousand years ago its population was far scantier.

The Viking ships were long open boats, raised at bow and stern, steered by a paddle fastened to the starboard quarter. They had one mast with a square sail, but were normally propelled by oars. In size they varied. At first they were certainly small, and though excellent in the fjords, were of little use for rough sea work. Doubtless the Scandinavian builders soon discovered this, and began to develop their craft, until they turned out Olaf Tryggvason's Long Serpent, the wonder of the North. But the average number of men to each ship can hardly have exceeded sixty, and it is doubtful whether the Vikings in England ever collected more than 20,000 men in one field.

The hosts were heterogeneous, unstable, and ill disciplined, liable to disown an unlucky or unpopular chief at a moment's notice.

The Vikings, however, began with at least three advantages. It is doubtful if the early English were ever, except from necessity, a maritime people. In any case, it is clear that in the ninth century they had almost entirely forgotten the nautical qualities of their ancestors, and that no English state possessed warships. The Franks appear to have allowed such squadrons as Charles the Great had constructed to check the Danes to decay.

Secondly, neither in England nor Frankland was there as yet any real sense of national union. The various English states were jealous and disunited. Wessex was slow to aid Mercia, and Northumbria, apart from its anarchic condition, disliked both. Concerted action was almost an impossibility. Even more so was this the case in Frankland. The Vikings, on landing, could generally rely upon having to meet only the local levies.

Thirdly, the invaders had for a long time at least an immense tactical superiority. They were for the most part trained fighting men, physically powerful, brave, ferocious, thoroughly inured to war and bloodshed, well equipped with arms offensive and defensive. The only troops on the English side equal to them were the 'thegns' and the royal bodyguard, and the Vikings could easily rout superior numbers of the ill-trained and ill-equipped country folk.

In 834 the Danes landed at the mouth of the Rhine and sacked Utrecht and Dorstadt. A detachment of this fleet ran across to Sheppey and made a hasty raid. In 836 they again wasted the delta of the Rhine, and thirty-five ships sailed down the English Channel to Charmouth, in Dorset. King Ecgberht came hastily against them, probably with only his personal following, and fought a bloody action. The Danes held their own, but apparently immediately re-embarked; at any rate, no more is heard of them. But a repulse inflicted on the Bretwalda of England by only the crews of thirty-five ships was an ominous event.

Two years later a Viking fleet touched in Cornwall. This last remnant of Damnonia had lately been subjugated by Ecgberht, and at once joined the invaders against him. The united forces, however, had scarcely time to unite on Hengestesdune (Hingston Down), west of the Tamar, when Ecgberht was upon them. They were entirely defeated. Cornwall was reconquered, and the old king returned home in triumph, to die in the following year.

He was succeeded by his son Aethelwulf, a curious counterpart of his contemporary the Frankish Emperor, Ludwig the Pious – brave and just, but weak and over conscientious, and cursed, like Ludwig, with undutiful sons and turbulent vassals. His troubles were soon upon him. In 840 a Viking fleet appeared on the south coast, and its land force fought an indecisive action with Wulfheard, Ealdorman of Hampshire, near South ampton. The raiders next landed on Portland, defeated and slew Aethelhelm, Ealdorman of Dorset, and sailed away with much booty.

Next year another squadron came into the Wash, defeated and slew Herebert, Ealdorman of Lindsey, wasted his territory, and then ravaged the coasts of East Anglia and Kent.

In 842 a great Viking fleet sailed into the Channel, and, apparently separating into detachments, attacked Quentovic in Picardy, London, and Rochester. These places seem to have ransomed themselves. In the next year a force landed once more at Charmouth, and repulsed Aethelwulf as they had repulsed his father, though, as they left Wessex alone for four years, it is to be assumed that they had lost heavily. In 844 a squadron touched probably in the Humber, and killed Redwulf, King of unhappy Northumbria.

So far as the Vikings had any settled strategic plan, it was to seek the point of least resistance. If they were beaten off in Frankland, they turned on England, and vice versa. For two years after 844 they were busy in France, and not until 846 are they found again landing in England, this time at the mouth of the Parret, where they were completely defeated by an English force, of which the most conspicuous leader was Ealhstane, the warrior bishop of Sherborne. It is possible that this band was composed of Norwegians from Ireland, for the main body of the Vikings was ravaging in France.

But in 851 the stress of the attack fell upon England. First a band landed in Devon, but was set upon by Ealdorman Ceorl and completely defeated. A second force attacked Sandwich, and was also defeated with heavy loss, including that of nine ships. But in the summer the main Viking fleet – three hundred and fifty ships under a chief named Rorik – came up the Thames. North Kent was wasted, and Canterbury taken and sacked. The victorious Danes then pressed up the river to London. Beorhtwulf, King of Mercia, was posted before the city, but he was defeated, and London stormed and sacked. Presumably its Roman walls were ruinous. The Vikings, flushed with success, pushed on to attack Wessex. Aethelwulf had failed to succour Beorhtwulf at London, but had now assembled the army of Wessex, and was ad vancing against the invaders. At Aclea (probably Oakley, near Basingstoke; see Appendix A) Northmen and Englishmen for the first time encountered in a great battle, and the Vikings were totally defeated. The greater part of their army was destroyed, the survivors fled to their effect in England was to strengthen the suzerainty of Wessex.

In 853 a Viking force entrenched itself in Thanet and defeated an attempt of the Kentishmen to dislodge them, but then abandoned the isle and sailed to fields where plunder was more easily gained than among the obstinate Englishmen. But in 854 they were again in England, and wintered in Sheppey; and Aethelwulf chose the next year to go on pilgrimage to Rome! His son Aethelbald seized the opportunity to practically oust his father – not without some justification in Aethelwulf's ill-timed religious enthusiasm. When the king came back he was content to acknowledge his son as king in Wessex, keeping only Kent, Sussex, and Essex for himself. The result of this dissension was, of course, a serious weakening of the suzerain power of Wessex.

Aethelwulf died in 858. His successor, the rebellious Aethelbald, reigned only two and a half years, and was then succeeded by his brother Aethelbert, who held the sceptre for six years. There were sporadic Viking raids at intervals after 855, but it was not until 860 that the danger again became serious. In that year a large Viking fleet, under a chief named Vcelund, was bribed to depart from France by the wretched Charles the Bald, and forthwith turned its dragon prows towards England. It sailed up Southampton Water, and its crews landed and marched upon Winchester. Its walls were ruinous, and it was taken and sacked; but immediately afterwards the Vikings were attacked by the men of Berkshire and Hampshire, under the Ealdormen Aethelwulf and Osric, and totally routed. This success of a hurried assemblage of country-folk shows that the military efficiency of the Wessex peasants was not to be despised.

For some five years the Northmen left England alone, but in 865 a great horde descended on Kent. An attempt was made to buy them off, and an armistice was declared, but they broke the truce and ravaged eastern Kent before assistance could be brought from Wessex. They then settled down for the winter in Thanet. Next spring King Aethelbert died, and was succeeded by his brother Aethelred I.

The success of 865 had apparently determined the whole Viking swarm in France to come over to England. Whether their leaders had any definite design of settlement it is impossible to ascertain, but the deliberation of their movements shows that they were carefully calculated. The people of Wessex had shown themselves to be warlike and patriotic, and its kings by no means despicable opponents. So the 'Great Army' poured into East Anglia, where they desisted from plunder after receiving a heavy subsidy, but wintered in the unhappy country and swept up its horses, so as to be able to move swiftly.

Very early in 867 the 'Great Army' swarmed out of East Anglia and passed through Eastern Mercia into Northumbria, which was torn between two claimants to the throne – Osbeorht and Ælla. The Northmen poured over the Humber and captured and sacked York, despite the fact that it was fortified – perhaps the walls of the Roman castra had been patched up. Ælla and Osbeorht thereupon, with surprising patriotism, came to terms and advanced together ·to recover York. The Northmen were driven back and forced to shut themselves up in the city, and the Northumbrians, impetuously pursuing, became involved in furious streetfighting and met with hideous disaster. Both kings were slain; the flower of the army perished in the streets and during the Viking pursuit; only a remnant escaped.

This annihilating defeat resulted in the destruction of Northumbria. For some years Deira remained in a miserable condition, in the power of the Northmen but not regularly ruled by them. North of the Tyne, for about ten years, some obscure princes called themselves kings at Bamborough.

Emboldened by this success, the greatest that any Viking host had hitherto gained, the 'Great Army' next year, under Ingvar and Hubba, sons of Ragnar Lodbrog, invaded Mercia from Deira and pushed up the Trent. King Aethelred of Wessex marched to the relief of his nominal vassal, Burhred of Mercia, and the two kings confronted the Danes before they had penetrated beyond Nottingham. It was the first positive sign of that hearty co-operation between the states in which lay the only hope of salvation; but on this occasion it was not very successful. The Northmen held out stoutly in Nottingham, and finally in the autumn a truce was concluded by which they agreed to leave Mercia in the spring if they were permitted to winter there without molestation. Whether they received a subsidy is unknown; it is at least possible.

During 869 the 'Army' streamed back to York, and it was now, perhaps, that they began to think of settling. But their restless and predatory instincts could not die down quickly, and in 870 the bulk of the host set forth again, 'rode over Mercia into East Anglia, and made their winter quarters at Thetford.' The great monasteries of the Fens, Peterborough, Ely, Crowland, and Bardney, went up in flames, and Eadmund of East Anglia, taken prisoner after a vain attempt at resistance, was murdered in cold blood. Though there is no authority earlier than Abbo (circa 980), the story is probably true, for shortly afterwards one finds his memory honoured, and churches raised to him by the very men who had murdered him, which could hardly have happened unless they had been deeply impressed by his heroic end. All East Anglia and Essex were soon in Danish hands, and the 'Great Army' prepared to advance against Wessex.

Ingvar and Hubba now pass from the scene, though Hubba reappears for a brief space some years later. The army that marched upon Wessex was led by Halfdene, another son of Ragnar, a second king named Baegsceg, and several jarls – a division of command which could hardly make for efficiency.

The defence of Wessex was in capable hands. The gallant King Aethelred was admirably assisted by his brother Alfred (the name Alfred has become so much a part of English history that the time-honoured orthography is retained), soon to be the greatest of English kings. Everything possible appears to have been done to facilitate mobilization, for the Wessex men were in the field with the least delay. Better still, there was no standing on the defensive; the royal brothers appear determined from the first to atttack their foes and drive them out of the country.

The Danish army advanced from Thetford to the Thames, contemptuously ignoring Mercia, and entrenched itself at Reading in the triangle formed by the junction of the Kennet with the Thames. The kings appear to have established this camp while the jarls began to ravage. But they were quickly to learn that they could not play the game with impunity. Three days after their arrival two of the jarls were attacked by the Berkshire *fyrd*, under Ealdorman Aethelwulf, at Englefield Green, in Windsor Forest, and defeated; one of them was slain. Four days afterwards the King and Alfred arrived at Reading unexpectedly with the army of Wessex. The Northmen were off their guard, and were driven back within the palisades. But when the English attempted to storm the camp they were heavily repulsed, with the loss of the brave Aethelwulf, and obliged to retreat westward.

The Viking host pursued. The retreat and pursuit went on for four days, until Aethelred and Alfred had called in reinforcements sufficient to enable them to fight again. Somewhere on AescDune (Ashdown) – i.e., the Berkshire Downs, a great battle was fought. It is impossible to locate the field; all that can be said is that it must have been a long distance west of Reading. The plan of the battle itself is quite clear, but the movements which preceded it are by no means so. It would appear that the army of Wessex, coming from the south or south-east, was halting before breasting the slopes of Aescdune when the Vikings suddenly crowned the heights. They were in two masses, one led by the kings, the other by the jarls. The English were also in two divisions, commanded respectively by Aethelred and Alfred. Alfred was already at the front, and he apparently made up his mind that it was far better to meet than to await a downhill charge. He gave the word for the whole army to advance, and informed his brother, who was hearing Mass in the rear. Aethelred, perhaps because he knew that matters were quite safe in his brother's hands, and because at the price of a few minutes' absence from the field he was quite ready to enhearten his superstitious followers by a little pious posing, declined to come until service was over. The story is probably true. Asser distinctly says that he had excellent authority for it, very likely that of Alfred himself.

The English uphill charge had the best effect. The Vikings were brought to a stand, and the fight raged furiously on the slopes of Aescdune, the focus of the fray being a stunted thorn, the only tree on the hillside. Alfred's tactical insight had its reward, and the day went steadily in favour of the English. King Baegsceg and five jarls were slain, and the Northmen broke and fled headlong. They were pursued all night and into the next day, and Asser says that 'many thousands' of them were slain.

It is sad to record that this splendid victory had no results. Halfdene and the surviving jarls succeeded in reaching Reading, and only a few days later they were joined by large reinforcements from the Continent. Thus recruited, Halfdene again took the offensive, and fourteen days after Aescdune was able to fight Aethelred at Basing, this time with success. Still no decisive victory had been gained, and two months later the armies are found confronting one another. at Marden, near Hungerford. Evidently the Northmen were still confined to the neighbourhood of Reading. The army of Wessex was formed in two divisions as at Aescdune, and for a great part of the day had the advantage, but in the end the Northmen were victorious. Aethelred himself was perhaps mortally wounded; certainly he died a few days after. His death would have been an irreparable loss but that his great brother was at hand to take up his sword.

The Northmen were now advancing into the heart of Wessex, and so heavy had been the losses in the campaign that it was a task of exceeding difficulty to reorganize the army. About a month after Marden Alfred took up a position at Wilton with the small force which he had been able to collect. Says Asser: 'The Saxons had been worn out by eight battles in one year against the pagans, of whom they had slain one king, nine dukes, and innumerable troops of soldiers.' Alfred and his little army made a gallant resistance, and for long beat back the assaults of their enemies; but the favourite Viking stratagem of a feigned retreat and a counter-attack turned the day against them. Defeated, and with the Northmen in the heart of his ancestral kingdom, Alfred was forced to sue for terms. The invaders also had suffered very severely, and were ready to depart for a time to some other more promising field of plunder. Asser and the Chronicle merely say that Alfred made peace with the pagans. We must assume that they were bought off with a subsidy. The respite could not be a long one the Northmen of the ninth and tenth centuries were the most perjured of mankind – but Alfred might be trusted to turn the interval in the fighting to the best advantage.

The position of England at the end of 871 could scarcely have been worse. The results of the lack of national unity were terribly apparent. Northumbria and East Anglia had practically disappeared from the roll of English kingdoms; Mercia was tottering. Only Wessex had succeeded in retaining its independence, and was still ready to fight fiercely for liberty. The situation was similar to what it had been four centuries before, when the first assaults of the English, after occupying the east, were checked by Ambrosius and Artorius. But while the British leaders left no successors worthy of them, it was otherwise with Ecgberht and Aethelwulf. The youngest son of the latter was to be the greatest and noblest of English kings, and to pass on his sceptre to successors worthy of his name.

ENGLISH AND NORTHMEN AT THE DEATH OF ALFRED, A.D. 900.
The 'Burhs' of Alfred and Eadward I. are shown as squares with a dot in the centre.

VI

Alfred and the Saving of Wessex

The stubborn resistance of Aethelred and Alfred had for the moment saved Wessex; but its immediate effect was to throw the whole force of the Northmen upon the rest of England. The host with which Alfred had been contending withdrew to London, and there it stayed through the winter. A most remarkable fact is that while there Halfdene minted coins, bearing his own name indeed, but distinctively Roman in type. In 873 the unhappy Burhred of Mercia subsidized the invaders to depart, but, as usual, they only shifted their quarters. This time they settled down at Torksey, in Lindsey. A second tribute induced them to move again, but with grim humour they now went forward into the very heart of Mercia and encamped at Repton, near Nottingham. This finally broke the spirit of Burhred, who, in despair, fled to Rome, where he died not long afterwards as a monk. The Danish host thereupon set up a puppet king of their own, in the person of Coelwulf, whom the Chronicle calls an 'unwise king's thegn,' and Asser 'a certain foolish minister.' With them he concluded a miserable arrangement, to the effect that when they called upon him he was to resign to them such of his lands as they needed to settle upon. So in utter ignominy the kingdom which had once been the greatest of the English states now dragged out its few remaining years.

The 'Great Army' now separated. One division under Halfdene went northward to complete the conquest of Northumbria. He wintered on the Tyne (875–876), and harried Bernicia, Strathclyde, and the lands beyond the Forth, now beginning to be known as Scotland, from the nationality of its reigning royal house. In 876 he took up his abode as king at York. Deira was parcelled out among the chiefs and warriors, and the Danish kingdom of York came into being. Bernicia was not annexed; it paid tribute, but lasted on – in a miserable fashion indeed – under the High-Reeves of Bamborough until better days arrived.

The rest of the Vikings – a vast force, says the Chronicle – under three war kings, Guthrum, Oskytel and Amund, wintered at Cambridge, where they appear to have been joined by fresh bands from abroad. Indeed, seeing that there is no record of Viking ravages either in France or Ireland for some years after 873, it seems that there was something like a grand concentration of all the Scandinavian pirate bands against Wessex. Aethelweard distinctly states that they had planned their attack in conjunction with the Viking hosts that were tormenting Ireland.

For four years Alfred had been unmolested by the Vikings, and had, beyond doubt, been working hard at the reorganization of his defences. Probably his military reforms were on the line of those which he effected later – recruiting the thegnbood, the military class, which was bound to follow the King to war, improving the arrangements for mobilizing the *land-fyrd*, and fortifying the chief towns and strategic points. But he did more than this. With a far-sightedness which raises him above all early mediaeval Western monarchs, save Charles the Great, he saw that the only sure way to curb the Vikings was to meet them at sea, and began to build a fleet. Under the date 875 the Chronicle says: 'This summer went! Ælfred the King out to sea with an armed fleet, and fought with seven pirate ships. One he took, and the others dispersed.' That obscure sea skirmish has a hallowed interest, for it was the first victory of the world-conquering British Navy.

But as yet Alfred's great reforms were in their infancy; his plans were only traced out, not yet executed. The flood was rising, and burst over devoted Wessex before the barriers which were to stay it had been raised.

As soon as the season permitted, the 'Great Army' left Cambridge, unopposed, rushed by forced marches across Wessex to Wareham, in Dorsetshire. It is to be noted that Winchester was avoided; evidently it had been fortified since the sack of 860. At Wareham the Danes were well placed for attacks on Wessex, and for a junction with their allies from Ireland, who came up immediately afterwards with a fleet of 120 ships. But Alfred was as prompt as his foes, and scarcely had the Vikings effected their junction when he blockaded Wareham with a large army. The result was that the Danes could only effect some sporadic raids of Dorset by sea. They finally extricated themselves by an act of treachery. They opened negotiations, and Alfred was ready to buy them off. Every year of immunity from pillage gained was to his advantage. The Viking chiefs swore a peculiarly solemn oath to observe the fact on a sacred ring or bracelet. Having thus thrown their enemies off their guard, the whole mounted part of the host sallied out from their entrenchments, cut their way through Alfred's lines, and dashed through Dorset into Devon. Alfred, leaving part of his force to continue the blockade, promptly pursued, and finally besieged his treacherous foes in Exeter.

We hear nothing all this time of naval operations, but now Asser appears to imply that an English squadron assisted in the blockade of Exeter. The Danes at Wareham embarked early in 877 on the ships from Ireland in order to join their comrades, but the fleet was caught in a storm and cast ashore near Swanage. Scarce a ship escaped, and almost all the crews were drowned or massacred. The army in Exeter was now isolated, and late in the summer, having exhausted its provisions, offered to treat. 'They gave him as many and as great hostages as he demanded, and swore solemn oaths to observe strictest friendship.' They retired to Cirencester.

The wretched Coelwulf II was now called upon to surrender his kingdom, according to the ignominious treaty of 874, and the Northmen proceeded to settle down. Ultimately they occupied the whole of Mercia, east of a line extending roughly from Macclesfield to Oxford; but probably only a beginning of the settlement was made in this year. A large portion of the host remained at Cirencester under Guthrum, and it now, in defiance of its solemn engagements, concerted a fresh attack on Alfred with the Vikings of Ireland. A force of the latter, under Hubba, was in South Wales, and communication was easy. The levies of Wessex had dispersed after their long service. Alfred was keeping his New Year festivities when the stunning tidings came that the treacherous horde had 'stolen' from Cirencester into Wessex, and was entrenching itself at Chippenham. Defence was impossible. Raiding bands at once began to burn and waste the heart out of the astounded peasantry; the foul treachery and suddenness of the attack made its success complete. It seemed as if all were lost. Many districts submitted; many people fled terrorstricken to France.

Yet it was but for a moment. Amid the panic and confusion there were brave men who kept their heads. The King, with his immediate following, retreated to the Isle of Athelney, in the marshes of the Parret, and there entrenched himself. His position was inaccessible, and he was able to rally the levies of the neighbourhood, and to commence a series of counter-attacks on the Danish raiding columns. Aethelnoth, Ealdorman of Somerset, suceeded in collecting some more of his country levies, and entrenched himself in the woods, while Ealdorman Odda gathered the men of North Devon at Cynuit, perhaps, as tradition indicates, Kenwith, or Henniborough (Cynuitburh), near Bideford. In the west, at least, there was no thought of surrender. The King was able to send out messengers to summon the fyrd, and though his position was critical, there is no reason whatever to believe that he was ever a solitary fugitive.

Still, it must not be forgotten that at this supreme moment the outlook was very black. Did the Danes hear of Alfred's intended mobilization, they might destroy the shire contingents in detail as they moved up to the rendezvous at 'Ecgberht's Stone,' by Selwood Forest. As a matter of fact, they appear to have been in a state of over-confident security. There is not a sign to indicate that they attempted to interfere with the concentration.

Meanwhile the first blow against the invaders had been struck. Hubba had duly made his attack. After ravaging the coast of Devon, he had sat down before Cynuit with twenty-three ships' crews. The place was strong by nature, though ill fortified with a rough palisade; and Hubba did not care to assault it, but trusted to a blockade. Odda and his following did not wait to be starved out. They made a desperate sortie upon the Viking camp, and gained a complete victory, slaying 840 or 1,200 men, with Hubba himself, and capturing the most famous of the Viking 'Land-ravager' standards, a raven banner that had been embroidered by Ragnar's three daughters for their three terrible brothers.

The victors probably then marched to join the King, and in the seventh week after Easter Alfred was able to move. The men of Somerset, Wiltshire, Hampshire, and Dorset, had at last gathered at 'Ecgberht's Stone,' and now they were joined by the King amid a scene of wild enthusiasm. Next day the united army marched to Iglea, near Warminster, and on the following morning encountered the Danes, who, hearing of the concentration, had advanced from Chippenham to Ethandune (probably Edington). The English were formed in a *detzsa testudo*, which, perhaps, means that Alfred concentrated a heavy column against part of the enemy's line. At any rate, his victory was complete; the Danish army was thoroughly broken. Its remains took refuge in the camp at Chippenham, where they were immediately blockaded, and, after fourteen days of siege, forced by famine to surrender.

Alfred's terms show how far he rose above his contemporaries. His beaten foes were to give hostages, Guthrum and the principal chiefs were to become Christians, and the army was to leave Wessex. That the terms were faithfully observed may be fairly ascribed not to any feeling of moral obligation on the part of the Northmen, but to the fact that they had been thoroughly defeated, and to the influence of the great King's personality.

So Wessex was safe, for it was probable that the Vikings would be very slow to attack the gallant state again. Though a fresh pirate horde arrived at Fulham in 879 while Guthrum was moving to settle in East Anglia, their predecessors would not join with them, and the newcomers returned across the Channel and attacked Flanders. Guthrum himself took his Christianity very seriously, and paid special honour to the name of St Eadmund; but his kingly power appears to have been somewhat vague, and his followers were unruly. Alfred was left in peaceful possession of his sorely-tried heritage, and set himself to that wonderful task of reorganization and civilization, the execution of which is his noblest title to fame.

The parts of England that still retained inde pendence were Wessex, Sussex, Kent, and Western Mercia, the latter under the rule of several ealdormen, of whom the chief was a certain Aethelred, who is usually given the quasi-royal title of 'Lord.' It is not quite certain, however, whether he did homage to Alfred until some years later.

Alfred's domestic reforms need not be more than mentioned here. His military reorganization included the enlargement of the thegnhood by admitting into it prosperous farmers and merchants, and organization of the *fyrd*, so that a competent force could take the field without allowing the land to fall out of cultivation – a most important matter in days when army and people were one. Fortification was systematically carried out, and garrisons were provided by a plan which was consciously or unconsciously based on that of the Roman military colonies. To each fortress were attached estates cultivated by military settlers, but the latter were regularly stationed in the burh, and probably had their residences there. They constituted the famous *burh-ware* (*lit.* fort-folk), which played a great part in the defence of England during the next century. Above all, Alfred steadily added to his fleet, though it was not until the end of his reign that it was able to play an important part.

For some years after 878 Alfred remained in peace, energetically pushing on his reforms, and drawing closer to Mercia and the distracted Christian states of Wales, which were beginning to find that the 'Saxon' was better as a friend than the Viking. The Vikings were ranging about Western Europe, inflicting upon it the direst misery that it had experienced since the Roman eagles flew away, but only once in fourteen years did they attack Alfred. In 885 a part of their main horde sailed up the Medway and besieged Rochester. It was gallantly defended by its burh-ware, and in the midst of the siege Alfred came up with a strong force and routed the Vikings, driving them to their ships and capturing their camp, horses, and baggage.

The effect of the raid, however, had been to unsettle some of the East Anglian Danes, who had given the besiegers of Rochester assistance. The English fleet made a retaliatory raid along the East Anglian coast, and captured sixteen ships at the mouth of the Stour, but was then defeated. It was clearly as yet too weak for its work.

Failing to obtain satisfaction from Guthrum or his jarls, Alfred next year attacked the 'Danelaw' by land. After severe fighting, London was retaken, and south-eastern Mercia overrun as far as the Lea and Great Ouse. Alfred's conquests were definitely confirmed to him next year by a treaty with Guthrum. The Roman walls of London were repaired, and the city occupied by a strong military colony.

The result of these successes was that not only the Mercians under Ealdorman Aethelred, but also the princes of Wales, formally paid homage to Alfred. He strengthened the tie with Mercia by giving Aethelred his daughter Aethelftaed to wife. He also placed him in charge of the reconquered districts, which had been mainly Mercian; but evidently not for that reason, but as a personal possession. The English were at last beginning to draw together. For six years Alfred was able to pursue his life-work in peace. The East Anglian Danes observed the treaty of 886; those of Northumbria also had a Christianized chief, Guthred by name, who kept the peace with Alfred, and when the Vikings again attacked him he was well prepared.

In 891 the Northmen were heavily defeated by Arnulf, King of the East Franks, at Louvain. Thereupon they resolved to turn upon England. They gathered from all quarters to Boulogne, and there remained for several months collecting and building ships. They now, on their short voyages, carried their horses with them, and had done so in the raid of 885. In all they mustered 250 ships, and, perhaps, 10,000 men. A second fleet of eighty ships under Hcesten, the most famous of the Scandinavian seakings, assembled farther south. The connection between the two hordes is not clear. Professor Oman suggests that while their action may have been concerted, it is possible that the leaders of the larger force held aloof from Hcesten owing to his selfishness and greed. The evidence of the campaign that followed gives the impression that the two forces acted in concert.

Alfred had also to fear that the settlers of the Danelaw would join the invaders against him. Guthrum of East Anglia had died in 890, and the friendly chief of Deira was associated with a certain Siegfred who was hostile to Alfred. For the present the settlers gave hostages to Alfred as a pledge that they would keep the peace, but they broke it without scruple when occasion offered.

The 'Great Army' landed at Lympne, in Kent, late in the autumn of 892. It was a bad base of operations, for it was practically shut off from the inland by the Andredsweald; but the ports were now so well defended that a landing-place was difficult to find. The Danes easily captured an old earthwork at Appledore which the local peasantry tried to defend, and, towing their ships up the harbour, entrenched themselves. 'Soon after,' says the Chronicle, 'came Haesten with eighty ships into the mouth of the Thames, and wrought him there a work at Middeltun.'

Serious fighting did not begin until the spring of 893. Alfred entrenched himself midway between the two Viking armies, and soon reduced Haesten to straits, perhaps by the aid of a fleet from London. Hcesten offered to depart and, as a proof of sincerity, handed over his two sons to be baptized. But with the usual Viking treachery, he merely transferred himself to Bemfleet, in Essex. The East Anglian Danes received him with open arms, and a great plan of operations was framed. While Hcesten 'contained' the English on the Thames, the 'Great Army' was to penetrate across the Weald into Wessex, ending a detachment with the fleet to Hcesten. Meanwhile forty Northumbrian Danish ships were to enter the Bristol Channel, and 100 more, partly Northumbrian, partly East Anglian, would sail down the east coast and attack Wessex from the south.

The 'Great Army' passed safely through the Weald, and began to waste eastern Wessex. Alfred himself seems to have been in the west; but the English army, under his son Eadward, abandoned its central position in Kent, and, hurrying through Surrey, overtook the Vikings at Farnham, and defeated them with great loss. Their chief 'king' was wounded, and they fled in disorder across the Thames into Herts, where they took refuge on Thorney Isle, in the Colne. Eadward followed and blockaded them; but then, hearing that his father was coming with fresh forces, allowed his half starved county levies to return home. Alfred was near at hand when he heard that the Anglo Danish fleets were attacking Exeter and northern Devon. Thereupon he turned back, sending only a detachment to Eadward. With these troops the prince resumed the blockade, and was soon joined by Ealdorman Aethelred and the Mercians. The Vikings then promised to depart, and gave hostages; but they only dispersed into the Danelaw, and were soon in arms again.

Haesten at Bemfleet had been joined by the main Viking fleet, and was wasting Mercia with part of his force, the rest being left to guard the camp. Aethelred and Eadward did not waste time in pursuing him; but turned back to London, gathered up its *burh-ware*, and marched against Bemfleet. 'Then came the King's men and defeated the enemy, broke down the work, took all that was therein – money, women, and children – and brought all to London.' Hundreds of ships must have been taken, and among the prisoners were Hresten's wife and his two sons. Hresten, returning from his raid, found only ruins at Bemfleet.

He must be credited at least with admirable pertinacity and courage. He established himself at Shoebury, and rallied there the broken sections of the·Viking host. Reinforced by East Anglians, he again made a dash westward, hurrying along the Thames Valley to the Lower Severn, and then turning northward. At Buttington, on the Severn, he was overtaken by the Mercians under Aethelred, supported by reinforcements brought up from Wessex by Ealdormen Aethelhelm, and Aethelnoth, and other troops from Wales. He was defeated and blockaded in his camp, only escaping to Shoebury after heavy loss. His hope appears to have been to join the Northumbrian fleet, but Alfred had relieved Exeter, and the discomfited squadrons had gone.

However, Shoebury had become the rendezvous of adventurers from all quarters, and Hcesten, late in the year, broke out once more. Marching night and day, he suddenly appeared in the desolate ruins of Deva, the 'Chester' where once Legio Valeria Victrix had made its home, and entrenched himself behind its ramparts. The Mercians were too late to overtake him, and could only waste the neighbourhood so as to straiten him for food.

The events of the next year, 894, are rather obscure. Hcesten, forced to evacuate Chester, wasted North Wales, and finally retreated to Northumbria, and so back to East Anglia. Evidently hoping to be safer so, the Danes established a new camp on Mersey Island, on the Essex coast. Meanwhile the Northumbrian fleet was at last coming to Hresten's aid. On its way from the west it attacked Chichester, but was handsomely repulsed, with the loss of several ships. The main force, however, reached Mersey safely, and late in the year the whole host proceeded up the Thames and entrenched itself twenty miles up the

Lea. One hears nothing of Alfred or the main English army all the year. It is possible that the King was trying to coerce the Northumbrians, and there is a terribly confused and probably misdated entry in Aethelweard's Chronicle which seems to point to something of the kind.

The winter of 894–895 passed away with the Danes and the Londoners watching each other on the Lea. So confident were the latter, that early in 895 they, with 'other folk,' marched to attack the camp. They were repulsed with loss, including that of four royal thegns. Still, however, the Danes dared not advance on London, and the English were able to cultivate the fields as usual. In the summer Alfred himself with the main English army encamped close to the city, and under his protection the harvest was safely gathered in. Forts were constructed some distance below the Danish camp and the Lea blocked with stockades. The enemy thereupon broke away northward, pursued by the English mounted troops, while the Londoners, for the second time, triumphantly towed a captured fleet into the Pool.

Meanwhile the retreating Danes had made a last dash into north-western Mercia, and entrenched themselves at Quatbridge-on-Severn. There they remained practically blockaded until the winter. The English army then, unable to maintain itself longer, dispersed; but the Danes were half starved and wholly dispirited, and in the spring of 896, when Alfred began to assemble the host to make an end of them, they broke up and scattered, some to the Danelaw: others who were penniless and desperate hired or built ships and went back to France. Alfred's victory was of far more than local importance. The Vikings had tried their fortune within a few years on both sides of the Channel, and both times had been beaten. The dogged resistance of Alfred had fairly broken up their main host, and it does not appear that so formidable a force was ever again collected by them.

Alfred's last years were comparatively peaceful. Small pirate squadrons, however, continued to annoy the coast of Wessex, and to cope with them he made great additions to his infant navy, employing in the work members of seafaring Frisians to train his crews. The new ships, however, appear to have been of his own designing-another instance of his wonderful versatility. The chronicler definitely states that they were built 'as he [Alfred] himself thought they might be most serviceable.' They were twice as long as the old vessels, swifter, steadier sea-boats, of higher free-board, and with sixty oars or more in addition to their sails. In 897 nine of the new ships fought in action with six Viking vessels in a Devonshire estuary, of which the Chronicle gives what almost reads like the official account.

Three of the Viking vessels were at anchor, the others beached higher up the inlet. Two of the three anchored vessels were immediately taken; the third escaped, but with only five sorely wounded men surviving out of her crew. Meanwhile the tide was ebbing, and seems to have compelled six of the English vessels to stand farther off the shore, leaving the other three aground in the rapidly retreating waves. The Danes on shore waded through shallow water and made desperate attempts to board the stranded ships. Lucomon, a royal reeve (perhaps the commodore of the squadron), was slain, and with him Aethelfrith, one of the King's herdsmen, three Frisian officers, and sixty-two seamen; but they accounted for one hundred and twenty Danes, and the Viking ships escaped only because the returning tide floated their light craft before the heavier English vessels. Only one of the three Danish vessels succeeded in reaching East Anglia, the other two went ashore on the coast of Sussex, and their crews were captured and hanged at Winchester, by order of the usually so merciful King.

The great King had now completed his gigantic task. He had welded together the unconquered half of England so firmly that there was no fear that the Vikings would overpower its united force. During his reign of over twenty-eight years he was, to a very large extent, occupied in resisting, and in organizing resistance to, the invaders. The success that attended his operations was emphatically due to his fine character, his capacity for organization, his steady concentration on the work of uniting England against the common foe, and his clear sighted vision that saw the necessity of being able to attack by sea as well as on land; and over and above all these qualities, his power of inspiring men with something of his own exalted ideals. On October 26, 900, he died; probably the greatest, beyond doubt the best and noblest, monarch who has reigned over England.

VII

The Conquest of the Danelaw

Alfred's death left Wessex and western Mercia still faced by a mass of more or less hostile Danish settlers in the Danelaw and Deira, but fairly well knit together by the consciousness of sufferings endured and victories gained in conjunction, and with a growing sense of national unity. At first it is doubtful whether Eadward I intended to subjugate the Danelaw; but he was quickly made aware that there was hardly any alternative. His cousin Aethelwald, son of Aethelred I, who had been passed over on account of his youth in favour of Alfred, and conceived himself to have a better title to the throne than Eadward, rose in revolt, and was supported by the Danish settlers.

Aethelwald succeeded in establishing himself as King of York, and invaded Mercia with a Danish army. Eadward promptly retaliated by invading East Anglia; this was precisely the plan laid down by 'Byzantine' tacticians for checking Saracen raids from Syria. It succeeded admirably – the Danes hurried back from Mercia to save their homes. By accident they came upon the Kentish troops isolated, and after a furious engagement gained a Pyrrhic success. Nearly every man of note on both sides fell, including, on the Danish side, both the English claimant and Eric, King of East Anglia. There was, perhaps, more indecisive fighting, but in 903 a treaty was made with Guthrum II of East Anglia on the basis of the *status quo ante*. For six years thereafter there was peace throughout England, except in anarchic Northumbria, which appears to have been a sort of dumping ground for everything that was restless and unsettled in north-western Europe.

In 910 the Danes, perhaps goaded into action by restless spirits from the Continent, again raided Mercia. Eadward apparently decided to repeat his strategy of 902, and collected a large army and a fleet of 100 ships in Kent, but the distress of the Mercians forced him to hasten to their aid. Having effected a junction with the Mercian forces, he intercepted the Danes as they returned from the Severn Valley, into which they had penetrated, and near Totanhael (Tottenhall), in Staffordshire, inflicted on them a heavy defeat. Three 'kings,' two jarls, and seven holdrs, or great landowners, fell, and the pillaging propensities of the settlers of the Danelaw received a rude check.

Aethelred, the 'Lord' of Mercia, died in the same year; but his widow, Aethelflaed, the sister of Eadward, took up his task with energy. Aethelflaed is one of the most remarkable figures in English history. She was not only an administrator, but a strategist and military organizer – a combination almost without parallel in a woman. How deeply her extraordinary qualities had impressed her contemporaries is shown by the fact that upon her husband's death she succeeded quietly to the exercise of his power. It is tantalizing that more is not told of Aethelflced, but even in the dry and scanty notices of the 'Anglo-Saxon Chronicle' she stands out as a great ruler, the worthy daughter of her heroic father.

Aethelflaed's capacity was soon to be displayed. The weakness of Mercia as compared with Wessex during the Danish wars lay in its lack of fortresses. It will have been noted that all Hcesten's raids were directed against it, obviously because there was little fear of being obstructed, as in Wessex, by thickly placed *burhs*, and attacked by the warlike and energetic *burh-ware*. Aethelred had evidently made some steps to remedy the deficiency of fortified places, and in 907 he repaired and occupied Deva, thenceforward to be pre-eminently the 'Chester' of England. Probably, however, the comparative poverty of Mercia retarded the systematic fortification of the towns, but now Aethelflaed took up the scheme with energy. In the preceding year she and her husband had built a burh at Bromesberrow, between Hereford and Tewkesbury, and in 911 she fortified Scargate (site doubtful) and Bridgenorth. Meanwhile Eadward fortified Hertford, conquered southern Essex, and fortified Maldon and Witham as advance posts against Colchester. So discouraged were the Danes that they sued for peace, but almost immediately broke it.

After Easter, in 912, the jarls of Northampton and Leicester raided Mercia. They wasted the country about Hocneratun (Hook Norton), but were repulsed at Lygton (Leighton Buzzard). Aethelflced guarded against further attacks by fortifying Tamworth and Stafford.

The Danes of England now summoned to their help some of the Vikings on the Continent, and a fleet under two jarls, Ohthere and Hroald, came over hither south from the Lidwiccians' (i.e., Brittany), and sailed up the Bristol Channel. They, as usual, shunned Wessex, where the watchful Eadward was guarding the coast with an army; but wasted South Wales, and captured Cimelauc, Bishop of Llandaff, whom Eadward ransomed for forty pounds of silver. They then pushed on to raid Mercia, but were quickly attacked by the levies of Hereford and Gloucester, and defeated, Jarl Hroald being slain. 'And they drove them into a park, and beset them there without until they gave them hostages that they would depart from the realm of King Eadward.' The fleet made two ineffectual raids at Watchet and Porlock, both of which were repulsed with slaughter; and after lying at Bradanrelice (Flat Holm) until its crews were wasting away with famine, retreated first to the Welsh coast and then to Ireland. The energetic King at once hastened eastward and besieged Bedford, which surrendered after a month's blockade; while the Lady of Mercia kept watch on Northumbria, and fortified Eddisburh and Warwick.

The not very effective intervention of the fleet of Ohthere and Hroald was the last attack on Wessex by Vikings from the Continent. Thenceforward Eadward and Aethelflaed were able to push forward the conquest of the Danelaw with little interference. During the next three years they steadily fortified, and practically shut up the Danelaw in a line of burhs. In 916 they made a great combined advance. Guthrum II, King of East Anglia, attempted to stem the attack by establishing a base on English soil at Tempsford, at the junction of the Great Ouse and the Ivel, while the jarls of Leicester and Northampton made a raid on the neighbourhood of Aylesbury. The counter-attack was a hopeless failure. Aethelflaed stormed Derby after a furious resistance, while Guthrum in vain attacked Bedford and Wiggingamere, and had to retreat on Temps ford, only to be assailed there by an English army of *burh-ware* from all the eastern fortresses. 'They beset the *burh* and fought against it until they broke into it, and slew the King and Earl Toglos, and Earl Manna his son, and his brother, and all them that were therein, and would defend themselves, and they took the others and all that was therein.' Eadward followed up the victory with energy. Though it was 'in harvest,' every available man in Kent and Surrey crossed the Thames, joined the men of Essex and the stormers of Tempsford, and marched upon Colchester. 'They took it, and slew all the garrison, and seized all that was therein, except those men who fled away there – from over the wall.'

The last hope for the independence of the Danes of England lay in a Viking fleet which had just appeared on the East Anglian coast. Its crews landed, rallied the broken levies of their kinsmen, and, in conjunction with them, besieged Maldon. Before they could complete their cordon, a strong body of English troops, probably part of the victors of Tempsford and Colchester, entered the *burh*, and the combined force made a sortie, repulsed the besiegers, and, by a vigorous pursuit, completely broke them. It was the beginning of the end. No time was given for the broken foe to recover. Late as was the season, Eadward kept the field; from every county the *land-fyrd* and *burh-ware* marched in hot haste to reinforce or relieve the army in Essex. Northampton, Huntingdon, and Cambridge surrendered, and with them all East Anglia.

This was practically the end of the independence of the Danelaw. Next year, 917, brother and sister made their last advance together, and captured Leicester and Stamford, and on June 12 Aethelflaed died. She had been her brother's right hand, and so well had she performed her part that little now remained to be done. By 919 Eadward had consolidated his rule as far as the Humber, had occupied and secured southern Lancashire, and had received homage from Regnald, the Danish ruler of Deira; Ealdred, the English chief of Bernicia; Constantine III, King of Scotland; and Donald, King of Strathclyde. Ealdred's submission was natural; the more shadowy allegiance of Constantine and Donald was obviously prompted by fear of the Vikings, whose settlements in Scotland included all the northern and western islands, and much of the adjacent mainland. When Eadward 'the Elder' died in 824 his supremacy over Britain was such as no monarch had yet enjoyed, and his power passed undiminished to his son Aethelstan.

Aethelstan's reign passed by largely in peace chequered by rebellions which were quickly suppressed. Aethelstan rather prematurely annexed Deira, deposing its Danish vassal king; but he was strong enough to keep down the turbulent Danes of Northumbria. He had more difficulty with Constantine of Scotland, who soon began to regret the engagement into which he had entered with the English 'Basileus' of all Britain. In 933 he threw off his allegiance; but Aethelstan proceeded northward with an army and fleet, marched through eastern Scotland to Dunnottar, and brought him to temporary submission. He was not cowed, however, and proceeded to organize underhand a great confederacy, which had as its object the destruction of the power of the overshadowing *Dispensator regni totius Britanniae*. His chief motive for this action was probably that he was hindered in his designs of absorbing Strathclyde and Northern Bernicia; but common fear of the now mighty English power had more than anything to do with the formation of the heterogeneous alliance, which included not only Scotland and Strathclyde, and probably the Galloway Picts no less than those of the North, but Anlaf Guthfrithson, King of Dublin, Anlaf Quaran, claimant to the Danish crown of York, and three more Viking sea-kings, with a great host of warriors.

The allied host gathered at Brunanburh, or Brunanwerc, a place the site of which is absolutely unknown. It must have been on the west or northwest of England, and, since a great part of the allied host consisted of Irish Vikings, probably on or near the coast. Professor Hodgkin, with whom Professor Oman agrees, is inclined to place it at Birrens, near Carlisle. But there is also a Bromborough near the mouth of the Mersey, which might be the *Brunanburh* of the Chronicle. Professor Oman's objection is that it is too far from the base of the Scots. On the other hand, it is as good a place of concentration for the Irish Vikings as Birrens, and, if the Northumbrians had revolted, as seems probable from the significant omission of any mention of them in the 'Song of Brunanburh,' the Scots and Britons may have penetrated so far south. In this case the Scots and Picts would have come through Lothian, joined the Strathclydians and Galwegians somewhere on the march, and, passing through Bernicia and Deira, gathered up the Danes of Yark, and moved westward to join the Irish Vikings in the Mersey. Still, it must be admitted that this implies a higher degree of efficiacy than can be supposed to have existed in the inchoate Picto-Scottish horde. Also, Constantine seems to have escaped by land, which would have been difficult had the battle been fought at Bromborough-in-Wirral. There is not a single topographical indication in the 'Song' to help the inquirer. Brunanburh may be Birrens and may be Bromborough – the probabilities are, perhaps, in favour of Birrens – but it is not certain that it is either.

However warily the cunning Constantine – 'the hoary warrior,' 'the old deceiver' – had gone to work, Aethelstan had good intelligence of the coming storm, and marched northward to meet the allies with all the forces of Wessex and Mercia, accompanied by his brother Eadmund. The battle that followed was the greatest that had been fought since the English Conquest. Details we have none, except that the struggle lasted from dawn to sunset, and that it ended in the destruction of the host that had gathered to undo the work of Alfred and his children. If the loss among the leaders be any criterion, the slaughter was fearful. Constantine himself escaped, but his son fell, and with him lay dead Eugenius, King of Strathclyde, three Viking sea-kings, seven jarls, and numberless crowds of lesser folk.

The battle of Brunanburh set the seal on the great task that Alfred had begun and that Eadward I and Aethelstan had so well continued. So long as the House of Ecgberht continued to bring forth strong rulers, the English Empire held together. The Danelaw was sometimes troublesome; the Northumbrians were always turbulent vassals; but Eadmund I and his successor, Eadred, coped successfully with all disturbances, and with the fifteen years' peaceful reign of Eadgar the ideal of English unity appeared to have been nearly accomplished. Yet it was not to be. A long minority, factious magnates, and a worthless king, were to accomplish between them what the mighty seakings of the ninth century had failed to achieve. The result of Brunanburh was to establish the 'Empire of the English,' and to awe foreign enemies for forty years and no more. Yet few battles of that age were so decisive, and it made a tremendous impression in Europe. Henry the Fowler of Germany requested the hand of the English king's sister for his son Otto, soon to add fresh lustre to the name of Roman Emperor of the West; and Aethelstan eventually became the brother-in-law of nearly all the monarchs of Western Europe. He also seems to have been in alliance with the famous Harald Harfaagr of Norway, who was working hard at the Sisyphean task of reducing his wild realm to some kind of peace and order. And yet it must regretfully be owned that we know hardly anything of one of the greatest and most successful of English kings –

Aethelstan King, Lord among Earls,
Bracelet – bestower and
Baron of Barons.

Tennyson's adaptation of 'The
Song of Brunallburk.'

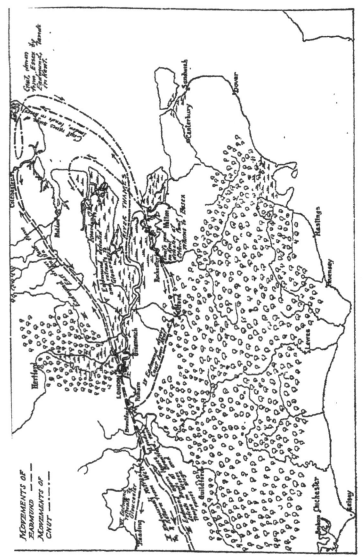

THE FINAL STRUGGLE BETWEEN EADMUND II. AND CNUT ROUND LONDON.

VIII

Later Viking Raids and the Danish Conquest

Men who had seen the famous triumphal procession on the Dee in 973, when Eadgar the Peaceful, rowed by eight vassal princes, passed in his boat by the venerable walls of the 'Chester' of Valeria Victrix, must have groaned in spirit at the wretchedness that overwhelmed England in the reign of his worthless son, Aethelred 'the Redeless.' (Aethelred is popularly known as 'the Unready,' but the Anglo-Saxon word rede means 'counsel' or 'advice,' and a better rendering of the king's nickname is 'ill-counselled' or 'wrong-headed.')

The story of how Aethelred's evil mother, Aelfthryth, contrived the murder of her stepson, Eadward II, 'the Martyr,' at Corfe is well known. He himself was at the time only ten years of age. For several years the kingdom was probably governed by his mother and her supporters, but they were not strong enough to oust the officials of Eadgar and Eadward II. The minority of the king left the rival ealdormen and reeves ill-controlled, and there is some reason to think that the monachizing religious policy of Eadgar and St Dunstan was greatly resented. At all events, there was much internal disorder; it is even possible that a state of modified civil war prevailed. Externally the country appeared great and powerful. Aethelred II at his accession was overlord of all Britain no less than his father. England possessed a navy as strong in numbers as the largest Viking fleet that had ever assailed the country. Yet when the crisis came everything was in hopeless disorder. It was not the people, but the ruling class that was in fault. The exasperation of

Corfe Castle, near the Dorset coast.

the nation glows fiercely through the bitter entries of the 'Anglo Saxon Chronicle,' whose compiler is thoroughly aware that sheer ineptitude, if not absolute treachery, was the cause of the national disasters.

Of the wretched monarch at whose door the blame for the downfall of the first 'English Empire' is usually laid little can be said that is favourable. Aethelred II is condemned for all time by the scathing epithet bestowed upon him of 'redeless.' He was not altogether devoid of courage and enterprise, but his instability and utter incapacity to adopt and execute any sensible plan of action were his bane.

In 980, after more than forty years of immunity, the shores of England were once more troubled by Vikings. Pirate squadrons raided Thanet, and the country round Southampton and Chester. Next year another, or the same force – apparently from Ireland – sacked St Petrocstow (Padstow), and Viking Raids and the Danish Conquest wasted on both shores of the Bristol Channel; and in 982 three pirate vessels touched at Portland for a hurried raid.

For five or six years thereafter nothing is heard of Vikings; but there was certainly unrest among the English nobles, and when the raids began again the country was utterly unprepared. Once again was repeated the weary tale of the ninth-century raids, growing ever more murderous and widespread, and met only by local resistance. But besides this there is the foul record of combined action repeatedly frustrated by jealousy, ineptitude, or treachery, and of frequent buying off after the invaders had done as much mischief as possible. In 988 there was another petty raid of Irish Vikings; and in the same year the great Archbishop Dunstan died, taken away betimes from the wrath to come.

At this period the famous Olaf Tryggvason, debarred from his ancestral Norway, which was held against him by Jarl Haakon, was roving about the Northern Seas. He appeared in English waters in 991 with, perhaps, fifty ships, sacked Ipswich, and, sailing down the coast, landed his followers at Maldon. He was gallantly opposed by Brihtnoth, Ealdorman of Essex; but, after a hard struggle, the day went against the English, Brihtnoth himself being slain. It was a mere local defeat, like that of Charmouth in 836; but the consequences were most disgraceful. 'In this same year,' says the Chronicle, 'it was decreed that tribute should be given to the Danish men for the great terror they occasioned by the seacoast; and that first [payment] was ten thousand pounds. The first who advised this was Archbishop Sigeric.'

Next year an attempt was made to collect a great fleet at London in order to 'entrap the army from without.' According to the Chronicle,

Ealdorman Aelfric, one of the admirals, deliberately betrayed the plan of campaign to the enemy, and then deserted his fleet. Olaf escaped with the loss of only one ship, and shortly afterwards was able to fight an indecisive action with the squadrons of London and East Anglia. The English flagship was taken; but, as far as we can see, the Vikings had the worst of it, and withdrew northward. In 993, however, they had recruited sufficiently to sack Bamborough, and then entered the Humber. 'They did much evil, both in Lindsey and Northumbria. There was collected a great force; but when the armies were to engage, then the leaders first commenced the flight – namely, Frcena and Godwin and Frithgot'. Two at least of the three bear Scandinavian names, and the suspicion must be strong that they deliberately deserted their men.

In 994 Olaf was joined by Sweyn Haraldson, 'Fork beard,' King of Denmark. He had been expelled from his kingdom by the Swedes, and compelled to take to the sea. He had been baptized as a Christian with his father, but had apostatized, and had an apostate's rancour against his former religion. The two fleets counted ninety-four ships, and Olaf and Sweyn determined to attack London. They were stoutly repulsed with great loss, though Olaf is said to have succeeded in breaking the bridge. The Vikings withdrew to the Channel, landed on the south coast, and horsing themselves in the old fashion, rode over Kent, Sussex, and Hampshire, committing 'unspeakable evil.' Again the shameful expedient of 991 was repeated, and the host was bought off with a tribute of 16,000 pounds of silver. The Vikings wintered at Southampton, and Olaf, who had been already converted to Christianity, visited Aethelred at Andover, was 'received at episcopal hands,' and swore that he would not again molest England. Next year he sailed to Norway, and recovered it for himself. Sweyn also went back to attempt to regain Denmark. Aethelred's silver was probably useful to both. For two years England was free from ravage.

But in 997 a new Viking fleet appeared, and wasted Devon, Cornwall, and Wales. This time it was not a half-political enterprise of two dispossessed princes, but a genuine plundering expedition of the old type. Next year the Vikings pillaged in Dorset, Hampshire, and

Sussex, without resistance from the cowardly ealdorman Aelfric, the betrayer of 992. In 999 they extended their ravages into Kent. An army and fleet were raised to fight them, but the generals put off a decision until the force broke up.

In the supposed world-ending year 1000 the Vikings tried their fortune in Normandy. One of their leaders, Pallig, husband of Sweyn's sister Gunhild, took service with Aethelred, and there in the Chronicle the surprising entry that the King took the offensive against the Irish Vikings with a great fleet and army and devastated Man and Cumberland.

But in 1001 the ravages again began on the south coast. The Hampshire levies were beaten by an advanced force, and the raiders were soon joined by the fleet which had been attacking Normandy. Jarl Pallig also deserted to his former comrades. Wiltshire and Dorset were ravaged, and the local levies defeated at Penselwood. The Vikings marched, devastating, along the coast to Southampton Water, and there the old miserable story was repeated. The invaders were again bought off with 24,000 pounds of silver. The year was marked by the famous massacre on St Brice's Day, of Danes settled in England. The fact is undoubted, but the nature and extent of the slaughter are not known. It is to be supposed that it affected only the mercenaries in Aethelred's service and the stragglers from the pirate fleets; but it is quite probable that many innocent persons were involved in it. The result was, of course, to add a natural exasperation to the thirst for plunder of the Vikings.

Sweyn 'Fork-beard' had established himself in Denmark. He had also defeated and slain Olaf Tryggvason at the famous battle of Svold, and now controlled Norway. In 1003 he appeared off the English coast with a large fleet, captured Exeter, and swept through Devon into Wiltshire. The cowardly ealdorman Aelfric once more deserted his troops, and Sweyn sacked Wilton and Sarum, withdrawing to his fleet unmolested, leaving in his wake a ghastly trail of smoking villages and farmsteads, desecrated and ruined churches, the mutilated bodies of the countryfolk, and the immediate prospect of famine and pestilence. He landed in the following year in East Anglia, and sacked Norwich and Thetford, though gallantly opposed by the local hrdunder Ealdorman

Ulfkytel, evidently an Anglo-Dane. 'If the main force had been there,' moans the Chronicle, 'never had the enemy returned to their ships ... they never met with worse hand play than Ulfkytel brought them.'

Conquest does not appear to have been yet in Sweyn's thoughts. In the spring of 1004 he returned home; but the wretched country, though free from foes, was stricken with famine during that year, and in 1006 Sweyn was back again. He landed at Sandwich, and swept unopposed through Wessex to Reading, defeated some local troops, and thence turned back to the sea. Aethelred fled to Shropshire, and the Witan decided that 'they must needs bribe the army with a tribute, though they were all loth to do it.' In the spring of 1007 36,000 pounds of silver were paid, and the satiated Danes retired for two years.

The respite was utilized for an apparently determined attempt to organize a great fleet. Every three hundred 'hides' of land was assessed at a ship; each ten hides at a boat, and for every eight hides a fully equipped soldier was to be furnished.

In 1009 a vast armament assembled at Sandwich, but to no purpose. Perhaps owing to the treachery of Eadric Streona, Aethelred's favourite, at any rate on account of disgraceful dissension among the leaders, the huge force broke up. The miserable story is told at length by the Chronicler, with bitter denunciation of Eadric.

The Vikings were led this year by Thorkil 'the Tall,' of Jomsborg, a famous Viking settlement on the Baltic coast of Germany. The beginning of the end was seen when Kent and Canterbury ransomed themselves from pillage. The Danes then raided Wessex as far as Oxford, and laid Essex and Hertfordshire under contribution, but were stoutly repulsed in an attack on London. They wintered in Kent, and, as usual, the wretched King began to contemplate another payment of tribute. Meanwhile Thorkil left his quarters in Kent and invaded East Anglia. Ipswich was sacked, the county levies defeatedt and the countryside wasted ruthlessly. 'Redeless' in everything, Aethelred did not open negotiations until 1011, by which time the raiders were completely out of hand. They disregarded their nominal chief Thorkil, 'and went everywhere in troops, plundering and slaying our miserable people.' They captured Canterbury through the treachery of the Abbot Aelfmar, and carried off Archbishop Aelfheah (Alphege), Godwin, Bishop of Rochester, and a multitude of captives. Not until the spring of 1012 was the huge 'gafol,' or 'Danegeld' – 48,000 pounds of silver – collected, and a hideous tragedy marked the final payment. A horde of drunken Danes dragged Archbishop Aelfheah, who had nobly refused to ransom himself, before their 'busting' (a Scandinavian word, meaning a general assembly of house holders; here used of an army, and today retained in connection with political elections) at Greenwich, and pelted him to death with the bones of the beasts which they had devoured. It may be questioned whether any deed more foul is recorded in history. And yet the brutality of these semi-savage destroyers has too frequently been held up to unstinted admiration. Thorkil himself was innocent of the Archbishop's blood, and next day he sent his body with honour to London. Soon after, oddly enough – perhaps the deed had sickened him – he entered Aethelred's service.

The humiliation had been in vain. Sweyn himself invaded England next year, and now at last the patience of the people with their incapable king was at an end. The whole north and east at once submitted to Sweyn. He then began to waste Wessex, and Wessex, too, yielded. All England was his almost without a blow, except London, which held its own 'in full fight against him, for therein was King Aethelred and Thorkil with him.' But the stout *burh-ware* were exasperated by the bad discipline of Thorkil's mercenaries, and when they withdrew to Greenwich, London, too, submitted. Aethelred fled to Normandy.

Sweyn himself lived only a few weeks, fortunately for England, for he was little more than a savage pirate leader. His army, and the English who were with it, elected as king his son Cnut, but the Witan of Wessex and Mercia sent to Aethelred – so hard to quench was English loyalty! – 'saying that no lord was clearer to them than their natural lord, if he would govern them better than he did before.' So at Lent Aethelred came home 'to his own people,' and for once acted with vigour. He promptly marched against Cnut, who was at

Gainsborough, caught him unprepared, and forced him to fly out to sea. He touched at Sandwich, and in his rage and disappointment committed the worst of the comparatively few crimes that stain his memory. He cut off the noses, hands, and ears of his hostages, put them ashore, and sailed away to Denmark.

For about a year England was free from invaders, but not from faction-strife. Money was needed for Thorkil's mercenary fleet – 21,000 pounds of silver. Eadric Streona murdered his personal foes without hindrance. Finally, the King's gallant son, Eadmund, sick of the endless disorder, took up a position of open hostility to his wretched father. Aethelred was already sickening to death, and when Cnut appeared again at Sandwich in the autumn the army raised to fight him broke up owing to the treachery of Streona, who deserted to Cnut, with Jarl Thorkil and his mercenaries. Wessex submitted to the Danes once more. Aethelred was carried to faithful London; Eadmund retreated northward. There he rallied the Anglo-Danish levies to punish Eadric, and early next year attacked West Mercia; but Cnut marched northward through the Danelaw upon York, and the Northumbrians, under Earl Uhtred, hurried back to defend their homes. Uhtred found the situation so hopeless that he submitted 'for need,' as the Chronicle pathetically says. But his submission was merely the signal for his murder – by the advice of Eadric, of course. Eadmund took refuge in London with the remains of his army, and Cnut, leaving Jarl Eric Haakonson in charge of Northumbria, prepared to follow him. Eadmund appears to have reached the faithful city early in April, and on the 16th the wretched Aethelred died.

The once mighty English Empire was now restricted to the walls of London, but Eadmund II made a splendid effort to recover it. Before ending this most wearisome and gloomy chapter of this story of invasion it is pleasant to chronicle one heroic attempt. Like Poland in the eighteenth century, the kingdom of Alfred was at least to die with honour.

Eadmund stayed only a few days in London. Its gallant inhabitants could be trusted to do their duty to the last, and the landless king sallied forth to rally adherents to his scanty following. Scarcely had he left London when Cnut beleaguered it. Being unable to force the bridge, he opened a passage for his ships round the fortifications of Southwark, probably by largely utilizing the water courses in the marsh. The popular impression that Cnut had with him a corps of engineers capable of carrying out such a formidable undertaking as that of excavating a ship canal something near a mile in length is certainly erroneous. It must be remembered that until quite modern times South London was liable to be flooded at every high tide, and it is more than probable that the only pioneering work imposed upon the Danish warriors consisted in making short cuts from one reed-grown watercourse to another, and in clearing a fairway. Cnut thus brought his lighter vessels above the bridge and completed the blockade; but the citizens held out stoutly, hoping for relief from Eadmund.

The King had reached Wessex safely, and the men of his dynasty's homeland soon began to rally to his banner. In June he was able to take the field and defeat a Danish force at Penselwood. Cnut sent off in haste an Anglo-Danish army under Thorkil and the traitor Eadric, but Eadmund defeated them at Sherston, and marched for London. He burst through Cnut's lines into the city and broke up the siege. Cnut collected his forces on the south bank of the Thames, but Eadrnund, two days later, slipped away up the river and forced a passage at Brentford. The Danes, however, though beaten, were not routed, and the English lost many men by drowning – apparently because they had scattered to plunder. The Danes still threatened London, but Eadmund's victories were attracting to him large reinforcements, and he was soon so strong that Cnut finally abandoned the siege and retreated to the mouth of the Orwell. Having collected provisions by systematic ravage, he transferred his base of operations to the Medway; but Eadmund, who was north of London, promptly crossed the Thames at Brentford and met him at Otford. For the fifth time he gained the day, and Cnut was driven back into Sheppey.

At this moment the double traitor Eadric deserted Cnut, and made his peace with the far too magnanimous Eadmund, apparently because he brought with him his Magesaetan (Hereford and Shropshire) levies, which had hitherto been aiding Cnut. The indefatigable Danish king, however, did not give up the game. He once more transferred his army into Essex, and when Eadmund advanced against him he stood to fight at Assandune (Ashington). He may have counted upon Eadric's treachery; it seems impossible that the abominable desertion that followed had not been concerted. In the heat of the battle the traitor left the line and 'began the flight with the Magesaetas, and so betrayed his true lord and all the people of England.' The result was fearful disaster. The whole English army was broken and destroyed; 'all the nobility of the English race was there undone.' Eadmund, undaunted still, retreated to Gloucestershire, and set to work to collect another army. But he must have been almost in despair, and it was well for him that the Danes were also wearied out and ready to come to terms. On the Isle of Alney, near Deerhurst, the kings met and concluded a treaty, by which the gallant English leader saved a part of his shattered realm, to be, as he might hope, a base for the future recovery of the whole. He kept Wessex, East Anglia, and West Mercia, while Cnut took Northumbria and the old Mercian 'Danelaw.'

The reconquest to which Eadmund must have looked forward was not to be. On November 30 the brave King died at Oxford. Cnut at once put forward his claim to be his successor, and was accepted by the Witan without opposition. It must have been general exhaustion and despair, as well as lack of leaders, that impelled the decision. Cnut proved an able and successful ruler, and identified. himself thoroughly with the nation which had accepted him under compulsion.

The deduction to be made from the melancholy story of the Danish Conquest is obviously that national unity was still lacking in England. Neither was patriotism other than a local feeling. So far as can be seen, the peasantry simply followed the magnates, and these latter, with some honourable exceptions, were clearly, as a class, worthless. A 'redeless' king was betrayed by contemptible and treacherous advisers and nobles, and the ill-compacted people, without national sentiment, and with no means of expressing its opinion, was unable then to redeem the blunders and cowardice of its nominal leaders.

Between 991 and 1018 the total payments made on account of 'Danegeld' amounted to 216,500 pounds of silver, probably equivalent to £7,000,000 in modern value.

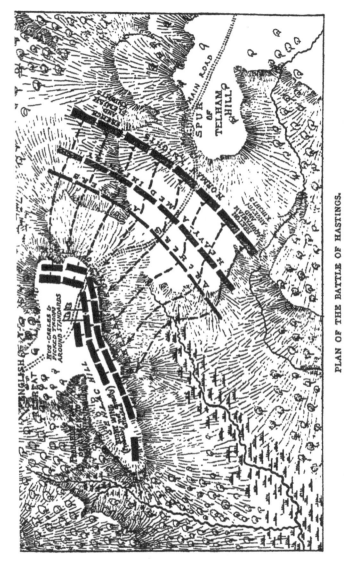

PLAN OF THE BATTLE OF HASTINGS.

The English are shown with black blocks, each representing approximately 1,000 men. The Normans are shown with shaded blocks, each indicating approximately 500 archers, 1,000 heavy infantry, or 500 cavalry.

IX

The Invasions of 1066

The passing from the scene of the strangely unsubstantial and shadowy figure of the sainted Eadward 'the Confessor' was the signal for the bursting of the storm that was to overwhelm Anglo Saxon England. For the last thirteen years of his reign the country had been practically governed by his great minister, Harold Godwineson, Earl of Wessex. Harold's character has suffered much at the hands of Norman chroniclers; there is no real reason to think that he was morally worse than most men of his age. His practical ability was of a high order, and while administering the realm with success, he also gave proof that he possessed tact and moderation. At the same time, his general success cannot hide the fact that England lacked political unity; it was a group of great family earldoms, whose heads looked upon each other with jealousy and distrust. Harold seems to have behaved with remarkable forbearance and friendliness towards the rival house of Leofric, and though he had more than one opportunity of aggrandizing his family at their expense, the death of Eadward the Confessor found Eadwine and Morkere, grandsons of Leofric, still ruling over his broad lands.

Eadward the Confessor's fondness for the Normans among whom he had been brought up was natural enough, and it is quite possible that the dominating personality of his cousin, William of Normandy, on the occasion of his visit, so impressed him that he made some sort of promise of leaving him his heir. At any rate when Harold, in 1064, after his shipwreck in the Channel, became William's unwilling guest, the Duke had no scruple in exacting from him an oath of support. The decorative adjuncts – 'holy' relics, and so forth – which he contrived in order to impress the superstitious bystanders, certainly had the desired effect on contemporary public opinion. Harold left as a hostage with William his hapless youngest brother Wulfnoth, destined to die in captivity.

But when Eadward the Confessor died on 5 January 1066, he, according to the 'Anglo-Saxon Chronicle,' left his realm to Harold. The 'Vita Eadwardi' says much the same. It seems, also, that the Witan had already chosen Harold, for he was crowned the next day in the new Abbey Church of Westminster. It is a curious reflection that the great church, which was consecrated as the old king lay dying, was, in a sense, the funeral monument of early English times.

Harold was threatened with attack from three quarters – perhaps four. It was certain that William of Normandy would attempt an invasion at the first opportunity. Harald Hardrada of Norway, the last of the great Viking monarchs, was known to be ready for any opportunity of aggrandizement. Sweyn Estrithson of Denmark, cousin of Harthacnut, might deem the moment favourable for advancing his claims. Finally,

Statue of William the Conqueror at Canterbury Cathedral. (Courtesy of Saforrest)

Tosti, Harold's worthless brother, was preparing to regain by force his forfeited Northumbrian earldom. Internally, the Northern earls were lukewarm in Harold's cause. They were men of little mark, but they controlled nearly half England, and their disaffection was a very serious matter. Truly, says the Chronicle of Harold, 'little quiet did he enjoy while he wielded the kingdom.'

When the news of Harold's coronation reached Normandy, William broke out into one of those terrible bursts of savage rage to which he was subject in times of stress. 'To no man spake he, and none dared speak to him,' says a chronicler. After his fit of passion was over he announced his intention of invading England. He called an assembly of his barons at Lillebonne on the Seine, and set forth his ideas, but they hung back; England seemed too strong. He then appealed to their individual loyalty, promising to reward them with English lands in proportion to the contingents that they furnished, and with this inducement practically the entire baronage of Normandy agreed to join in the enterprise. But the forces of Normandy alone were not strong enough, and William used every means to induce neighbouring princes and adventurers to join his standard. Eustace, Count of Boulogne, who had a private grudge against England, and Alan Fergent, cousin of the Duke of Brittany, were the most notable of these foreign allies; but adventurers from all France came in numbers, and even, so Guy of Amiens says, some of the Normans who were conquering Southern Italy from the Eastern Empire. Many months were needed before the miscellaneous host could be gathered, and hundreds of ships had to be built and launched for the transport of the fighting men, followers, the provisions, and, above all, the thousands of horses, without which the mailed knights would lose three-quarters of their efficiency. Wace tells us that the number of vessels that actually sailed was 696; other chroniclers raise it to 3,000. In this conflict of evidence the figures given by Wace have a strong appearance of veracity. Most of the vessels were doubtless small.

The number of the army is stated at from 40,000 to 60,000 by medieval chroniclers. Some modern estimates put it as low as 112,000. There are no solid grounds upon which to base a reasoned estimate. After the Conquest there were about 4,300 knight's fiefs in England.

The casualties among the invaders were enormous, but the gaps were filled by fresh adventurers, and certainly not all the English landowners were dispossessed. We are, perhaps, justified in assuming 4,000 cavalry, about 4,000 archers, and possibly 7,000 mail-clad infantry – say 15,000 men in all.

William had the support of religion in his enterprise in so far as it could be given by a papal bull. There had been, even under the pious Confessor, irregularity in the filling up of the episcopal sees; in particular, the position of Stigand, Archbishop of Canterbury, was a scandal. This, and Harold's perjury, induced the support of Alexander II, and a consecrated banner was sent to William with the bull.

The gathering-place of the army of invasion was at the mouth of the Dive. The Norman writers are eloquent upon the admirable order and discipline that prevailed in the camp, and, beyond doubt, William did keep his own subjects well in hand; but that the same was the case with the motley throng of allies is hardly possible. Still, knowing what manner of man William was, it is likely enough that his standard of discipline was, for the time, a very creditable one. Moreover, when the army came to fight it showed itself to be very different from the usual disorderly mediceval horde – highly trained, flexible, precise in manoeuvre, and under excellent discipline. Its organization was clearly Byzantine. The three East-Roman arms – archers, heavy infantry, and mailed cavalry – were all there. An East-Roman army would have had nearly as many cavalry as infantry, if it had used infantry at all to back its masses of mail-clad horsebowmen and lancers, but William's resources were unequal to putting many thousands of mounted men in the field. As it is, it is evident that his army was by far the finest force that had ever invaded England.

By about 10 August the concentration appears to have been almost complete, but for a month no move could be made owing to persistently contrary winds. The difficulties of supply must have become greater and greater, and in September William moved to the Abbey of St Walaric, now St Valery, in Caux. Still for a fortnight longer the favouring wind did not come.

Meanwhile Tosti had long since sailed. His attack was made apparently in conjunction with Harald Hardrada. He had in Flanders collected enough miscellaneous adventurers to man sixty ships, but his impatience – probably he could not keep his plundering bands together – wrecked the design of co-operation with Hardrada. The Norwegian king was collecting a great armament, and probably its concentration took time. At any rate, he did not appear in English waters until August

Harold, meanwhile, was organizing for defence. His only standing force consisted of the HusCarles, or royal household troops – 4,000 men at the utmost. They were, unquestionably, a magnificent body of men, fully equal in quality to William's knighthood, equipped like them with helmet and mail-shirt, kite-shaped shield, and armed with the terrible battle axe, which England had adopted from Denmark. Unfortunately, however, though they habitually used horses on the march, they had no experience of, or training in, fighting on horseback – a fatal defect.

The *land fyrd*, on the other hand, was difficult to move. It is easy to under-estimate its value; there must have been a large number of men in it fully armed and equipped for war; but they were never properly drilled and exercised together, and were mingled with half-armed peasantry. Still, considering the large numbers of the men liable for service, it must have been comparatively easy to collect a considerable force of properly equipped troops, but it entirely lacked cavalry and archers.

Medieval feudal armies practically depended for supplies on plunder, and were consequently always liable to dissolve. Here and there we find men – great generals like William I and Edward I – who understood how to organize a proper commissariat, but they were few and far between. Apparently Harold II was one of them, for there is no doubt that he kept a large army together on the south coast for several months.

The defence of the north was, of course, entrusted to the earls Eadwine and Morkere; no other course was possible. Nor, upon the whole, does it seem that they failed to do their duty. Harold was in Northumbria early in the year, and no doubt did his best to conciliate them. Otherwise he seems to have been very active, and Florence of Worcester says that his activity was highly beneficial, but significantly adds that his chief efforts were for the defence of the country. In April Halley's Comet made one of its recurring appearances, and, needless to say, was looked upon as the forerunner of coming evil.

Under the great West Saxon kings, as we have seen, England possessed an effective navy, but it is very doubtful whether under Eadward the Confessor any large force had been kept up. Harold's defensive armada must have consisted largely of levied merchant craft. It collected off the Isle of Wight – obviously in Spithead – and there awaited the coming of the invaders. The forces of the south were stationed 'by the sea' – presumably in divisions within easy reach of one another – and the King himself with his guards formed a reserve which could be transferred north or south at will.

The defects of this strategy are obvious enough. It was solely defensive. No attempt was made to stop the sailing of the hostile fleets; even Tosti's puny armament was allowed to reach England without molestation. The splendid marching and fighting feats of the royal guards show that their efficiency was high. A commissariat sufficient to supply a large force for several months had evidently been organized; but all this proved useless owing to the bad initial strategy of standing purely on the defensive.

In May Tosti appeared on the coast of Kent. Apparently Harold was already on the south coast, for we are told that he at once moved against him with a fleet and an army such as no King of England had ever gathered. Tosti, who had made plundering descents on the coast and had also endeavoured to increase his small force by forced impressment, did not await the onslaught, but fled. His second descent was made in the Humber. Earl Eadwine promptly set upon and defeated him; his miscellaneous force broke up, and Tosti himself fled northward to Scotland with only twelve ships. Here he seems to have been sheltered by Malcolm Canmore; presumably the Scottish king dared not eject him, when at any moment the formidable Harald Hardrada might appear.

Harold and William lay watching each other across the Channel all through the summer. When William's host had at last gathered, the wind, as we have seen, was contrary, and for nearly two months he could not stir. This was fortunate for him; had he sailed in August, he would have been attacked by Harold's fleet, and his own flotilla, crowded with troops and thousands of horses, would have fared badly. Even had the Normans gained the day they would have hardly been able to land. It was a trial of endurance. On September 8 the English fleet had exhausted its stores, and was forced to return to London to reprovision and refit. Still the land army remained in the south, but a week later came the news that Harald Hardrada was in the Humber.

The consequences of Harold's purely defensive strategy now stared him in the face. The fleet was for the time entirely off the board, but to concentrate against Hardrada was a vital necessity.

Harold marched northward without delay, and certainly strove to make up for strategic errors by activity. From Portsmouth to York is over 250 miles, but the distance was covered in ten days. Obviously Harold's whole corps must have been mounted; but even so it was a remarkable performance.

Hardrada, having picked up Tosti and the remains of his expedition, proceeded southward along the coast of Northumbria, landing and ravaging in the old Viking fashion. Scarborough was taken and sacked, and the Norwegian fleet sailed up the Humber and landed its army, which marched upon York. Eadwine and Morkere had united their forces, and stood to fight at Fulford, two miles south of the Northumbrian capital, where they were attacked by Hardrada on September 20, and completely defeated. The remains of their army took refuge in York, and so cowed were the Northumbrians that they offered 150 hostages as a pledge of their submission. Hardrada probably thought himself secure; he withdrew to the Derwent, seven miles east of York, and was encamped carelessly on both its banks, about Stamford Bridge, when on September 25 Harold, having passed through York, came upon him. No hint of his approach seems to have preceded him. The speed and secrecy of the march are alike remarkable.

The attack fell like a thunderbolt on the unprepared Norwegians. Scattered, astounded, and without time to form order of battle, they were massacred right and left, and driven towards the Derwent in a confusion that can only have tended to grow greater. The bridge was desperately defended, and under cover of the stand Hardrada's personal following seems to have been able to rally on the 'Land-ravager' – the raven standard of the Vikings. After a series of fierce attacks the shield ring was broken, Hardrada and Tosti were slain, and Olaf, the king's son, surrendered, on promise of being allowed to depart with the survivors. They are said to have been able to man only 24 ships of the original 300. We may suspect exaggeration.

Harold returned in triumph to York, where he seems to have delayed for a week or so; doubtless his troops, after their exertions, needed a rest. The northern levies also must have required reorganization. In the midst of toils and rejoicings came the terrible news that William was in Sussex.

On September 27 the long-sought-for south wind blew at last, and the huge unwieldy Norman fleet put out from St Walaric. William's flagship was the Mora, a gallant vessel given to him by his wife Matilda. She bore on her stern a gilded figure of a boy bearing a banner, as the Bayeux tapestry clearly indicates.

From St Valery-en-Caux to Pevensey is less than sixty-five miles, and the fact that the flotilla took, apparently, nearly two days to cover it, gives some index to its encumbered condition. None the less, it sailed in something like order, guided by a huge lantern at the masthead of the Mora. On the 28th it reached Pevensey, and the disembarkation was quietly effected. William himself stumbled and fell on his face as he sprang ashore. A murmur of dismay rose from the superstition-ridden barons behind, but he sprang to his feet and showed them that as he fell he had clutched up the sand with both hands. 'See how I have taken possession of England!' he cried, and his followers hailed the omen of good as readily as they had trembled at the accident. It was one of those incidents that mark the born leader of men.

From Pevensey William moved to Hastings, which he occupied without resistance. A palisaded fort is said to have been constructed; one wonders why William did not encamp within the splendid Roman walls of Pevensey. He then began to waste the coast districts in the neighbourhood, partly perhaps in order to provoke his rival to an engagement, but also, probably, in part for purposes of supply.

Wonderful as had been Harold's march to York, his rush back to London was yet more so. He covered the distance of over 190 miles in seven days at the outside, perhaps in six, an average of 27 or 32 miles a day! On 7 October he was in London. Eadwine and Morkere were still far behind. They have been severely blamed for their slowness; but it is only fair to point out that their levies had been sorely thinned at Fulford and Stamford Bridge, and that the collec tion and organization of reinforcements can have been no easy task. If the northern troops started only a day behind Harold and marched at the very fair rate of eighteen miles a day, they must have still been some distance from London when he left it for the south. Probably Eadwine and Morkere failed to realize the urgency of the crisis; but, on the other hand, Harold's precipitancy must have been dis concerting.

The King stayed only some four days in London. On the 11th he marched again, presumably with the royal guards and the men of London and the home counties. He again pressed forward with great speed; the rate of marching was over eighteen miles a day. On the afternoon of the 13th the head of the column was on Senlac Hill, eight miles from Hastings, and there, no doubt, the King could question peasants and could ascertain that William had concentrated his army.

That he had had hopes of repeating his feat at Stamford Bridge seems almost certain. The authorities are practically unanimous in stating or implying that his army would have been strongly reinforced had he delayed a little, and that he did not do so is best explained by his anxiety to execute another surprise attack on an unprepared enemy. As this plan had obviously failed, it was to his interest to avoid a battle; and the general opinion at the time evidently was that he was unwise to risk one. The story that his brother Gyrth would have dissuaded him from engaging, but that he declined to look on while his people were pillaged by the Norman raiders, may be taken for what it is worth, but it points to the prevalence of this opinion. The most probable explanation is that the weary and illdisciplined army could not be withdrawn in the darkness from the ridge on which it was bivouacking, and it was therefore necessary to remain there for the night. William on his side was obliged to fight. His army subsisted by pillage, and would starve if it were forced to remain long in a state of close concentration. He had early notice of his rival's advance, and had his army in hand about Hastings. He was at Telham so early on the morning of the 9th that to decline a battle was difficult, if not

impossible, for Harold. With disciplined troops a retreat would have
been practicable enough, but it was not so for the cumbrous English
host. Perhaps, too, Harold overrated the fighting power of his axemen.
In any case, it is clear that he stood to receive battle when retreat was
his wisest strategy.

Senlac Hill is an outlying spur of the South Downs, roughly parallel to
them, and connected with them by a short saddleback. The main ridge
is about 280 feet above the sea at its culminating point, and nearly 1,200
yards long. The road from London passes along the saddleback, over the
ridge towards its eastern end, and across a valley to Telham Hill, about
a mile distant. The slope of the ridge in front is fairly gentle, but where
the remains of the Abbey now stand it rises steeply to a commanding
knoll. The exact gradient is difficult to estimate, for when the Abbey was
built the slope was much altered by terracing, which exists today. On
both flanks – especially the left – and on the rear, except where the road
approaches, the slopes are steep. For over half its length the front face of
the ridge is covered by a brook and a line of ponds. In 1066 in their place
there was most probably a marsh, almost impassable for cavalry. Even
at the present day the ground just below the ponds becomes extremely
difficult for a horseman. The western half of the position could probably
only have been assailed by the very dangerous process of filing horsemen
round the end of the marsh, and advancing them in front of it. This
actually appears to have been attempted by part of the Norman army;
but it was only possible to deliver direct attacks on a front of about 750
yards. In this narrow space the deadliest fighting took place. Behind all
was the forest of the Andredsweald.

The strength of the English army can only be guessed at. According
to the earlier writers it was densely massed along the ridge, but it is
probable that the almost unassailable western end was not held in
force. On the other hand, the eastward portions were probably very
strongly held. There may have been in all about 5,000 men. About
half the troops were probably fully equipped men, and in their strong
position were capable of beating off an attack of any other army in
Western Europe, except the one that now faced them. As compared
with it the English, without archers or cavalry, were at a hopeless
disadvantage, but even as it was they came very near success.

The question of fortification has been often discussed. None of the earlier writers mention any, nor are any shown on the Bayeux tapestry, the workers of which would very probably have had William's own personal account to go upon. Wace appears to describe a sort of wicker breastwork. So much is certain, that the English troops reached the ground too late and too fatigued to be able to account much entrenching work. The cries of 'Ut! Ut!' (Out! Out!), attributed to the English, may perhaps indicate that they conceived themselves to occupy an entrenched enclosure: but it may just as well refer to the impatience of men pent up in the shield-ring under a storm of arrows.

The Norman army advancing from Hastings reached Telham early in the morning. An interesting detail is that the knights rode in their tunics and did not don their armour until they reached the field. At the foot of Telham the army deployed in three divisions, each of three lines classified according to arms. The front line consisted of archers and crossbow-men – there were some of these latter present; the second of mail-clad infantry; the third of the cavalry. The right wing consisted mainly of the French and Flemish mercenaries under Eustace of Boulogne and the Norman baron Roger de Montgomerie. On the left

Hastings.

were the Breton Angevin and Aquitanian troops. William himself was in the centre with his Normans. Ralph de Toesny, the hereditary standard-bearer of Normandy, bad begged to be allowed to 'fight with both hands' on that day; and Walter Giffard declined to bear the Pope's banner. He was old, he said, and would like to do a last good day's fighting. So the standard was borne at William's side by Toustain de Bec-en-Caux. William himself bore on this day not the lance, which was still a light weapon often used for throwing, but a ponderous iron mace, and with him rode his brothers Odo of Bayeux and Robert of Mortain.

As the Normans marched down Telham, Senlac suddenly appeared to be crowned with a dense line of axes and shields. The English seemed to spring out of the wood, says Guy of Amiens. This may indicate that they were taken by surprise, and hastily faced about to meet the unexpected approach of the Normans. The royal guards were on the left centre, with the Dragon of Wessex and the King's Warrior banner planted where the altar of Battle Abbey afterwards rose. With the guards almost certainly were the Londoners, who were probably the best equipped troops of the fyrd. They were under Esegar, the first 'Staller' (Marshal). Everything seems to show that there was a solid mass of picked troops in the centre. The King, with his brothers Gyrth and Leofwine, was on foot by his standards surrounded by his incomparable footguards.

The Norman host advanced across the valley and began to breast Senlac Hill, the archers shooting furiously as soon as they came within range. For a while it was attack without defence, and it is odd that William does not appear to have seen that the bowmen could be left to prepare the way. The English could only suffer, and already, perhaps, impatient warriors were beginning to cry 'Out! Out!' yearning to exchange blows with their exasperating enemies. The archers, emboldened by their bloodless progress, pressed forward to close range, and then came the English reply. The leading ranks of the Normans were overwhelmed with a perfect hail of miscellaneous missiles – spears, javelins, casting-axes, and stones, some of the latter tied to clubs and hurled like hammers. The archers came to a stand, still plying their bows; and the heavy infantry pushed up between their intervals and came to handgrips with the English. Their charge broke vainly upon the shield-wall; not a gap could the Norman footsoldiers tear in it. Javelins, taper-axes, and stone hammers crashed among them fast and furiously; the great axes swayed and fell with terrible effect. Do what they would they could make no progress.

Probably the Norman infantry were already falling back when William let loose his cavalry. No doubt the chivalry of France and Normandy expected to ride down the English infantry with ease. Out in front of the long moving line of horsemen, bright in their ringed mail shirts, rode the minstrel Taillefer, chanting verses from the 'Song of Roland', playing with his sword as be pricked up the slope. He was the first of the knighthood to penetrate the shield-wall – also the first to fall. The long lines of horsemen crashed against the shields; the shock must have been tremendous, but their fortune was no better than that of their despised infantry. The English front may have been pressed back, even pierced in places, but the gaps were at once restored; man and horse went down beneath the tremendous strokes of the great axes, while from the rearward ranks of the English host the same tempest of darts, throwing-axes, and stone clubs crashed upon the mail and helmets of the charging cavaliers. After a furious struggle the Bretons and Angevins were repulsed and driven downhill. After them poured the ill-disciplined levies of the English right. The retreating horsemen blundered into the marsh, which they had avoided without difficulty as they advanced, and, with the English pressing furiously on their rear, were in wild disorder, when the victors were suddenly charged in flank by part of the Norman centre, turned against them by the watchful Duke. The results were terrible. The scattered warriors, many of them half-armed peasants, were over ridden and cut down by hundreds, and only a remnant regained the position which they had so rashly left.

This, however, was only the beginning. William rallied the broken left wing, and again and again the fierce horsemen charged the immovable English line – in vain. Never had the knights seen or heard of such footsoldiers as these. One tremendous charge led by William himself did burst through the shield wall; and the brave Gyrth went down beneath the Duke's terrible mace. Leofwine, too, was slain; but the charge was beaten off by a rally of the English axemen, and hurled downhill, and the cry went up that the Duke was slain. William flung himself among the panic-stricken knights: 'I live! I live!' he thundered, tearing off his helmet. By God's aid I will conquer yet!' Out of evil came good – for Normandy.

Nearly the whole Norman line was apparently in disorder, but William rallied it again and brought it up to the charge, though it is evident that the attacks must have grown less and less effective as time went on, owing to the fatigue of the horses. At his wits' end, William tried the expedient of a feigned retreat; and the French on the right recoiled, to all seeming broken and beaten, down the slope. This was too much for the greatly enduring Englishmen, and a great part of their left and centre came pouring down in pursuit. The retreating horsemen turned upon them; William assailed them in flank with troops from his centre. The carnage was great, and apparently the whole English left wing was annihilated. But the pursuing horsemen appear to have met with disaster in an unexpected trench or watercourse, and Bishop Odo of Bayeux had to ride among and steady them.

Still, the battle was far from over. The best part of the English army, including the royal household, was still ranged in dense masses on the crown of the hill. But their line was sorely reduced by the disaster of the wings, and the Norman cavalry could charge in front and flank. Inspired by the hope of victory, the knights hurled themselves again to the attack, but still in vain. The line of shields was an impregnable barrier; charge after charge recoiled from the steadfast front and to the fierce Norman war-cry of '*Dex aie!*' (Dieu aide!) the English shouts of 'Holy Cross!' still thundered in defiant answer.

The Norman cavalry was growing more and more wearied and ineffective; the victory was far from decisive as long as the English centre still fought on. Then at last William did what he should have attempted long before, and brought his archers to the front. Any East-Roman tactician would have told him that the cavalry should never have attacked until the English masses had been thoroughly shattered by their fire, and the fact shows how low the art of war had fallen in the West. Between the cavalry attacks the bowmen poured in their volleys, shooting with a high trajectory so that the arrows were not wasted on the shield-wall, but made havoc in the heart of the dense mass. The device had terrible success. The picked warriors of England fell fast before the pitiless rain to which they cou d not reply. For the most part they could but suffer. Once or twice it seems that small bodies tried to charge out; now and again desperate warriors sprang forth to contend hand-to-hand with the Norman knights, but they only hastened their end. The splendid guards stood shoulder to shoulder in the mass, never wavering or faltering, but the losses were all on one side. Behind the unbroken shield wall was an ever-increasing weltering confusion of dead and dying upon which the arrows beat pitilessly; and the King, mortally wounded in the eye, lay in agony beneath the standards. The position was desperate; but so long as the banners waved and the King lived there was no thought of yielding. But at last the fatal gaps could not be closed fast enough, and the Normans burst through the shield-wall. A band of knights hewed their way through the dissolving mass, cut down the faithful few round Harold, tore down the Dragon and the Warrior, and literally hacked the dying King to pieces at the foot of his banners.

And now the end had come. The noble English infantry, who had defied the Norman chivalry all day, and but for the archery would have beaten them to their ships, began – all that remained of them – to withdraw sullenly but hopelessly. Even yet they were not demoralized, and some were still in good order. As the little remnant got away across the saddleback into Andredsweald they saw the Normans plunging rashly in pursuit down the steep rearward slopes of Senlac. Turning to bay, true even in that hour of despair, to their noble warrior strain, they set upon the overweening horsemen, cut their leading squadrons to pieces, and drove them back on Senlac. Panic spread through the Norman army; Eustace of Boulogne is said to have counselled retreat, and it was only when William himself rallied his squadrons and brought them along the ridge in a properly ordered pursuit that the English finally melted away into the woods.

Looking at the battle after this length of time, it is clear that William only gained the day by desperate exertions, and that more than once success hung in the balance. Had the English army possessed a proportion of archers the day would have been Harold's. It has been pointed out that not even a great fleet saved England from an attack by an invader prepared to take the risk of destruction. But it should be remembered that Harold's flotilla was not a properly organized force, and cannot be compared to a modern fleet able to keep the sea for several months at a time. Even as it was, William was very near destruction though, so far as we can see, he caught Harold at a disadvantage. By calmly taking such risks as few men could contemplate unshaken, William did land in England, but his success was due to a very remarkable combination of circumstances which it would be well to recapitulate.

1. The English fleet, owing to its urgent need to revictual, was absent from the chief danger-point at the crucial moment, and at the rate of sailing in those days the Thames, even with favourable winds, was farther from Pevensey than Rosyth is today from Portsmouth.

2. The English army at the moment when the invasion was imminent was called to the defence of the north.

3. The wind which had baffled William for some six weeks shifted in his favour at the precise moment when the English fleet and army were absent.

4. The extraordinary rapidity of Harold's southward march after his defeat of Hardrada left the disorganized Northumbrian and Mercian levies far in the rear.

5. The English were probably surprised into giving battle when Harold would have preferred to await support.

6. The English army was at a fatal tactical disadvantage owing to its lack of archers.

William's losses had been exceedingly heavy. The medieval chroniclers estimate that he lost 12,000 to 15,000 men out of 40,000 to 60,000, and we may fairly estimate from this that his casualties were about a fourth of his fighting strength. But only a mere remnant of the English host survived the day, and with the King fell every man of note in southern England, except Esegar the Marshal, who was desperately wounded. This awful destruction of the leaders was the most disastrous feature of the battle. There was, as after-events showed, a complete dearth of men about whom the English might rally.

In many ways the Battle of Hastings was itself the Norman

Conquest, though the events of the following two or three years are rather those which gave William his title of 'Conqueror.' The whole southeast of England had been utterly crushed; there remained for William only the conquest piecemeal of the west and north. Kent was conquered with scarcely any resistance, and William, advancing to the Thames, beat back a sortie of the Londoners, burned Southwark, and moved up the river feeling for a passage. Detachments from his army occupied Winchester and the neighbouring towns, and William, crossing the Thames at Wallingford, marched upon London. Eadwine and Morkere, who were there with the forces which had been too late for Senlac, lost their nerve when the Normans threatened their line of retreat to the north. They hurriedly withdrew, and the Londoners bowed to necessity. 'They submitted then for need, when the most harm was done,' mourns the 'Anglo-Saxon Chronicle.'

There is no reason to doubt that William, when he promised to govern England well, had every intention of keeping his word. But he probably found it difficult from the outset to control the greedy adventurers who followed him; and in any case he was bound to reward them. When his strong hand was temporarily removed by his return to Normandy, the tyranny of Odo of Bayeux and the excesses of the foreign nobles and soldiers soon produced revolt. Yet there was nothing national in the various uprisings; north, east, and west acted independently, and of cordial co-operation there was not a sign. In 1067 William, returning from Normandy, subdued the west and captured Exeter. Then, marching northward, he overran Mercia and Northumbria. Nowhere was there anything like an effective resistance; such opposition as was made appears to have been mainly inspired by King Malcolm of Scotland. Strong garrisons were placed at York, Lincoln, Nottingham, and other places, and earthworks thrown up, which later were to grow into the frowning castles that have somewhat incorrectly been associated with the Norman Conquest.

The year 1069 saw the only serious and determined attempt to overthrow the Norman rule. A great Danish fleet, sent by Sweyn Estrithson, arrived in the Humber, joined the Northumbrians, and marched on York. It was stormed and captured, and 30,000 foreign soldiers, it is said, were slain or taken. But that was all, and the peril died down before William's vehement energy. The Danish fleet was bought off – William was as ready as Philip of Macedonia to use 'silver spears'. Then the King reoccupied York, and, lest any succeeding Scandinavian invasion should find a foothold, wrought the awful devastation of the north – the worst deed that stains his otherwise not ignoble character. The north, wasted and ruined, was at his feet, and the reappearance next year of Sweyn with a great fleet ended in a mere fiasco. The Danes and the East Anglian rebels did little but plunder abbeys, and after sundry useless demonstrations the Danes returned home.

There now remained in all England in arms against William only the gathering in the Isle of Ely under the famous outlaw Hereward. Thither came sundry English leaders, powerless and discredited, who now could only swell the band of an erstwhile obscure chief. Eadwine had already disappeared-slain, so says the 'Anglo-Saxon Chronicle', by his own men. Morkere succeeded in reaching Ely; but at best the leaders were but a poor remnant. The position of Ely, surrounded by its waters, was strong; but the garrison was not sufficiently numerous to take the offensive with any hope of success. William fixed his headquarters at Cambridge; a fleet was collected and brought up the Wash, and the lines of investment were steadily drawn round the doomed stronghold. A causeway was driven across the fens, and when at last it reached firm land, after many checks and surprises inflicted by the watchful Hereward, Ely was forced to surrender. Legends have clustered thickly about the figure of Hereward 'the Wake'. He was certainly taken into William's favour, and was commanding troops for him on the Continent some years later. The mass of the rank and file, however, were treated with what seems to us horrible barbarity, being maimed and mutilated wholesale. The punishment of death the 'stark' and terrible Conqueror was always very chary of inflicting. Famous as the defence of Ely has become, it is noteworthy that the Chronicle does not seem to regard it as other than an isolated incident in the struggle. It is at any rate clear that it could never have done more than temporarily check the progress of the Conqueror, just as eighteen centuries before the defence of Eira could only delay the Spartan conquest of Messenia. With the fall of Ely the Norman Conquest of England was complete.

The country settled down beneath the yoke of William with resignation if not cheerfulness, and the lack of further outbreaks seems to indicate that after all his rule was not worse than that of his immediate predecessors. Perhaps one explanation of this submissiveness is that the English thegnhood emigrated to Constantinople in large numbers, so that the nation lacked its natural leaders, but something must be set to William's credit despite his many faults and crimes. The fear of foreign invasion died away; the Danish attacks in 1075 and 1085 were utterly futile. Englishmen, while they hated William as the destroyer of their independence, could not forget 'the good peace that he made in this land; so that a man of any account might fare over his kingdom unhurt with his bosom full of gold.' To keep the peace in a land was no slight thing in those days of feudal anarchy; and if the Norman Conquest was very far from being an unmixed benefit, it at least brought about a better sense of unity than had hitherto prevailed in England.

X

Continental Invasions
1066–1545

Since 1066 – a period of over eight centuries – there have been, apart from many sporadic raids, no great successful invasions of England. On two occasions relatively large forces have landed on these shores, but in both cases they had the support of a considerable part of the nation.

The first of these occasions was in 1216. King John's tyranny had at last produced something like a general revolt – at any rate among his barons. His assent to Magna Carta, given on 15 June 1215, had proved a farce, and his mercenary armies were too strong for disorderly feudal and civic levies. Further, John had declared himself the vassal of Pope Innocent III, and thus ensured his support. The men of London, the chief baronial stronghold, stoutly withstood the thunders of Rome; but their military weakness forced them to apply for help to the Dauphin Louis, son of John's great enemy, Philip Augustus of France, whom they acknowledged as King. Despite the opposition of the Pope, who finally excommunicated him, Louis invaded England early in 1216.

England had possessed no regular standing navy since the days of Edward the Confessor. The ports, however, had steadily increased in prosperity during the generally peaceful period 1066–1216; and John, living in fear of invasion, had kept up a large naval force collected from them. It is at this time that the association of the Cinque Ports becomes prominent, and, besides London, Yarmouth, Fowey, Bristol, and other places, could send out hundreds of small but well-manned craft. In 1214, under John's gallant half-brother, William 'Long sword,' they had gained the famous victory of Damme. Their effectiveness was much diminished by their lack of discipline and bloody feuds, but when united they were formidable. John had suc ceeded in conciliating them, and had they met Louis at sea he would hardly have landed. But in 1216, as in 1066, the English fleet was wind-bound, and Louis landed in Thanet on 21 May.

The operations that followed are devoid of interest, owing to their aimlessness. Most of the south-east submitted to Louis, except Dover, which made a magnificent resistance under Hubert de Burgh. A memento of Louis's domination survives in the name of a row of ancient houses at St Albans, which are said to have lodged some of his followers. King John made an attempt to come to the relief of his faithful officer, but lost his baggage and treasure in the treacherous shallows of the Wash, and died at Newark on 19 October.

His son Henry, a boy of ten, was crowned king at Gloucester by Cardinal Gualo, the Pope's legate. His chief supporter was William the Marshal, Earl of Pembroke, an aged warrior, who had held his present rank under Henry II. He was also supported by a strong remnant of his father's mercenaries, under the fierce chief Faukes de Breaute, as well as by greedy but talented officials of the type of Peter des Roches. Gualo and the Marshal made great efforts to satisfy the mercenary generals, and to keep their ruffianly troops in hand.

Louis, on his side, distrusted his English supporters, regarding them as traitors, and was short of money to pay his own mercenaries. For a while he continued to gain ground, but the dissensions among his followers increased. The Royalists promised that all past desertions should be forgiven to those who returned to their allegiance, and barons began to change sides once more. The Cinque Ports, which had submitted to Louis, now repented. The Wealden peasants rose against him under an esquire named William de Cassingham ('Wilkin of the Weald'), and practically besieged Louis in Winchelsea, which was patriotically deserted by its inhabitants. He was at last relieved by a French fleet, but the Royalists meanwhile regained most of the south. Meanwhile, however, his lieutenant in London, Enguerrand de Coucy, had organized a force under Gilbert of Ghent, which marched northward and besieged Lincoln.

Louis, much disheartened, went to France for reinforcements; but as he was now under the ban of the Pope, he obtained little support, since his cautious father dared not act openly. He was, however, joined by the Counts of Brittany and Perche and other nobles, with some 120 knights and their followings, and brought back with him to England a train of siege engines. The engines, however, made no impression on Dover; and Lincoln Castle, gallantly defended by its chatelaine, Nicola de Camville, was defiant.

Blanche of Castille, Louis's wife, regardless of Papal thunders, was collecting fresh forces in France to aid her husband. Louis, in London, had the choice of moving either north or south. In the south the Royalists were very strong, though Winchester still was Louis's, and the Prince resolved to turn his strength northward. A force under the Count of Perche, Robert Fitzwalter, who had been the Marshal of the baronial army in the preceding year, and Saer de Quincy, Earl of Winchester, accordingly marched to assist Gilbert of Ghent at Lincoln. The fall of the Castle now appeared imminent. The besieging army consisted of over 600 knights and their followers. William the Marshal came in haste from the south and joined Peter des Roches and Faukes de Breaute at Newark.

The Royalist army consisted of 400 knights' retinues, and 300 mercenary – crossbowmen – i.e., probably only about 700 really effective troops. They wore white crosses on their garments as the army of Holy Church, and were solemnly blessed before they set out by Cardinal Gualo – a ceremony which may or may not have appealed to Breaute's swashbucklers. On May 20 they were outside Lincoln. The crossbowmen were passed safely into the Castle, and the knights charged into the town by the north gate. The French seem to have had no proper guard at any of the entrances. They fought gallantly in the streets, but were finally driven out by Bargate. It became blocked, and hundreds of knights, including Robert Fitzwalter, were taken. The Count of Perche was slain by a spear-thrust in the eye. Only a few knights fell, but there was a frightful massacre of their followers and the hapless citizens, while so much plunder was gained that the Royalists called the combat 'The Fair of Lincoln.'

This defeat was a severe blow to the hopes of Louis, but he still held firm at London, watching for his reinforcements. The Dauphiness had collected several hundred knights and large supplies, which were to be conveyed to England by Eustace the Monk, a renegade ecclesiastic, now a noted pirate chief, with a fleet of 100 sail. On August 23 it sailed from Calais, but as all the south eastern ports were hostile, and were held in force by the Marshal, who had his headquarters at Sandwich, it turned up Dover Straits to round the North Foreland and put into the Thames. As it passed Dover, the Cinque Ports squadron, some forty vessels under Hubert de Burgh himself, put out to the attack. The ships were well manned with bowmen (or crossbowrnen) under Philip d'Albini, and quicklime was provided for use against boarders. The heavily laden French ships were at a hopeless disadvantage. The English seamen manoeuvred for the wind, and, having gained it, bore down on their encumbered foes. The result was an overwhelming victory. Robert de Courtenay, the leader of the reinforcements, was taken prisoner. So, too, was the Monk, who, having been in the English service, was immediately beheaded. Many knights were slain, others drowned themselves in despair, and only fifteen ships escaped. The victory had decisive results. Louis at once made peace, submitting to the Pope's legate, and abandoning all hopes of the English crown. Hubert de Burgh became the darling of England. Years later, when he had fallen into disgrace with Henry III, a smith who was ordered to fetter him threw down hammer and chains and swore that he would never put iron upon the man who had saved England from a foreign yoke.

For more than three centuries there was little that can be described as a serious invasion of England from the sea. The constant raids and counter-raids of the more than half-piratical seamen of the Channel ports, indeed, went on unchecked. The State Papers afford ample evidence that piracy was rife among the seamen of the English ports. During the 'Hundred Years' War' with France these raids became of national significance. At first the English held the command of the sea by their famous victories of Sluys in 1340 and 'L'Espagnols sur Mer' in 1350, but after 1372 it passed to the allied French and Castilians. As early as 1360 Winchelsea was sacked – a fate it again suffered in 1361. In 1369 Portsmouth was burned. In 1372 the French and Spaniards gained a complete victory over the English off La Rochelle. France had now a capable admiral in Jean de Vienne, and in 1377 he carried devastation along the English coast. The Isle of Wight was wasted, and Dartmouth, Plymouth, Yarmouth, Rye, Hastings, and Portsmouth, sacked one after another. The English were helpless, and the French sailed up the Thames to Gravesend, which shared the fate of the other ports. The Patent Rolls of this period are full of records of the prevailing panic and disaster.

Something was done to retaliate by raids on France, but with little success. In 1380 the main Franco-Spanish fleet endeavoured to raid Ireland, but was severely defeated by the ships of Devon and Bristol at Kinsale. Yet in the same year Winchelsea was again destroyed. It never recovered, and its once splendid church was reduced to the fragment which still survives. In 1385 De Vienne sailed to the Forth, and helped the Scots to invade England. A great effort, however, in 1386, to equip a vast fleet for the invasion of England failed utterly, and the English port squadrons made lucrative raids upon the French ships as they lay rotting on the coasts. This failure practically put an end to active French operations, but they still retained to a great extent the command of the sea. In 1403 a French squadron sacked Plymouth, and landed a few men to assist the great Welsh rebel, Owen Glendower. Another squadron raided the Isle of Wight, but was repulsed by the men of Hampshire.

In August, 1405, a large French fleet appeared in Milford Haven, and landed 800 horsemen and 1,800 infantry, under the Marechal Jean de Rieux and Jean de Hangest, Master of the Crossbows. Glendower joined them with 10, 000 men. The allies took Tenby, Haverfordwest, and Caermarthen, and brought Henry IV westward with a large army. Glendower starved him into a retreat, and captured much of the royal baggage, including Henry's crown and robes. But the French fleet was defeated by Lord Berkeley, and the French soldiers worked as ill with the Welsh as with the Scots (see Chapter XI). They drifted home in detachments during 1405 and 1406, and Glendower was left to maintain alone his gallant but hopeless contest with England.

For over a hundred years Franee made no further attempt. She interfered at different times in the English dynastic broils, but not until 1545 was there any attempt at a great invasion. During this period, despite civil and foreign war, the idea of a true royal navy had never been really lost sight of. Henry VII had given the question serious attention, and his vigorous son took a strong personal interest in naval matters. The consequence was that by 1543, when war threatened with France, he had a really formidable naval force.

When war broke out England was in alliance with the Emperor Charles V, while France's only supporter was gallant but feeble Scotland. The result was that the English Navy wasted the Scottish and French coasts, and swept French commerce off the sea. But in 1545 Francois I succeeded in detaching Charles from the alliance. He then slowly collected a huge fleet. There finally assembled nearly 150 great ships (*gros vaisseaux ronds*), 60 oared vessels of 40 or so tons (*flouins*), and 25 galleys from the Mediterranean. Besides the crews, there were 10,000 troops on board under the Marechal Biez. The Commanderin-Chief was Admiral d'Annibault. Paulin, Baron de la Garde, and Leone Strozzi, Admiral of the Galleys of Rhodes, commanded the galleys.

Henry had ample intelligence of the intended invasion. The whole of the available naval strength of England was concentrated at Spithead under the command of John, Lord Lisle, High Admiral of England, afterwards Duke of Northumberland. It consisted of 'great-ships' built in England or purchased abroad, 'galleasses' – really galleons, or ships built on finer lines than the ordinary great ship (see Chapter XIII), and small craft. To deal with the free-moving galleys Henry had himself designed thirteen row-barges, fast, handy little vessels of about 20 tons, armed with several small guns, and propelled by sweeps as well as sails. The flagship was an unwieldy giant of 1,000 tons, the *Harry Grace-à-Dieu*. The total number of vessels was over 100. The majority of the crews were soldiers; the supreme importance of the seaman was not yet realized. In view of the apparent superiority of the enemy Lisle was ordered to remain on the defensive. No less than 120,000 men were levied for land defence, organized in four armies.

D'Annibault sailed from Havre on 14 July. On the 16th he was off the coast of Sussex, where be wasted time in pillaging fishing villages. He then moved on to the Isle of Wight, and anchored off St Helens. Next day the galleys engaged the English fleet at long range without result. On the 18th the French threatened an attack in three divisions of ships, with the galleys as an advance guard. There was a dead calm, and for a while the long 60-pounders of the galleys made good practice. But before long a breeze sprang up, and Lisle weighed so smartly that the galleys were nearly caught before they could put about. They succeeded in doing so, however, and retired slowly, with the object of drawing on the English great-ships. Lisle, however, would not be enticed, and sent the rowbarges in pursuit. They chased with great daring, and before the long galleys could turn on their nimble tormentors they had been well peppered. Had the French made a serious attack, Lisle had formed an able plan for their discomfiture. He designed to fall with his whole force on their right wing and drive them upon the dangerous shoals of the 'Owers' which stretch eastward from the Isle of Wight. The wind, however, was unfavourable, and without it he would not abandon his strong position.

As it was obvious that Lisle was not to be drawn out, the French landed raiding parties in the Isle of Wight. They were roughly handled by the Continental Invasions garrison, and then D'Annibault gave up and retired. Disease was already breaking out in the crowded and dirty ships. The English lost the great-ship *Marie Rose*, which capsized owing to her bad construction and over-armament, carrying with her Captain Grenville, (father of the hero of Elizabeth's reign), Sir George Carew, and 500 men.

D'Annibault made some more irritating and futile raids on Sussex, and then went back· to Havre, landed 7,000 of his scurvy-stricken troops, and returned to sail aimlessly about the Channel. Meanwhile Henry, annoyed at finding that the galleys could thus beard him at his very door, had ordered some of his lighter ships to be fitted with sweeps. Having effected this, Lisle cleared from Spithead about 11 August, with 104 sail. He had carefully organized his fleet, and the flagships all carried special flags by day and lights at night. The watchword was 'God save King Henry!' the countersign 'And long to reign over us!' The order of battle was –

'Vawarde': 24 great-ships; 3,800 men. Sir Thomas Clere, Vice-Admiral of England.
'Battle': 40 great-ships; 6,846 men. Viscount Lisle, Lord High Admiral of England.

'Wing': 40 galleasses, shallops, and war-boats; 2,092 men.
Rear-Admiral William Tyrrell.

On the 15th the two fleets encountered off Shoreham. Lisle intended to attack the French great-ships, which were close inshore, with the 'Battle' and the 'Vawarde,' while the 'Wing' of oared craft kept off the galleys. Before he could close, however, the wind fell. The fighting was only between the galleys and Tyrrell. The advantage rested with the English. Lisle stated that the oared craft 'did so handle the galleys, as well with their sides as with their prows, that your great ships in a manner had little to do;' and in the night the French drew off. They went home and dispersed, and so in this impotent fashion the greatest invasion of England that had yet been planned flickered out. Lisle was able to burn Treport, and retaliate for the raids on Sussex; and towards the close of the war an action was fought off Ambleteuse, south of Cape Gris-Nez. There were eight French galleys against four English 'galleasses' and four pinnaces. It is notable because the English declined to close, and relied chiefly upon steady gun-fire. The galleys were severely mauled, and one of them taken.

The attack of François I was the first serious attempt at an invasion of England by France from the sea since the abortive effort in 386. It was not to be the last, though all were to be fruitless; but not for more than 250 years was a hostile French soldier to set foot on English soil, and then but for a moment.

XI

Scottish Invasions

Shakespeare in *King Henry V* puts into the King's mouth the following lines:

> For you shall read that my great-grandfather
> Never went with his forces into France,
> But that the Scot on his unfurnish'd kingdom
> Came pouring like the tide into a breach.

And the words express sufficiently well the popular opinion of Scotland as the especial and persevering enemy of England. Like a good many popular opinions, it is only partly true. Yet it has a foundation of fact, in so far that for some three centuries England and Scotland were generally at war. Still, this condition of chronic hostility was not reached until the reign of Edward I, and before then the two countries had no more than the amount of warfare that might have been expected of two adjacent and warlike peoples.

It has already been noticed that Constantine III's vague acknowledgment of English suzerainty had had less success from the political point of view than he had hoped for, and that his attempt to unite the disaffected sections of the English Empire had met with crushing disaster. The old King, bereaved and broken-hearted, withdrew to 'his northland,' and for many years the Scottish kingdom, slowly growing together out of its discordant elements of Scots, Picts, and Strathclyde Britons, was content to remain a sort of appendage of its powerful neighbour.

But with the break-up of the English Empire in the beginning of the eleventh century, the unsubstantial allegiance of Scotland grew more than ever shadowy. In 1018 occurred an event which had consequences of profound importance. England had just come under the rule of Cnut. Deira was governed by Eric Haakonson, but the Bernicians held out against him under Eardwulf 'Cudel.' Malcolm II of Scotland, a vigorous ruler, saw his chance. He had long coveted Lothian, and had made various futile attacks upon it. In 1006 he had pushed southward as far as Durham, and had there been defeated by Earl Uhtred. But this time he was more fortunate. Eardwulf, attacked by Eric, had more upon his hands than he could cope with, when Malcolm with his vassal, Eugenius of Strathclyde, invaded Bernicia. He overran Lothian without assistance, and at Carham, on the Tweed, gained a crushing victory over the weak Bernician host, almost exterminating it. The result of the victory was the permanent union of Lothian to Scotland. To Cnut it was a matter of small importance; probably he regarded it as better that Lothian should belong to the apparently loyal Scot than the rebellious Eardwulf. In 1027 Malcolm paid a formal homage to the Emperor of the North. But the Lothians and the Merse became an integral part of Scotland, and their sturdy Teutonic population proved the nucleus about which the inchoate and distracted realm eventually solidified into a single state.

It is almost unnecessary to say that, as soon as Cnut was in his grave, Malcolm's successor Duncan threw off his allegiance. In 1040 he invaded Bernicia. The line of the Tyne was as yet undefended, and he pressed on to Dunholm (Durham), where the south Bernician levies had taken refuge. Making a gallant sortie, they completely routed the disorderly swarm of Picts, Scots, and Britons, and celebrated their victory by raising a bloody trophy of severed heads.

Duncan's prestige as successor of the conqueror Malcolm II was shattered by this defeat, and he was at once involved in war with his many unruly vassals. Soon after the battle of Dunholm he was defeated, and slain by his general Macbeth, 'Mormaer' (hereditary chief) of Moray, who assumed the crown, and ruled very successfully for seventeen years. It was not until 1057 that he was slain in battle by Malcolm 'Canmore,' the son and heir of Duncan.

Durham.

Malcolm early began to interfere in English affairs. He may be very fairly compared to those early kings of Parthia, whose single object was to add territory to their own narrow lands. Malcolm's power, however, was not equal to his energy and ambition. Like the kings of Bulgaria in their relations with the Eastern Empire, he might gain temporary successes, but in the end the victory inclined to the larger and more powerful state; nor, despite the courage of her people and their stubborn pride in their nationality, was Scotland ever a dangerous rival. At her best she was a troublesome neighbour, and as England naturally moved faster on the path of progress than her poor and politically hampered foe, the chances were more and more against the latter ever gaining a decisive success.

Scotland has been well served by her poets. The average Englishman is generally serenely ignorant of the very names of his ancestors' victories; while not merely Bannockburn, but a score of minor matters – mostly mere Border skirmishes are celebrated by Scott, and referred to with pride. This radical difference between the standpoints of the two nations can hardly be ignored.

The hope of making further acquisitions of Northumbrian territory was undoubtedly the main motive of Scots kings for two centuries after Carham. Malcolm III made a raid on Northumberland in 1061, but the savagery of his followers can hardly have helped his cause.

Later he is found in alliance with Tosti, the rebellious brother of Harold II.

Malcolm's hopes were rudely checked by the events of 1066. William's introduction of a highly centralized rule ensured that for the future Northumbria would not be left to fight her own battles unaided, or, at least, unavenged. Yet for a time Malcolm's marriage to Margaret, sister of Eadgar the Aetheling, and the considerable immigration into Scotland of fugitive Englishmen, seemed to promise otherwise. Cumberland, it must be remembered, was at present a part of Scotland, having been granted by Eadmund I, after his conquest of it, as a fief to Malcolm I, and Carlisle was an excellent base of operations. In 1070 Malcolm, starting thence, made another savage raid into Northumberland. William thereupon proceeded northward next year, with a great army and a fleet, and penetrated to the Tay. Malcolm made a vague submission, but in 1079, during William's absence in Normandy, he made a third raid, which was replied to by a counter raid under Prince Robert. A fortress was then constructed on the Tyne to defend southern Bernicia, called the 'New Castle'. The result was immediate. Malcolm made no further attack for twelve years, and was then checked by the garrison of Newcastle. He made some kind of submission, but Cumberland was conquered by a treacherous attack of William Rufus, and the English king's insults drove him to madness. He once more invaded Northumberland, and near Alnwick was defeated and slain.

For many years after the famous king's death there were no Scottish invasions. Scotland was much troubled with civil war, and afterwards divided between two sons of Malcolm. It was not until 1124 that David I reunited the country under his rule. For eleven years his relations with England were peaceful, but when Stephen of Blois usurped the English throne, the Scottish king invaded Northumberland, nominally to support his niece, the Empress Matilda, really, of course, to make his profit out of the situation. Northumberland and Durham readily submitted to him as the representative of Matilda, and Stephen, pressed by many difficulties, was glad to purchase his withdrawal by the retrocession of Carlisle, nominally to David's son Henry, who also received Doncaster and the Earldom of Huntingdon. But the great

English magnates were bitterly indignant, and in 1138 war again broke out.

David invaded Northumberland at the very beginning of the year. Already castles were arising, and he failed to take Wark, but wasted the open country, his hordes of wild mountaineers committing terrible atrocities. Stephen hastened northward, and David retreated; but the English king, with rebellion in the south, could only waste Lothian and withdraw. David thereupon reassembled his forces and again advanced. Norham Castle was taken, Wark again besieged, the levies of Lancashire defeated by the King's nephew William at Clitheroe, and the Scottish host poured over Tees into Yorkshire. There it encountered solid resistance. Its barbarities had exasperated the country-folk, and they rallied *en masse* to oppose the invaders. The nominal commander-in-chief was the young William of Albemarle, but Thurstan, Archbishop of York, and Sir Walter Espec, the High Sheriff, were the real leaders.

The men of Yorkshire, with reinforcements from Durham, Derby, and Nottingham, assembled at Northallerton, and took up a position on Cowton Moor some distance to the northward. On August 22 they were attacked by the Scots. David had with him a heterogeneous host from all parts of his dominions - said, with considerable probability, to have been 26,000 strong. But it was very unstable. The Picts of Alban were jealous of the 'Saxons' of Lothian, and neither were inclined to work well with the Britons of Strathclyde. The Niduarian Picts of Galloway were uncontrollable, and all the old elements of the realm disliked the new Norman-Teutonic immigrants, although their small force of about 500 mailed horsemen was to show itself the one thoroughly reliable arm of the host

The English army was, without any doubt, greatly inferior in number, as is shown by the fact that it maintained a passive defensive – the last plan of action likely to be adopted by the fiery Norman English knights unless there had been compelling reason for it. The bulk of the force consisted of the country levies, but the whole knighthood of Yorkshire were there, and there was a strong contingent of archers. Albemarle and Espec formed their army into one solid mass, probably with the mail-clad knights and their followers dismounted as a front rank. In the centre of the line was a waggon with a tall mast stepped in it, from which flew the sacred banners of St Peter of York, St Cuthbert of Durham, St Wilfrid of Ripon, and St John of Beverley; and beneath their shadow old Walter Espec and Albemarle took their stand, with a band of chosen warriors as a guard. The horses were sent to the rear, and the barons and knights promised to stand and die with the country folk.

There was a hot and unfriendly debate in the Scottish host, which shows how incoherent it was. David, according to Aelred of Rievaulx, had intended to attack in one huge column, with the mailed cavalry in front; but the Picts violently objected. Malise, Earl of Strathearn, declared that the 'Saxons' were no better than cowards, and that he himself, though he wore no mail, would outstrip the best of them in the charge. Alan Percy hotly replied, and the King was obliged to part the two. The Galwegians, who had distinguished themselves at Clitheroe, were equally furious and insubordinate, and eventually David had to consent to deliver his attack in territorial divisions. On the right, under the King's gallant son Henry, were the Strathclydians with two hundred knights at their head. On the left were the men of Lothian, with some Argyll and Isles men; and in the centre, in advance of the wings, were the Galwegians with, probably, other Pictish contingents. Behind the centre King David led a reserve consisting of the men of Moray and other Highland regions, with all the knights not on the wings.

As the Scottish masses moved forward they were assailed with showers of arrows, and the wild Galwegians raced to handgrips just as, for centuries thereafter, the Highland clans were to charge, brandishing their swords and yelling 'Albanach! Albanach!' as they dashed through the deadly hail. The English line gave back for a moment before the impact of the rush, but rallied at once and stood firm – a wall of steel upon which the Celtic billows beat fiercely, but without avail. On the left the men of Lothian and Lorn did badly. They had never agreed together. Perhaps the Lowlanders had little heart in the fight against their Northumbrian kinsmen. Their leader was killed in the advance, and the whole wing gave back after the first charge, taking no further part in the battle.

On the Scottish right matters went differently. The Strathclydians charged gallantly, and the knights in front burst right through the

English line, penetrating to. the baggage and horses in the rear. But so fine was the spirit of the Yorkshire men, that they rallied and re-formed in the very face of the enemy, and cut off the Strathclydian infantry from Henry's squadron. The fight raged fiercely along the line, the Scots rallying again and again, and hurling themselves in repeated charges against the close English ranks. The hardest and best fighting seems to have been done by the Galwegians in the centre. They held on to the English line for two hours, and made three furious assaults. Not until the third had been repelled; and their chiefs Donald and Ulgarich slain, did they sullenly give back, many of them, as Aelred says, 'looking like hedgehogs with the arrows sticking in them.' The Strathclyde men also were in retreat, and Prince Henry, cut off with the remnant of his gallant band, was vainly endeavouring to rejoin the main body. The King's reserve was demoralized by the sight of the retreat of the left and the repeated repulse of the Picts and Strathclydians, refused to advance, and broke up. David was left among his dissolving host with only his few hundred horsemen. He fell back some way, and raised his banner on a hill. Around it the ruins of the right and centre, with the disgraced left and reserve, gradually rallied, unmolested by the English, who knew that only half the Scottish host had been seriously engaged, and were unaware of the dissensions that had rendered it ineffective. Then David began his retreat to Carlisle, cautiously pursued by Espec and Albemarle. At Carlisle Prince Henry at last rejoined, having given away his encumbering mail to a peasant, and with only nineteen of his two hundred horsemen still with him.

The result of the 'Battle of the Standards' was highly honourable to the English Northerners, but it is easy to see that the hopeless lack of cordial cooperation between the various sections of the Scottish host ensured its defeat. In a modified form this want of cohesion continued to the last to affect the efficiency of Scottish armies of invasion. David continued to fish in the agitated waters of English politics, and during his reign retained practical possession of Northumberland and Durham, save for a few castles; but he made no more invasions in force, and after his death Henry II recovered the northern counties.

The invasion of William the Lion, in 1174, was made ostensibly to aid the rebellious sons of Henry II against their father. William's true object was, no doubt, to recover the border counties. Perhaps. no invasion of England has ever appeared so threatening, and proved so completely 'the fleeting shadow of a dream.' William's army was large – perhaps the largest that a Scots king had hitherto gathered – but he could not control his wild followers. His advance was marked by ravage and destruction – peculiarly stupid in view of the fact that he hoped to annex the country which he was ruining. Several fortresses were captured, and in July he besieged Alnwick. He kept only a very small force about him, and allowed the main portion of his probably unruly host to spread over the country for purpose of pillage. The consequences of the dispersion were disastrous. The troops of the North had already assembled under Robert d'Estuteville, Sheriff of Yorkshire, and were marching against the invaders. A body of some four hundred horsemen was scouting ahead of the main body, and so hopelessly were the Scots scattered that they passed, apparently unchallenged, through the enemy's line into his rear. Before the walls of Alnwick they saw a small body of about a hundred horsemen engaged in exercising and tilting. They can hardly have expected that they would be so rash as to charge their own superior numbers. Yet so it was. Practically the whole of the tilting band were taken, and the astonishment of the victors may be imagined when they found that they had captured the King of Scots. The Scottish army melted away across the Border. The King paid dearly for his recklessness. He was forced to become Henry's vassal, and so remained until the death of the Angevin king. Richard I very wisely freed him from this humiliation in return for a money payment, but there were no more Scottish invasions of England for many years. The Scottish kings never gave up their hopes of gaining Northumberland, and more than once hostilities appeared to threaten; but on the whole the relations between the two countries were peaceful, and when Alexander III died in 1286 there had been no real outbreak of war for a century.

This peaceful period came to an end when Edward I made his attempt to unite the two countries. That his aim was wise and statesman-like is not to be doubted. There was no strong dividing line between the great mass of the English nation and the Scots Lowlanders, who, for all practical purposes, formed one race. The two countries had been in close and generally peaceful connection for over a century; the estates of many of the magnates lay on both sides of the Border. On the subject of the repeated 'commendations' of the Scottish kings to those of England, opinion will always be divided; but to Edward's legal mind they must have appeared to constitute a strong body of precedents. Nor does it, on the whole, appear that there was at first any great disinclination to the union among the Scots. It was Edward's highhandedness, and the blundering violence of his officials, who were foolish enough to treat the country like a conquered land, that slowly roused the pride and courage of the Scots.

In 1297 Scotland was in full revolt under William Wallace, and after his famous victory at Cambuskenneth he invaded northern England while Edward was absent in France. For some three months the Scots ranged over the English Border counties. Newcastle and Carlisle successfully held out, but the open country was swept bare. The chronicler Hemingburgh accuses the Scots of committing unmentionable atrocities, but practically admits that Wallace was not to blame for them, being unable to control his followers. There exists a letter of protection granted by him and his colleagues to Hexham Abbey, and doubtless there were others. Still, great barbarities appear to have been perpetrated, and it was largely owing to them that Edward conceived his furious animosity against the Scottish patriot.

In the stress of their struggle for independence with Edward I the Scots contrived to make a raid on Cumberland in 1299, but by 1305 the country was at the feet of the English king. Not until Robert Bruce had taken the lead in Scotland, and the worthless Edward II had succeeded his great father, were the northern borders again troubled. In 1310, and again in 1311, Robert raided Northumberland, and in 1313 he swept through Cumberland, joined a fleet which he had sent from the Isles and the Clyde, and annexed the Norse principality of Man. In 1314 he gained the supreme victory of Bannockburn. The independence of Scotland appeared assured and the way open for invasions of England.

Between 1314 to 1323 the Scots invaded England repeatedly. All their operations were of a guerrilla type, and rarely appear to have aimed at more than the devastation of the countryside. Robert, himself one of the ablest generals of medieval days, had no illusions as to the ability of Scotland to cope singlehanded with her strong antagonist, and his famous testamentary counsel to always avoid action and to endeavour to starve invaders out of the country is well known.

The armies which carried out the invasions of England during this heyday of Scotland's renown were well adapted for their purpose. They included a force of mail-clad men-at-arms strong enough to overcome any local resistance which might be offered, and a much larger contingent of light-armed men mounted on rough, hardy, country ponies. Each man carried a bag of oatmeal on his horse, and an iron plate whereon to bake it. Otherwise men and beasts lived on the country through which they passed. The hardy, frugal Scots were quite at home in this rough-and-ready campaigning, and for several years they rode at will over northern England.

There is generally a lack of interest about the invasions themselves, which all bore almost the same image and superscription. Once the Border was crossed, the Scots rode far and wide over the northern counties, ravaging, plundering, or ransoming villages, towns, and castles, much as the Vikings had done four centuries before. There was little fighting as a rule. England was at war with herself. And when once or twice English armies did assemble, the Scots simply avoided an action until they were starved into dispersion.

In 1314 Edward Bruce and the 'Good Lord' James Douglas wasted the English Border. In 1315 Bruce himself attacked Carlisle, but it repulsed him. For the next two years the main energy of Scotland was devoted to Edward Bruce's attempted conquest of Ireland, but Douglas was busy on the Border; and such was the dread of him in the North that his name was used to frighten disobedient children, and the humiliation of the times is depicted in the lullaby:

'Hush thee, baby, do not fret thee;
The Black Douglas shall not get thee !'

In 1318 Berwick was taken, and a large English army was driven in ruinous retreat from an attempted counter-invasion of Scotland in the following year. In 1320 the best of Robert's captains, the famous Thomas Randolph, Earl of Moray, assisted by Douglas, retaliated. They pressed on across Northumberland and Durham into Yorkshire, and at Myton-on-Swale encountered the local levies under the Archbishop of York. Perhaps the Primate hoped to repeat the famous day of the 'Standards.' But the results were far otherwise. The Yorkshiremen were totally routed; 3,000 men were slain and so many of the ecclesiastics, who were present to encourage the peasants, that the fray was called 'Myton Chapter' by the victors.

The result was that King Robert planned a campaign in 1322 which should be more than a mere marauding expedition. The English obtained intelligence, and Edward II collected a large army at Newcastle. The Scottish king, therefore, stood on the defensive in Lothian, while a strong detachment crossed the western border and penetrated into mid Lancashire. Edward found Lothian desolate, and effected nothing but the destruction of some abbeys – notably those of Melrose and Dryburgh. Bruce declined to fight, and the English army, perishing from famine and disease, melted away over the Border. So ruined were the northern counties of England that Edward could not halt until he reached Byland Abbey in Yorkshire. There so much as remained of the dissolving host lay in security, when, on October 14, like a bolt from the blue, the royal army of Scotland was upon them!

When the English army broke up, Bruce had followed from across the Forth, and had passed through Northumberland, Durham, and Yorkshire so swiftly that no tidings of his march seem to have reached the astounded English. Early on October 14 the Scots fell upon the scattered English divisions. There was little effective resistance; a connected line of battle was never indeed formed. Edward fled in haste, abandoning his baggage and military chest. A part of his army attempted to make a stand at a good position in the rear of their cantonments. Douglas, whose division was leading the pursuit, attacked in front, assisted by Moray, who hurried in advance of his troops to serve under 'Good Lord James.' For a time the English held their own, but when the Highlanders arrived on the field the end came swiftly. The barefooted mountaineers scrambled up the crags which covered the English wings, and charged in flank and rear. The English fled in panic-stricken rout, and Walter the Steward took up the pursuit, chasing the fugitives to the gates of York.

On May 30, 1323, Edward at last bowed his pride to calling a truce. It was time, for the suffering North was already making terms of its own with King Robert. The truce was ill-kept, and in 1327 broken by the Scots. This was a diplomatic blunder on the part of King Robert; but the disorder in England at the deposition of the witless Edward II was so great that he can hardly be blamed for seizing the opportunity. He himself was already dying, but Moray and Douglas led the army across the Border on this last great successful Scottish invasion of England. Its strength is stated at 24,000 men, but it was probably less. The English Regency assembled a strong force at York under the nominal command of the boy-King Edward III, but its operations were utterly futile. It literally lost its way in the Border wilderness, and only ascertained the whereabouts of the Scots from a released prisoner, Thomas of Rokeby. Even then the Scottish position was found too strong to be assailed, and though Douglas would have accepted young Edward's proposal – fantastic, but quite in the spirit of the times – to withdraw far enough to allow him to form order of battle, the able and prudent Moray rightly refused to listen. For fifteen days the armies confronted each other, the English suffering far more than their foes; and then Moray quietly retreated under cover of a daring night surprise of the English camp executed by Douglas. Three hundred men were killed, and Edward's tent was almost cut down over his head before the bold warrior was obliged to retire. The supplies left behind by the Scots saved the English from immediate starvation, and that was all. The expense of the armament had, for the moment, exhausted England, and by the 'Shameful Treaty' of Northampton, April 24, 1328, the independence of Scotland was formally recognized.

From the high position to which she had been raised by Robert I Scotland fell fast. The anarchy which followed his death bade fair to undo his lifework. Edward III of England assisted Edward Balliol, son of the ill-omened John, to attack Scotland, and himself made repeated attempts to destroy her newly-gained independence. In these he was baffled, but numerous strong places on the Border remained in English hands. The need of an ally against England drove Scotland into the arms of France, and the country became little better than an appendage of the Continental Power. The ill effects of this are to be traced in Scottish history for two centuries.

In 1346 King David II, the weak successor of his great father, determined to invade England as a diversion in favour of France. Edward III was besieging Calais, and David appears to have been certain of success. His army is said to have included 2,000 men-at-arms, 20,000 light cavalry, and 10,000 infantry. He invaded England by the Western Marches, and sacked Lanercost Priory, a circumstance which evoked bitter denunciations of him and his from the Lanercost Chronicle. Moving on westward, David stormed the 'Pyle' (Obviously another rendering of the well-known term 'Peel' – Border stronghold.) of Liddell, hanging its commander, Walter de Selby, and advanced to Bearpark, about six miles from Bishop Auckland, where he encamped on October 16.

Meanwhile the levies of the North had gathered to oppose his farther advance. Edward's youthful son, Lionel, was the nominal guardian of the realm, but the real head of the government was Queen Philippa, who herself was in the North to expedite measures of defence. Though it is probably untrue that she accompanied the army to the field, it is highly probable that she personally directed the levying of the troops. By October 16 an army of some 10,000 men, under those barons of the North who were in England, was collected in Bishop Auckland Park. The Scots were quite unaware of its proximity, and a marauding column, under Sir William Douglas, blundered into it on the evening of the 16th, losing heavily before it could withdraw. David, young and hot-blooded, at once resolved to attack, though his swarm of spearmen, without archers, and weak in heavy cavalry, was at a great disadvantage beside the English force.

On the morning of the 17th the English army was strongly posted on the hills north of Bishop Auckland. The ground in its front was broken and intersected by hedges. The Archbishop of York was on the field, and the banners of the northern saints, suspended to a great cross, were carried into action, as they had been at Northallerton two centuries before. The centre was commanded by Ralph Neville, the right by Henry Percy and the northern barons, the left, of Lancashire men, by Thomas of Rokeby. The Scots advanced in three divisions, the centre under the King, the right under the Earl of Moray, the left under Robert, the High Steward of Scotland, afterwards the first Stuart King. From the first everything went ill with the Scots. Entangled among the enclosures and ditches, their heavy, cumbrous columns, as at Halidon Hill, were tormented and disordered by a rain of arrows, to which they could make no reply. Sir John Graham in vain charged with a body of horsemen in the endeavour to ride down the bowmen. He and his band were all shot down. Seeing the disorder among their adversaries, the English army came on to a counter attack, with the sacred banners waving in their van. The Scots' right, striving vainly to form in order amid the hedges and obstacles, was charged by the men-at-arms, broken and driven back in utter rout, with the loss of its leader; the Steward's division was forced away, and cut off from the King, and the whole English force closed upon the centre. For some three hours the Scots fought desperately, but their mass was finally pierced through and shattered, and David himself wounded and taken prisoner by John of Coupland, a Northumbrian squire.

Robert the Steward appears to have been accused of having made no effort to save the King. David certainly seems to have suspected him; but it must be said that had he brought up his division again, he would probably have only added to the greatness of the disaster. He retreated in tolerable order, drawing to him as many as possible of the survivors from the other divisions, and the English were too weary to pursue. With David were taken the Archbishop of St Andrews and several nobles, while the death-roll included more than thirty barons, including the Lord Marischal Keith and the Constable Hay.

This great disaster brought about a cessation of Scottish invasions for many years. David II became more or less Anglicized during his long residence in England, and Robert the Steward, both as regent and monarch, was inclined to peace. The nobles, however, were warlike and turbulent, and the people did not love England. Several Border strongholds were still held by the English, and there was continuous skirmishing on the frontier, which, however, rarely assumed the dignity of national strife. The Black Death weakened both nations, and not until 1377 was the war renewed in earnest. Berwick-on-Tweed was taken and retaken. There was fighting on the sea, ending in the destruction of the Scottish piratical fleet under Andrew Mercer by the London merchant Philpot. The English invaded the Lothians more than once with no permanent results.

In 1385 Jean de Vienne, Admiral of France, landed in Scotland with 2,000 men-at-arms, 50,000 francs of gold, and a large supply of arms and armour. A great invasion of England was organized, and 30,000 men under De Vienne, James, Earl of Douglas, and other lords, entered Northumberland. So formidable did the invasion appear that the young King Richard II himself took the command against the Scots. To the disgust of the French, the Scots retreated into Clydesdale, and, while the English burned Edinburgh, Perth, and Dundee, made a retaliatory raid into Cumberland. They did not agree well with their allies, who, on their side, conceived a great dislike for the poverty of the country, as well as for the keenness of the people in respect of monetary transactions. They went home sulkily, De Vienne himself being pledge that the cost of their maintenance should be paid by France. Chance made the two nations allies, but the French themselves never seem to have made a good impression in Scotland.

In 1388 the Scottish nobles arranged – behind the King's back be it noted – an attack on England to revenge the devastation of 1385. An army, vaguely said to have been 40,000 strong, under Robert, Earl of Fife, the second son of the King, invaded Cumberland, with the usual negative result; while a body of about 5,000, under Douglas, crossed the Tweed, and carried devastation to the gates of Durham. The Earl of Northumberland and his son Henry, the celebrated 'Hotspur,' were driven into Newcastle, and Douglas retired unmolested as far as Otterburn, some twenty miles from the Border. Here he was overtaken by a force under 'Hotspur,' and a furious engagement took place, which has been celebrated by Froissart in prose and in the famous ballad of

'Chevy Chase.' In the end the English were beaten off, and Percy and other knights fell into the hands of the Scots, who, however, had to lament the death of their leader.

In the following year Robert II died. His feeble son John, 'Robert III,' was anxious to keep the peace with England, and in this was backed by his brother and co-regent, Robert, Duke of Albany. In 1398 the heir-apparent, David, Duke of Rothesay, supplanted his uncle for a while, and inaugurated a vigorous anti-English policy. He alienated the powerful Earl of March by breaking off his betrothal to his daughter, and March fled to England. Henry IV was anxious for peace, but the Scots appear to have been determined on war, and he made a brief expedition into Scotland in 1399. In 1402, after much desultory skirmishing, the Scots, taking advantage of Henry's preoccupations, invaded England with a considerable army under Murdoch, Earl of Fife, son of Albany (who had overthrown and murdered Rothesay), and Archibald, Earl of Douglas, grandson of the hero of Otterburn. They advanced, ravaging in the usual manner, as far as the Tyne, and then turned homeward, pursued by a force under 'Hotspur' and the fugitive Earl of March. They were overtaken while encamped on Homildon, or Humbledon, Hill, near Wooler. Percy and March, adopting tactics curiously similar to those employed a century later almost at the same spot by Surrey, moved round the Scots' position, and, by placing themselves on their line of retreat, forced them to abandon their booty and disperse, or fight.

The battle presents few features of interest; it was a mere counterpart in tactics of Halidon Hill and Neville's Cross. The Scots were tormented in the old fashion by the archers, and Fife and Douglas failed to attempt the only possible, if forlorn, expedient to stay them – a determined charge of cavalry. Seeing the increasing disorder, Sir John Swinton, one of the bravest knights in the army, begged permission to advance, though only with his following of 100 lances. Adam, Lord Gordon, his personal enemy, thereupon sought reconciliation with him, and the erstwhile foes, embracing on the field, placed themselves at the head of the band, which rode downhill among the archers, and perished to the last man. Driven to desperation by the murderous discharge, the Scottish masses at last lumbered clumsily down the hill, only to be massacred by the pitiless arrow flight, until in despair they broke and fled. The English men at arms hardly struck a blow. Fife and Douglas were both taken; the latter had received five wounds, and owed his life solely to his well-tempered armour.

Disastrous as Homildon had been, it cannot be said to have any decisive effects. The old frontier strife went on unchecked. The Scots recovered Jedburgh, one of the few posts still held by the English in 1409. A great invasion, organized by Albany in 1416, ended in a fiasco; and when James I returned in 1424 from his captivity in England, hostilities had almost died away. This was largely due to the fact that several of the chief Scottish nobles, including Douglas, had gone to fight in the service of France against England. The result was that direct warfare on the Border tended to die out.

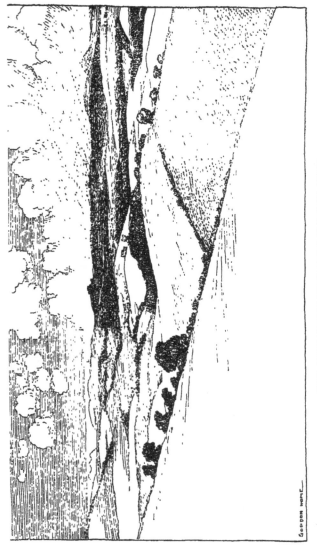

GORDON HOME

THE VIEW NORTH-WEST FROM FLODDEN FIELD.

Across the slope in the foreground the Scots probably advanced to meet the English, moving past Branxton Church, which is below the hill to the right. This was the panorama which presented itself to the eyes of the Scottish left wing. On the left are the Eildon Hills, in the centre is Home Castle and a bend of the Tweed near Coldstream, and on the right Dirrington Great and Little Laws.

XII

Later Scottish Invasions
1424–1542

When in 1424 James I, after his long captivity in England, took over the government of Scotland, his energies were mainly directed to internal reform, though he made in 1436 a fruitless attempt to recover Roxburgh. James II attacked Berwick in 1455, and raided the Border next year. In 1460 Roxburgh was recovered, though James himself was killed by a bursting cannon. England, involved in the Wars of the Roses, could do little. As the price of assistance rendered to the Lancastrians, Scotland regained Berwick, which was retained until 1482, when Prince Richard, afterwards King Richard III, finally recovered it for England.

For thirty years thereafter a precarious peace subsisted between the two kingdoms, but dread and dislike of England were always strong in Scotland, which was also more or less attached to England's old enemy, France. James IV interfered in the cause of the adventurer Perkin Warbeck in 1497 without effect, and the Earl of Surrey retaliated by a raid. Hostilities were ended by the Peace of Ayton. In 1503 James married Henry VII's daughter Margaret.

For ten years the peace subsisted, but the chronic Border feuds were a constant source of trouble. Henry was suspicious of the frequent passage through his realm of Scotsmen proceeding to France. James was busy endeavouring to form a navy, and his captains, Andrew and Robert Barton and Sir Andrew Wood, were often in conflict with English vessels. It was the rule of those days that navy ships must support themselves, and the English, who were often probably little better, regarded the Scots admirals as pirates. There is little doubt that they did occasionally behave as such.

Up to 1511 the peace lasted, though the fierce and resolute Henry VIII was a more dangerous neighbour than his father. But in August came an event which precipitated hostilities. It appears that Andrew Barton had made prize of English ships, and Lord Edward Howard, High Admiral of England, with his brother Thomas, attacked him as he was cruising in the English Channel. After a fierce struggle Barton was slain, and his two ships, the *Lion* and the *Jennet Perwyn*, were taken. James protested, but Henry haughtily declined to treat upon a matter of piracy. Yet it seems that he released the prisoners, and certainly offered to make fair compensation for the unjustifiable actions of Englishmen. In May, 1512, Lord Dacre and Dr. West appeared in Edinburgh, but at the same time came the French Ambassador, De la Matte, with instructions to enlist, if possible, Scotland on the side of France in the impending struggle with England. The wisdom of making a diversion on England's rear was obvious. James informed Henry that he could consent to no peace which did not include France. De la Matte came and went between Paris and Edinburgh, and supplies of all kinds were sent from France. To James's romantic nature Queen Anne's ring and the message to 'her true knight,' begging him to invade England for her sake, were perhaps clearer.

On June 30 Henry VIII crossed to Calais to invade France, and on July 26 James sent Lyon King-at-Arms to declare war. A squadron of thirteen ships, under the Earl of Arran, was sent into the Irish Sea, perhaps to make a diversion by attacking Ireland. This attempt was a failure. A futile attack was made on Carrickfergus, and then the Scottish fleet disappears from the scene.

The whole fighting population of Scotland was ordered to assemble on the Boroughmuir of Edinburgh. Today the population of England is eight times that of Scotland. In 1801 it was only five and a half times as great, and in 1513 the discrepancy may have been less. Assuming it to have been the same, and taking the population of England at 4,000,000, that of Scotland would be about 700,000, and the number of fighting men perhaps 100,000; but though this is the figure given by Hall, it is unlikely that more than 500,000 took the field. The English chronicler would naturally incline to exaggeration.

Still, the army was the most formidable that Scotland had ever sent forth. Thanks to France, the Lowlanders were well equipped as regards defensive armour. Hall says that the English arrows had less effect than of old. The Highlanders however, as a whole, lacked mail and consequently efficiency; and the Borderers were unstable and turbulent, and attached more importance to pillage than fighting. The grand Lowland foot-spearmen were, as ever, the backbone of the army, but it lacked anything like a proper proportion of archers and arquebusiers. The artillery was largely composed of fine cast pieces, the work of Robert Borthwick, James's famous master-gunner. It appears to have included some forty guns in all, but there were few trained artillerymen.

To cover his concentration, James ordered a raid into Northumberland under Lord Home, High Chamberlain of Scotland and Warden of all the Marches. Home has gained a bad reputation in the annals of his country, but it would seem that his fault was not treachery, but mere lack of military capacity. He collected a force estimated by the English writers – probably with exaggeration – at 7,000 men, and did much damage; but on his retreat he was overtaken by a small English force under Sir William Bulmer at Milfield-on-Till, and routed with a loss of 1,000 men.

Henry, to use Hall's quaint language, had not forgotten 'ye olde pranks of ye Scottes,' and had made dispositions for the adequate defence of the realm during his absence. His general in the north was Thomas Howard, Earl of Surrey, Lord Treasurer and High Marshal of England, a veteran nearly seventy years of age, who had fought for Richard III at Bosworth, but had become reconciled to the new conditions and commanded against James sixteen years before. Henry was undoubtedly wise in leaving him to watch over England, but the old warrior himself was disappointed at losing a chance of distinguishing himself in France. He grumbled in good English fashion, and growled that, if James did invade, he should meet more than he had bargained for. 'Sory may I se hym or I dye that is the cause of mye abydynge behynde, and if ever hee and I mete, I shall doe that inne mee lyeth to make hyme as sory if I canne.' In July, as the danger became more imminent, he established himself at Pontefract to organize the defence of the north. The efficacy of his measures is apparent in the remarkable rapidity of his concentration.

On August 22 the Scottish army occupied Twisel, and on the following day began the siege of Norham, which had often defied the strength of Scotland in bygone days. But James brought his guns to bear upon the walls, and breaches soon began to appear. The garrison fought desperately and repelled three assaults, but, in the effort to keep down the Scottish cannonade, rapidly expended their stock of ammunition. On the 29th, without further means of defence, the castle surrendered. This was a considerable success for James, and was improved by the capture of Etal and Ford Castles. The next object of attack would probably have been Berwick, but already the English Army of the North was on the way. James therefore took up a strong position west of the Till, and awaited attack, his own quarters being for some days at Ford. Round this latter circumstance has gathered the time honoured but baseless legend that he wasted weeks in dalliance with Lady Heron.

Surrey heard of the Scottish advance on August 25, and promptly ordered his forces to assemble at Newcastle. He directed his son Thomas, who commanded the fleet on the coast, to join him with his marines. On September 1 he advanced, but the weather was so bad that not until the 3rd did he reach Alnwick, where he halted to close up. On the 4th the Admiral joined with 1,000 men. The army was now 26,000 strong.

Surrey organized his force in two corps. The Vanguard was commanded by the Admiral, who led his main body in person, with his brother Edmund in charge of his right wing and the venerable Sir Marmaduke Constable (this ancient warrior was buried in Flamborough Church seven years later, and in his long and quaint epitaph appear the lines: 'At Brankiston feld, wher the kyng of Scottys was slayne, He, then beyng of the age of three score and tene, With the gode duke of Northefolke yt jurney be haye tayn.') leading his left. The Rearguard was under Surrey's personal control. Lord Dacre led its right wing, composed mainly of Border horsemen; and Sir Edward

Stanley its left, consisting chiefly of the fine archers of Lancashire and Cheshire. The artillery train was under Sir Nicholas Appleyard. For the last time the famous banner of St Cuthbert was carried into action.

On September 6 Surrey reached Wooler, 'three lytel miles, from the King of Scots,' says Hall. Counting upon James's reputation for rash chivalry, he sent him a formal challenge to fight on the 9th. The Admiral added a provocative message of his own, informing James that he was there in person to answer for the death of Barton. All this 'quarrelling by the book' was quite in the style of the times, a fact which Mr. Andrew Lang and other modern writers who have commented upon the 'insolence' of the Howards, appear to have forgotten.

The Scots were encamped upon a mass of hilly ground lying three miles above the junction of the Glen with the Till. The southern portion of this mass is roughly circular at the base, from two to three miles across in every direction and 700 feet high. On the north and north-east it sinks somewhat sharply 400 feet to a valley, across which a saddle-back runs to a second mass, roughly quadrangular, nearly four miles long and two in breadth. The western portion is 800 feet high; Barley Hill, the southern spur, is 582; Flodden Edge, on the north-east, overlooking the Till, is 509. The northern spur is called Branxton Hill; it drops from 500 feet to 227 feet at Branxton Church, just below.

If only three miles separated the armies, the Scots must have been stationed on the southern mass, between Milfield and Kirknewton. The artillery was at the foot of the slope. On the 7th there was a distant cannonade, but no further fighting. The Scottish position was far too strong to be attacked. On the 8th, therefore, Surrey moved to his right across the Till to Barmoor. He was, so Hall says, only two miles from the Scottish front. This must mean that the English outposts on the ridge between Ford and Doddington were about two miles from the Till. The English main army, however, was behind the ridge, out of view of the Scots.

From the ridge – perhaps the part above Ford wood – Surrey and his son reconnoitred James's position. Holinshed says that it was the Admiral who advised his father to make a turning movement across Twisel Bridge, and so plant himself on the Scottish communications. Hall, who is very detailed as to the Admiral's doings, does not say so;

in any case, the decision rested with Surrey. The momentous resolution was taken, and at daybreak the English army marched for Twisel.

The Scots committed a fatal blunder in leaving Twisel Bridge unguarded. It can, of course, be said for them that strategy so bold as that of Surrey was almost unheard of in medieval warfare. But there does not appear to have been a picket at the bridge, nor does any attempt seem to have been made to keep in touch with the English army by means of the light Border moss-troopers. Either the Scottish leaders were incapable of penetrating a skilful but hazardous design, or the Borderers were surprisingly useless for scouting.

From Barmoor to Twisel Bridge is about nine miles. Wet weather had rendered the tracks very difficult, and progress was doubtless slow. Hall also says that the English were starving, but this statement cannot be accepted; the vigour with which they acted sufficiently disproves it. The bridge was found unguarded, and the Vanguard began to stream across. The artillery train followed. The Rearguard appears to have crossed chiefly by Mill Ford, a mile above Twisel. As the armies were not in contact until about 4 p.m., it cannot be doubted that the passage was not detected by the Scots until after midday.

The Scottish army was probably watching the line of the Till above Ford, with its artillery at the foot of its strong position. Its order of battle can only be surmised. The common idea that it was ill supplied seems to be baseless; the Bishop of Durham, who had means of knowing, stated that the Scottish camps were full of provisions. France had sent shiploads of supplies, and the army had only been eighteen days in the field. Assuming that James had commenced the campaign with 50,000 men, he must still have had 40,000 at least.

The Scottish scouts appear to have interpreted the English movement as a counter-invasion of Scotland, and so it was reported to James. Tents were hurriedly struck and parked, and the unwieldy host proceeded to change front to the north. The varied and undisciplined character of the Scottish army must have rendered the complicated manoeuvre slow and difficult. It is possible that James intended to recross the Tweed at Coldstream in order to deal with the supposed invasion. On the other hand, it is probable that Surrey hoped to encamp for the night on Branxton Hill, and not to engage until next day.

About 3:30 p.m. the English Vanguard was passing Branxton Church. The Scots were still scattered over the upland in five great masses, three of which were moving over Branxton Hill. A division under Lords Home and Huntly was leading on the left; next came another under the Earls of Crawford and Montrose. On its right rear was the centre, under King James, with Lord Sinclair in command of the artillery. The Earl of Bothwell's division, and the Highlanders under the Earls of Lennox and Argyll, were still far behind. The English order of battle has already been given. There was a considerable interval between the Vanguard and Rearguard. The artillery was with the Vanguard.

James, seeing from the heights the English passing Branxton, ordered the rubbish in the camps to be fired, that the acrid smoke, borne on the south-west breeze, might drive in the face of the foe, and under cover of it the three Scottish divisions began to advance. Probably the smoke confused them as well; it must have put the English on the alert. Still, the silent advance was to some extent a surprise. As the English van reached the Branxton brook the smoke cleared away, and they saw the Scottish 'battles' bristling with pikes in their front. The peril was imminent. Taking the Agnus Dei from his neck, Lord Thomas sent it to his father, begging him to hasten into line, and hurriedly fronted up the Vanguard. The artillery, coming into action on the left, pounded furiously at the Scots pouring down the hill.

Howard's bold show had good effects. James halted to allow his guns to come into action, but Borthwick's beautiful pieces, worked by ill-trained gunners, and badly placed on a slippery hillside, were rapidly silenced or dismounted. Lord Sinclair was slain directing his batteries, and the English guns soon gained the complete mastery. Then Surrey hurried into line with his son, and James's great opportunity was gone. The English main battle closed up on the Admiral and Constable; Dacre took post behind Howard; Sir Edward Stanley was hurrying to form on Surrey's left. The English fire was directed with deadly effect on the heavy masses of the Scottish centre; the Scottish artillery was almost all out of action. Much has been said of the rashness of the Scots in charging, but in truth there was little alternative.

At first, all went well for Scotland. Home and Huntly bore down on Edmund Howard's division, while Crawford and Montrose charged the Admiral. The two English divisions became separated from one another, and Lord Edmund's was completely broken and scattered, though he himself cut his way through a body of Homes (this body was commanded by Sir David Home, the father of the famous 'Seven Spears of Wedderbum.' He himself was slain by Howard in single combat, and with him fell his eldest son. At Wedderburn Castle is a portion of a standard which was probably the rallying-point of this unfortunate detachment. After the fight it is said to have served as Sir David's winding-sheet), who endeavoured to stay him, and joined his brother. The success of Home and Huntly was locally complete; but they could not control their undisciplined followers, many of whom scattered to plunder. Dacre hurried up his reserves, and, though his Bamboroughshire and Tynemouth troops wavered and broke, succeeded in checking the Chamberlain's advance, and kept him at bay throughout the battle.

The Scottish centre, moving down the hill, was met with a hail of cannon-balls and arrows, but the sturdy yeomen came on with the finest spirit, doffing their shoes to obtain firmer footing, never halting or wavering. They closed upon the English centre, despite its heavy fire, and under the weight and impetus of the charge it was forced backward. But it was not broken, and the fight raged fiercely along the line, James and his picked troops making repeated and desperate attempts to pierce the stubborn English front. The non-arrival of Bothwell and the Highlanders left James's right entirely uncovered, and Sir Edward Stanley, coming up from the Mill Ford, was directed against it. His left reached the crown of Branxton Hill without meeting any foe, but before he could develop his attack he was charged by the Highlanders, who had at last arrived, while Bothwell passed behind them down the slope to support the King.

It was bow against claymore. Again and again the wild Highlanders, stripped to their shirts after their fashion, 'like wave with crest of sparkling foam,' hurled themselves with fiery impulse upon Stanley's division – in vain. Their desperate courage availed nothing against the deadly arrow flight of the best archers of England and, after both their earls had fallen, they broke and fled westward over the space on which the Scottish centre had stood, leaving the hillside heaped with slain.

Somewhere about the same time, as it would seem, the Admiral had succeeded in breaking the division of Crawford and Montrose; the earls had fallen, and their followers were streaming away to the rear, and becoming intermingled with the fleeing Highlanders. The sight of the crowd of fugitives cannot but have had a fatal effect upon such troops as Home and Huntly had succeeded in keeping together. Howard turned the bulk of his victorious division against the uncovered left of the Scots' centre, while Stanley wheeled round upon its right and rear. These movements decided the battle. The Scottish centre and Bothwell's division were probably equal in number to the troops that assailed them; but they were practically surrounded, destitute of artillery, and with few arquebusiers and archers to respond to the steady fire from the English guns, matchlocks, and bows, while the unwieldy dimensions and density of their defensive formation made manoeuvring impossible. Possibly the mass made endeavours to move to its left, but for all practical purposes it was stationary, and nothing was left to the gallant spearmen but to fight to the last. King James was in the front rank, and so long as he lived he never ceased to lead desperate attempts to break the English line. If he was no general, at least he wielded his vain 'knights-errant's brand' as became a king. Wounded again and again, he was slain at last, within a few yards of where his aged opponent sat in his chariot (Pitscottie calls him 'an old crooked carle lying in a chariot') directing the battle. Still his followers fought on desperately. Scott has told the story of their great stand in glowing verse. The last stages of the battle must have taken place in ever growing gloom, and when there was no longer light to direct the charges Surrey drew off his troops. Under cover of night the Scottish centre, shattered and broken, but unconquered still, struggled away to Coldstream and so across Tweed, to tell Scotland the story of disaster.

The English passed the night in bivouac on the field. All around the Borderers of both armies were plundering indiscriminately, stripping the dead, and committing, doubtless, nameless atrocities. They impartially made prize of Surrey's tents and baggage and the Scottish artillery oxen, for want of which nearly the whole train had to be abandoned. When morning came it was seen that the Scots' centre had disappeared. Home had got some of his troops in hand again, and was in line towards the west, perhaps covering the retreat of the centre. His demoralized and half-hearted men were scattered by artillery fire, and drifted away across Tweed; and then Surrey 'could take stock of his victory'. On the slope of Branxton Hill the victors found dead the King of Scots, his natural son Alexander, Archbishop of St Andrews, two bishops, two mitred abbots, twelve earls, fourteen lords, and hundreds of scions of every noble house in Scotland. The whole Scottish loss can hardly have been less than 10,000; the unmailed Highlanders had been mown down in thousands. The English superiority in troops armed with missile weapons must have had terrible results; and it should be remembered that as a rule quarter was neither asked for nor given. The English put their own losses as low as 1,500. Except in Edmund Howard's division, they must have been far lower in proportion than those of the Scots; perhaps 4,000 in all is a fair estimate. Prisoners in such a conflict could not have been numerous; the only definite record is that of about sixty taken by the Scottish left wing. Surrey took possession of nearly all the Scottish artillery: five 'great drakes' (24-pounders), seven 'great culverins' (18-pounders) four 'sakers' (5-pounders), and six 'serpentines' (4-pounders) – all beautiful brass pieces wrought by Borthwick's skilled hand besides light guns. (Hall gives the total of large pieces at seventeen, including two culverins; but Holinshed says that the 'Seven Sisters ' were all taken, and it is most unlikely that the Scots could have saved any of these heavy guns.)

So ended the Battle of Flodden. On the Scots' side it was a magnificent display of fruitless courage, very little aided by military skill. On the part of England, all the commanders on the field worked together as one man to gain the victory; and though some of the hasty county levies showed unsteadiness, on the whole they admirably seconded their leaders. The boldness of Surrey's strategy is remarkable in such an aged man. Napoleon was emphatically of opinion that military leaders lose their boldness with advancing age. Tried by this standard, the only modern leader who can challenge comparison with Surrey is Suvórov, whose greatest triumphs were gained when he was almost seventy.

In Scotland the tendency has been to throw the blame for the catastrophe upon Lord Home. That his Borderers and Huntly's Highlanders largely dispersed after their successful charge is no doubt true; but seeing how entirely unstable and unreliable they always were in battle, the chiefs can hardly be blamed. After Flodden Home became a partisan of the English alliance, and has therefore been condemned by many writers who regard his action from a narrowly patriotic standpoint. He was clearly not a man of military ability, but there is no reason to doubt that he did his duty. Lord Dacre's letter to his Government, dated May 17, 1514, effectually disposes of the idea that Home looked on at the defeat of the Scottish centre and right. It was unfortunate for him that he survived the battle only to be put out of the way by the Regent Albany three years later.

Flodden as regards the courage displayed on the field was honourable to both nations. In a sense it was a decisive battle, for it seems to have brought home to public opinion in Scotland that the country might do better than sacrifice itself for France. There were no more great invasions of England. In 1522, and again in the following year, the Scottish nobles refused point-blank to cross the Border against England. But James V was still disposed to adhere to the French alliance, and Henry VIII's somewhat truculent diplomacy did not tend to improve matters. With brief intervals of truce, the weary Border warfare went on for many years. James's marriage to Marie de Lorraine in 1538 accentuated his leaning to France. In 1542, in order to make a diversion in favour of François I, James drifted into open war. A small English force invaded Scotland, but was badly beaten at Haddon Rigg in Teviotdale. A larger expedition under the Duke of Norfolk (the Admiral of Flodden) was more successful, but had no great results.

To cope with Norfolk, James collected a large army on Fala Muir. Finding that Norfolk had already retired, he would have invaded England; but once more the nobles declined to rush into disaster for the sake of France. Bitterly mortified, James fell back on the assistance of the great Churchmen, upon whom his Gallicizing policy chiefly depended, and raised a new army, variously estimated at from 10,000 to 18,000 men strong. In November 24 it crossed the Border north of Carlisle. The result was the disaster of Solway Moss, the most melancholy affair in Scottish military annals.

James himself did not accompany his army, but remained at Lochmaben. It was thus without a responsible commander, and not apparently until the last moment was it announced that the King's choice was Sir Oliver Sinclair, Standard-Bearer of Scotland. The effect was disastrous. The nobles present were exasperated at being placed under a mere knight, whose only distinction was that he was his master's favourite, and the army became an incoherent mass of ill-disciplined contingents without a responsible head. In this condition the Scots were attacked by the English. Sir Thomas Wharton, Deputy-Warden of the Western Marches, had collected 3,000 men at Carlisle; and informed by Thomas, a bastard Dacre, and 'Jacke' of Musgrave, of the state of the Scots, advanced against them.

The demoralized Scottish force was in a very dangerous position. Some miles behind them were the Esk and the dangerous bogs of Solway Moss. Their van was charged by a detachment of English cavalry and thrown into disorder, and then the whole army, as it seems, began to retreat in a huddled mass to the Esk. In vain the nobles present endeavoured to rally their followers, and dismounted to set them an example. 'In a shake all the way,' the demoralized Scots crowded back towards the only point of passage across the Esk, a narrow ford near the hill of Arthuret. The confusion grew worse and worse: prisoners were taken and men lost in the marshes. At the ford every trace of order was lost, and the English, making a final charge, thrust the army into the river and Solway Moss. The rout was piteous. Only twenty men are said to have been slain in fight, but hundreds were drowned and suffocated in the bogs; and 1,200 prisoners taken, including the unfortunate Sinclair, two earls, five barons, and hundreds of gentlemen. Twenty-four cannon, the Royal Standard of Scotland, and all the Scots' baggage fell into the hands of the victors.

Solway Moss was the cause of the premature death of James V, and more than ever must have convinced the Scots that the French alliance was the ruin of the country. But the blundering violence of England roused the spirit of the nation, and repeated harryings of Lothian and the disastrous defeat of Pinkie only fired its stubborn pride. For thirty years, thanks to the blunders of her rulers, England was still to have Scotland as a potential enemy. But after 1550 hostilities practically ceased, and the growing strength of Protestantism in Scotland drew the two countries slowly together. The Border disturbances gradually died down; the presence of French mercenaries taught the Scottish Protestants that French domination was more to be feared than that of England. After the expulsion of Mary, a succession of rulers worked steadily towards a closer friendship with England, and when the last and greatest of the Tudors ended her life, the sceptre which she had wielded so well passed quietly to the King of Scotland.

While the Scottish invasions were a perpetual menace to the peace of the North, they cannot be said, in the slightest degree, to have really threatened the national stability. Man for man, Scot and Englishman were well matched, and in minor frays, in which individual and reckless courage counted for much, the honours were fairly divided. In the great invasions the political and economic conditions in Scotland were never sufficiently favourable to allow of the formation of a properly organized and equipped army large enough to make a serious impression. The most effective Scottish invasions were those of Robert Bruce, but the most dangerous of these only penetrated as far as York. After Halidon Hill had taught the English generals what an effective weapon they possessed in their archery, they never hesitated to give battle, however great might be the odds against them.

GREAT GALLEASSE
CASTILLE & PORTUGAL
(DUQUE DE MEDINA SIDONIA & DON DIEGO FLORES DE VALDES)

LIGHT SQUADRON
(DON AGOSTIN DE OJEDA)

ARMED "URCAS"
(DON JUAN GOMEZ DE MEDINA)

3 GREAT GALLEASSES
(DON HUGO DE MONÇADA)

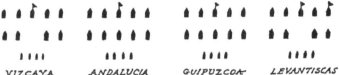

VIZCAYA	ANDALUCIA	GUIPUZCOA	LEVANTISCAS
(RECALDE)	(P DE VALDES)	(OQUENDO)	(BERTENDONA)
REARGUARD		VANGUARD	
(DON JUAN MARTINEZ DE RECALDE)		(DON ALONSO MARTINEZ DE LEYVA)	

ORDER OF SAILING OF THE SPANISH ARMADA.

Constructed from Spanish documentary material. The English idea of a crescent formation was due to their attacking the rear squadron which sailed in line abreast. If the ships at the extremities did not keep station well the crescent form would no doubt have appeared.

XIII

The Spanish Armada

The Spanish attacks upon England during the reign of Elizabeth were hardly invasions in the strict sense of the word, since only once was a small force actually landed. Nevertheless, they cannot be ignored, if only for the reason that they came nearer to effecting a landing in force than any other of England's oversea foes since that period. They furnish the spectacle of a remarkable display of patience and ill-directed determination, brought to nought by the might of sea power, happily guided at the critical moment by the first of England's modern scientific admirals. Finally, it is not generally realized that more than one attack was made.

'To Castille and to Leon, Colón (Columbus) gave a new world,' but his gift was to be the ruin of Spain. The preposterous papal decree which divided all the new discoveries between Spain and Portugal was hardly likely to be respected by powerful states like France and England.

It was the French who led the way. The Franco-Spanish wars of the sixteenth century gave them their opportunity, and the fine seamen of Normandy, Brittany, and La Rochelle began to harry the ports of the West Indies. Matters became worse when the persecuted French Protestants took to the sea. In 1553 Sores, a Huguenot captain, with the help of escaped negro slaves, sacked all the chief Spanish settlements except San Domingo. The corsairs were assisted by the utter rottenness of the Spanish colonial system. It was also in their favour that the social organization of Spain was still completely medieval, and that mercantile and trade interests were entirely subordinated to those of the military aristocracy.

The English came later. The relations between England and Spain were for long friendly, and their commercial intercourse was of old standing. But after the Reformation the religious factor came to complicate the situation. Though the Governments strove to maintain peace, the Protestant rovers from the West Country preyed on Spanish commerce, and the Holy Inquisition ignored all the laws of nations in its treatment of heretic seamen. Nor was it in human nature to stand idly and see the trade of half the world monopolized by two countries merely on the authority of a papal bull. The colonists themselves were quite willing to trade, and English merchants soon began to endeavour to establish markets. To describe them as pirates is totally inaccurate, but the Spanish officials did not – perhaps in their ignorance could not – realize the comparative innocence of the English merchants. In 1568 John Hawkins, the most prominent of the pioneers, was treacherously attacked in the Mexican port of San Juan de Ulua by the Viceroy and Francisco de Luxan, General of the Fleet of New Spain. The result was to deeply embitter the relations of the two Powers, and thenceforth English seamen went to the West Indies determined, since the Spaniards would not trade, to make their profit out of them otherwise.

At sea the two states were most unequally matched. The power of Spain on land was great, but her strength at sea has been ludicrously misrepresented. Spain at this time had no sea-going navy at all! In the Mediterranean she had some 100 war-galleys, but galleys were useless for ocean work. On the other hand, England had, for the time, a considerable Royal Navy, and the number of armed merchantmen liable for service in time of war was very large. Portugal had a considerable oceanic squadron. But Spain, for two generations, was content to leave her Atlantic trade entirely unprotected, until the depredations of the French corsairs forced the situation upon the notice of her Government.

It was Pero Menendez de Aviles, perhaps the greatest of all Spanish seamen, who goaded his slow moving and short-sighted government into creating an oceanic navy. Menendez was a fanatically religious man, and regarding, as he did, the heretic corsairs as the enemies of mankind, he was frequently guilty of acts of ferocious cruelty. That he, as sincerely as his English antitype Francis Drake, believed himself to be the chosen instrument of Heaven cannot be doubted; but he certainly lacked Drake's kindly nature.

In 1555 Menendez is found with an armed squadron guarding the trade fleets. He built at his own cost three 'galleons' – the battleships of the day – and in 1561 was appointed Captain-General of the Indian Trade. The French were checked, and by strenuous endeavour something had been done when the English appeared on the scene. The Huguenots, driven from the West Indian Islands, established themselves at St Augustine in Florida. Menendez's untiring energy pursued them there, and in 1565 the colony was wiped out. Menendez's grim cruelty was bitterly remembered. The Spanish Government, now beginning to rouse itself, issued orders that the principal vessels of the trade fleets were always to be armed, and twelve galleons were built for further protection, for the maintenance of which a special tax was

The Spanish Armada.

levied on the Indies merchants. These galleons were the beginnings of the Spanish oceanic navy.

The Spanish sea service was full of grave defects. A Spanish warship was commanded by a military officer, whose special charge was the soldiery; gunnery was neglected and the seamen treated like galley-slaves. In these circumstances the Spanish galleon was comparatively ineffective against ships provided with good guns and gunners. Spain's seafaring population, also, was not large, and since it was impossible to commandeer and arm a powerful force of her own merchant ships on an emergency, the government was wont to seize foreign ships for the purpose, whose crews naturally embraced every opportunity of deserting.

On the other hand, the English Navy was the natural product of seafaring instincts. It was not the outcome of policy, and was ruled by no jealously devised legal code comparable to that of Louis XIV of France. It grew up almost imperceptibly without any clear conception of the process. The old feudal traditions gave way slowly, and in 1588 they still so far prevailed that a noble had to be made nominal Commander-in-Chief over the head of Drake, though, thanks to both, no disaster followed. But there has usually been a spirit of comradeship in English armaments largely or entirely lacking elsewhere, and this spirit was beginning to be felt under Elizabeth.

During the early years of Elizabeth there was a tendency to neglect the Royal Navy. The country was so strong in privateers and merchant craft available for war, and so devoid were her possible antagonists, France and Spain, of true naval power, that little was done. But about 1570 the news of Menendez's untiring efforts brought about a new shipbuilding programme under the direction of John Hawkins, who in 1569 became Treasurer of the Navy. Several new ships were built under his supervision, and were the most formidable fighting engines that had yet appeared on the seas. They were of moderate size, but very seaworthy, heavily armed, and almost entirely lacking the high fore- and stern-castles which had encumbered the earlier vessels. In 1574 a Spanish agent, reporting to his government, noted their great fighting value.

The word 'galleon' has been frequently misinterpreted. The galleon was a ship fit for ocean work, built with something of the fine lines of a galley, hence its name. The very long, narrow, lightly built galley was useless in the Atlantic; on the other hand, the short, broad, oceanic trading vessels were too slow and unwieldy to be of use in war. Trimming between these two extremes, the French shipwrights evolved a vessel at once seaworthy and comparatively fast, and the model was adopted by England and the Peninsular States. Its essential characteristics were that it was three beams or more long, with a draft two-fifths of its beam. By an extraordinary series of misconceptions the galleon has come to be regarded as a heavy, clumsy vessel peculiar to Spain. As a fact, Spain was perhaps the last of the great powers of the sixteenth century to adopt it. This conclusion has been very convincingly set forth by Mr. Julian Corbett in his 'Drake and the Tudor Navy.'

In 1574, Philip II, whose bigotry and absolutist tendencies had created a terrible enemy to Spain in her Netherland possessions, began to collect a fleet of light vessels at Santander. The Duke of Alva had failed in the Low Countries, and had been succeeded by Don Luis de Requesens, who found that he could do nothing while Admiral Boisot and his flotillas held the sea. The command of the force at Santander was conferred upon Pero Menendez de Aviles, and by the summer it was nearly ready to sail. There were 24 large ships and 188 light vessels of various classes, manned by 12,000 men. Menendez, impressed by the danger in the Atlantic, was anxious to do something more than merely support Requesens. He conceived the design of seizing the Scillies and Falmouth Haven, and occupying them as naval stations. In this way he hoped, with his powerful force, to be able at once to intercept the privateers at the outset of their Atlantic voyage, and establish a solid check upon England.

Though Requesens himself was aware of the danger of provoking England, Philip gave his assent. On Elizabeth's side the now reorganized Royal Navy was prepared for mobilization, together with some fifty sail of armed merchantmen. But so great was the dissension in the Council that Requesens told Menendez that he could sail up the Channel unopposed. The attempt, made in the teeth of England's sea power, would probably have failed in the end; yet it might easily have had grave results, and Menendez was a commander of real genius.

But he died in the midst of his final preparations, and so much had the armament depended upon his single dominating personality that it broke up.

Thus a great danger to England passed away with the man who perhaps of all was best fitted to direct an attack upon her; and, as Mr. Julian Corbett points out, it is worthy of note that almost at the moment when the greatest of the Spanish ocean admirals vanishes from the scene, Francis Drake, the protagonist on the English side, comes to the front.

For ten years after the death of Menendez peace nominally subsisted between England and Spain, but it was a peace that was violated every day. England, officially and unofficially, continued to assist the revolted Netherlands, and to raid Spanish and Portuguese commerce. It became an everyday affair for young Englishmen who wanted some fighting to slip across to the Low Countries. Philip countenanced plots against Elizabeth, and intrigued in England and Ireland. The exiled Queen Mary of Scotland was an ever present source of danger. Above all, the religious side of the struggle became accentuated as time went on. In no man was militant Protestantism more incarnate than in Drake. In 1577 Elizabeth permitted him to sail on his famous raid on the Spanish Pacific Settlements, and his striking success was a new stay to the war party. He became at once the leading figure on the English side.

In 1580 the King of Portugal died, and Philip at once seized his country, forcing Prince Antonio, the last (illegitimate) scion of the House of Avis, to flee to England. Terceira, in the Azores, held out for some years; but in 1583 it was reduced by Philip's famous Admiral, Alvaro de Bazan, Marques de Santa Cruz, after a naval victory off St Michael's. The possession of Portugal and its colonies vastly enhanced Philip's power. The most important acquisition was that of the Portuguese Navy – eleven fine galleons, besides galleys and small craft. The Spanish Empire was now for the first time a real naval power.

After his reduction of Terceira, Santa Cruz wrote to Philip. He suggested that his victorious squadron should be made the nucleus of a great fleet, and an attempt made to settle the English Question.

His suggestions, if acted upon, would have meant the assembly of a far larger force than did actually sail against England five years later. Santa Cruz thoroughly understood that the English power was very formidable. Philip did not see his way to immediate action, but he issued orders in accordance with his Admiral's suggestions. They were only very partially carried out, but something was done, and in this way began the 'Enterprise of England.' Certain aspects of the situation must be carefully held in mind. England and Spain, though still nominally at peace, were being steadily drawn into war by religious feeling, the jealously exclusive trade policy of Spain, and the determination of the English to thwart it. Philip, despite his religious fanaticism, was very loth to plunge into a war that was clearly against his interests, since the deposition of Elizabeth would mean the accession to the English throne of the half-French Mary Stuart. England, under Mary, might become by dint of sword and stake Roman Catholic in faith, but would lean to France in policy. The Pope believed that Philip must perforce conquer England, but Philip thought that he could gain the upper hand at sea without wiping England off the map. Though he was clumsily putting Santa Cruz's precepts into practice and conniving at plots against Elizabeth, he did not wish for war, nor was he ready.

On her side Elizabeth personally desired peace. Sir James Crofts, the Controller of the Household, was Spain's paid spy. The Lord Treasurer, Burghley, was a man of peace, and especially detested the technically dubious means by which the war party and its instruments were teaching the world that Spain was but 'a colossus stuffed with clouts.' He entirely failed to see that religious ardour had cleft an impassable chasm between the nations, quite apart from the formidable trade question. The real force which was driving England into war was the intense Protestant (or Puritan) feeling of a great part of the nation, of which the war party in the Royal Council – Walsingham, Leicester, Hatton, and others – were the chief exponents, and whose strongest helper was the famous seaman, Sir Francis Drake. The London merchants, however, to a considerable extent, were opposed to war.

In 1585, an egregious blunder on Philip's part precipitated hostilities. There had been a failure of harvest in the Biscayan provinces. Under special safe conduct a fleet of English corn-ships sailed to relieve the distress, but once in port they were all seized and the crews imprisoned. One ship, the *Primrose*, of London, escaped, carrying off with her the Corregidor (Sheriff) of Biscay, who had endeavoured to seize her. On the Biscayan official were found his directions, proving beyond all doubt that Spain was really preparing to invade England.

The country now was resolute for war, and Elizabeth determined to give Philip a sharp lesson. A fleet of royal and private ships, commanded by Drake, was ordered to sail to the rescue. Philip had already released the ships, apparently because he realized that the action had been a blunder, but this made no difference to Drake. On September 27 he appeared off Vigo, and for more than a week blockaded the port, extorting from the humiliated and helpless local authorities all that he needed, and plundering in the neighbourhood. Then he went on to the Canaries and the West Indies. Santa Cruz was ordered to prepare a squadron to pursue him, but not for six months could he sail; and Drake sacked Santiago in the Cape Verde Islands, San Domingo, Carthagena, and St Augustine in the Spanish Main,

Statue of Sir Francis Drake on Plymouth Hoe, Devon. According to legend, he had time to play bowls on the Hoe while preparing for battle in 1558. (*Courtesy of Jackofhearts101*)

returning in triumph to England in the summer of 1586.

After this open defiance, war seemed inevitable, and nothing but the strange diplomacy of those days still deferred it. Elizabeth was, at last, interfering officially in the Netherlands. In 1586 the 'Babington' plot was discovered, and its result was the execution of Mary Stuart in 1587. One of Philip's deterring motives was thus obviated. By 1587 the work on the Armada was in full swing, when Elizabeth again let Drake loose with a powerful squadron. On April 18 he broke into Cadiz Harbour, worked havoc with the store ships which crowded it, and came out again in spite of all that the Spaniards could do. Then, with magnificent strategic insight, he stationed himself off Cape St Vincent, and threw the entire Spanish mobilization into utter disorder. Santa Cruz and Admiral de Recalde in the Tagus could not move, and were cut off from the other Spanish squadrons in Cadiz and elsewhere. For a month Drake held his ground, and when forced to leave his station, owing to disease in his insanitary ships, he sailed to the Azores and captured one of Philip's great trading carracks, with a cargo worth £110,000, or about £800,000 in modern value. He said that his cruise had singed Philip's beard. In fact, it had dislocated all the Spanish plans, and done damage to the amount of millions of ducats.

Had the blow been followed up, Philip's scattered squadrons could hardly have concentrated. But Elizabeth now fell into a fit of indecision, which was encouraged by the unscrupulous Crofts, who actually suggested that for his services Drake should be disgraced and his property confiscated!

After Drake's return, the Spanish preparations were able, slowly and painfully, to go forward. The Prince of Parma, Philip's General in the Netherlands, said afterwards that had the Armada sailed in September, it would have encountered no opposition. But the point is that it did not sail, and that the English Government was well informed of its backward state of preparation. Santa Cruz was still at sea hunting for Drake, who was already safe at home, and he did not return until September. By that time the Spanish squadrons were at Lisbon under General de Leyva, but still in a very unready state, while Santa Cruz's vessels needed a complete refit. After repeated efforts, the Marquis succeeded in inducing the King to defer the expedition until March.

But he was broken by anxiety and thankless toil, harassed by unjust attacks, and early in 1588 died. His death robbed the expedition of most of its chances of success.

At Santa Cruz's death the Armada was still hopelessly unready. Guns, ammunition, food – everything was wanting. The men were unpaid, ragged, and often dying of hunger. According to feudal notions, the command of so great an expedition must be given to a great prince, and a harmless Spanish grandee, Alonso Perez de Guzman, Duke of Medina Sidonia, was appointed nominal General. The fleet was slowly patched into an appearance of efficiency, but it could not sail until the middle of May, 1588. To strengthen it nearly all the galleons of the Indian Guard were added to it, leaving the Atlantic trade route almost unprotected.

Meanwhile in England, on December 21, 1587, Lord Howard of Effingham, Lord High Admiral, had received his commission as Commander-in-Chief at sea. His official rank was rather civil than naval, and he was placed in chief command for much the same reason as Medina Sidonia had been. He was, however, greatly superior to the Spaniard in moral qualities, and, though somewhat lacking in firmness of character, was always ready to yield to the advice of the experienced seamen with whom the navy swarmed. Drake, the guiding spirit of the resistance, was given the command of an independent squadron at Plymouth. When the news of Santa Cruz's death came in February, there appeared to be some chance of peace, and commissioners from the contending powers met at Flushing. Howard's fleet was partly demobilized, but he himself, with a picked force, was ordered to make a demonstration off Flushing. In March, however, news came that the Armada would sail on the 20th, and the whole Navy was mobilized.

Drake himself was full of contempt for the Spanish sea power, and endeavoured to induce the government to allow him to attack the Armada in port. After repeated representations, he triumphed. Lord Howard was ordered to leave a force to watch Parma, who was making a precedent for Napoleon in 1804, by building a flotilla for the transport of his army, and to join Drake with the bulk of his fleet. This practically amounted to giving Drake the command of the English Navy. With Howard present he was nominally only second, but there is ample evidence that he was the real chief. Abroad Howard's name was hardly mentioned. Drake was recognized as the English leader by everybody, from the Pope downwards. Howard was much addicted to nepotism. To command the Channel Squadron he appointed his nephew, Lord Henry Seymour, to guide whose inexperience two veteran admirals, Sir Henry Palmer and Sir William Wynter, had to be left behind. Seymour had under his command three of the finest galleons of the Royal Navy, five smaller ones, several pinnaces, and the whole of the ships supplied by the East Coast and Cinque Ports. As Parma's flotilla was already closely blockaded by Dutch ships, this large force was practically wasted. Howard took off to the West eleven splendid galleons and eight pinnaces of the Royal Navy, with some forty private ships and pinnaces, half of them furnished by London. Drake at Plymouth had five galleons specially chosen by himself for their sailing qualities, twenty of the finest private ships in the country, and a number of pinnaces.

The English Navy ships were very heavily armed, largely owing to the influence of Drake. Some were, indeed, so over gunned that they could not use their lower tiers in a swell, and there was a lack of trained gunners. The government also, unused to warfare on a great scale, failed to send supplies and ammunition in sufficient quantity.

On May 23 Howard and Drake effected a junction off Plymouth, and now had a united fleet of about 100 sail, manned by 10,000 men. At once Drake began to urge the necessity of sailing to attack the Armada in port. On May 30 the whole fleet put out, but encountered gales, and was obliged to return on June 6. Meanwhile, on May 18, the Spanish fleet had sailed from Lisbon, but by June 9 had to put into Coruña with half its stores spoilt, short of water, crews down in hundreds with sickness, and with a third of its numbers missing. Medina Sidonia and his staff, except Don Pedro de Valdes, Admiral of the Andalucian Squadron, considered that to continue the attempt was hopeless. Philip refused to listen to them, and for a month the fleet lay huddled in Coruña, collecting its stray ships, painfully refitting, revictualling, and recruiting its crews with raw peasants from Galicia. Some of the store ships had drifted almost to the English coast, perilously near Howard's clutches, before they were recalled.

Meanwhile at Plymouth Drake and Howard were also struggling with difficulties, the chief of which was shortage of supplies. The unlettered genius at the head of the fleet never ceased to endeavour to impress upon his Admiral his aggressive tactics. After much argument the whole fleet took up the station off Ushant, which was afterwards to be so famous; and on July 7 the wind blew fair for Spain. Drake insisted on a Council being called, and set forth his arguments more urgently than ever. After a long debate the sea admirals prevailed over the hesitation of the half-feudal entourage of Howard, and at eight o'clock in the evening the English Navy made sail for Spain. Had Drake never done anything else, this splendid dash would stamp him for all time as a captain of the first order. What would have happened to the Armada had Drake attacked it in Coruña is not doubtful. But almost within sight of the Spanish coast the breeze died away, and then turned against the English. They were forced to put about, and on the 12th were back at Plymouth. There they lay for a week, straining every nerve to revictual, dismissing some of the ships so as to fully man others whose crews were weakened by disease. On the afternoon of the 20th the officers, after a hard day's work, were on the Hoe of Plymouth, some of them amusing themselves with a game of bowls, when Captain Fleming burst upon them with the news that the Armada was off the Lizard!

It was a staggering blow. The English were caught in the same predicament as the Spaniards would have been a week before. Everybody turned to the short, sturdy, thick-set 'pirate' captain upon whom England pinned her faith, and Drake replied by one of those little bits of posing by which great captains so often encourage their followers. 'Plenty of time – plenty of time!' he remarked with studied coolness. 'We'll finish the game, and then go and finish the Spaniards!' – or words to that effect. It may be imagined that the great seaman's nonchalance had an excellent effect in steadying the nerves of his excited and less tried colleagues.

None the less, the situation was critical. The Spaniards were a few miles to the windward of Plymouth. There was but one remedy – to put to sea at once in the teeth of the wind. It says volumes for the efficiency of the captains and crews that it was successfully done.

Everyone worked to such excellent purpose that by next morning 54 ships, under Drake and Howard, were clear of the Sound and beating out to sea, while Hawkins, the Rear-Admiral, was warping out the remaining 10. Besides these 64 ships, there were some 20 light craft. Other vessels were in harbour, but not immediately available owing to lack of hands. The 64 ships included 16 Royal Navy galleons of from 250 to 1,000 tons, 5 private galleons from 300 to 400 tons, and 43 between 140 and 200 tons.

Turning to the Spaniards, the original organization of their fleet had been in six ship squadrons, one galleasse (giant galley) squadron, one galley squadron, one light squadron, and one *urca* (cargo vessel) squadron, the last being mainly intended for store carrying, though its vessels were armed. The six ship squadrons included two of war galleons and four of armed merchantmen and private ships. Each consisted nominally of ten ships, except the Castillian squadron, which contained four armed merchantmen besides its ten galleons.

Between May and July ships lost company and did not all rejoin, while to replace them others were added. So far as can be ascertained, the Spanish fleet, when it arrived off the Lizard, included 19 galleons, 4 galleasses, 41 armed merchantmen, 27 *urcas*, 16 water and salvage vessels, and about 40 small craft. The real commander, who was to Medina Sidonia what Drake was to Howard, was Don Diego Flares de Valdes, Admiral of the Castillian galleons. The better to discharge his duties, he sailed with the Duke on the flagship San Martin. It is characteristic of Philip that he had chosen for the substantial command a man inferior in every respect to some of the other admirals. The squadrons and commanders were as follows:

Portugal: Alonso Perez de Guzman, Duque de Medina Sidonia. Castille: Don Diego Flores de Valdes.

Vizcaya (Biscay): Don Juan Martinez de Recalde (Vice-Admiralof the Armada).

Andalucia: Don Pedro de Valdes. Guipuzcoa: Don Miguel de Oquendo.

Levantiscas (Italy): Don Martin de Bertendona.

Don Alonso Martinez de Leyva (Lieutenant General of the Armada).

Naples: Don Hugo de Moncada.

Light Squadron: Don Agostin de Ojeda.

Squadron of Urcas (heavy supply ships): Don Juan Gomez de Medina.

Pedro de Valdes told Drake that the total force included 110 armed vessels and 32 non-effective craft. There were between 7,000 and 8,000 sea men and perhaps 17,000 soldiers, besides gentlemen and slaves; but the seamen were of many races and some raw recruits. Many of the soldiers were also raw, though there were five Tercios, or brigades, of veterans on board.

The Spanish ships were of more antiquated pattern than those of the English, and looked to amateur observers very large and formidable. As a fact, the Spanish galleons were no larger, ship for ship, than those of their adversaries, and were much more lightly armed. All the armed merchantmen were of over 300 tons, but they carried no armament of guns in proportion to their size. Some of the Italian ships were wretchedly armed. Still, it is possible to labour this point too much. The English galleons were undoubtedly by far the best fighting ships in the two fleets, and the fine London trading galleons were also formidably armed; but so far as can be seen, the bulk of the English private craft were armed mainly with 4 and 5 pounders. The inferiority of the Spaniards chiefly lay in the fact that they were even weaker in gunners than the English, as well as badly supplied with ammunition. The military officers who commanded most of the ships were too ignorant and too self-satisfied to trouble about the guns, relying instead upon their soldiers. The result was that no effective reply could be made to the often ill-directed but rapid English fire, while the soldiers crowded in the ships were slaughtered helplessly.

Philip's strategic orders were faulty. No actual point of junction with Parma was named. The fleet was to go to the Downs, avoiding an action if possible until the two forces had united – a difficult and indeed impossible task. The division of the English fleet was known or anticipated, but not Howard's junction with Drake. On the basis that Howard with the Royal Navy was in the Downs, and Drake with a fleet chiefly of privateers in the west, the Armada was tactically organized in three main divisions. At its head sailed the vessels of Portugal and Castille in one squadron under Medina Sidonia and Diego de Valdes. The position of the galleasses is a little uncertain. It has been thought that they sailed separately with the chief flagships; but they are generally found acting together. Behind this vanguard was the Light Division, and behind it again the *urcas*. Behind the *urcas* was the rearguard in two divisions: the 'Rearguard,' or left wing, consisting of Recalde's and Pedro de Valdes' squadrons, under the chief command of the former; the Vanguard, or right wing, comprising the squadrons of Oquerido and Bertendona, under Leyva. Sidonia and Diego de Valdes flew their flags together on the Portuguese galleon *San Martin*. Recalde was on the Portuguese galleon *San Juan*, and Leyva on an Italian ship, the *Rata Encoronada*. The ships generally were badly found. The tactical formation by line abreast, too, was faulty, since the broadsides were masked – a proof of how little the Spanish officers realized that their best weapon was the gun. But the squadronal organization was excellent for manoeuvring, and discipline was good.

The ships seen by Fleming were not the whole Armada, but Pedro de Valdes with his squadron, and about twenty other ships. The rest of the fleet had been scattered in a gale, but on the 20th it reunited and proceeded up the Cornish coast towards Plymouth. Along the shore the Spaniards could see the beacons signalling their approach. The Pope's consecrated banner was hoisted on the *San Martin* and everyone knelt at the signal to pray for victory.

The experienced Spanish admirals, no less than the impetuous Lieutenant General de Leyva, urged their commander-in-chief to push into Plymouth and destroy the English fleet at its anchorage; but while they deliberated ships were made out ahead. It became obvious to the astonished Spaniards that the English had slipped out of the trap. Presently a scouting pinnace arrived confirming the unwelcome impression, and also bringing tidings that the ships were the united fleets of Howard and Drake. Sidonia, at a complete loss, anchored his fleet to wait for daybreak.

Meanwhile Drake and Howard had reached out to the Eddystone, and at dawn on the 21st they bore boldly down to attack the Armada, which was formed in the squadronal order of battle already described.

The English fleet, coming from seaward in a long line ahead, passed Leyva's division, and developed a fierce attack upon Recalde. The Vizcayan squadron was panic stricken, Recalde's flagship completely disabled, and not for two hours did Sidonia and Leyva succeed in supporting him. Howard, thereupon, drew off. As the fleets lay watching each other, however, the Guipuzcoan *San Salvador* was disabled by an explosion. Howard again threatened an attack. Pedro de Vaides' flagship, the *Nuestra Senora del Rosario*, was also disabled by a collision as she put about, but the Spanish squadrons came up to the rescue in such admirable order that Howard again drew off. The injured Spanish ships were taken in tow, and the Armada made sail to continue its voyage, as an attack on Plymouth was obviously now out of the question.

The English pursued. The leading of the van was given to Drake, who flew his flag on the far famed Revenge, the smartest ship and fastest sailor in the English navy. His attention was, however, distracted in the night by some strange lights, and with a somewhat imperfect appreciation of his duty, for which he was afterwards unduly blamed, he turned aside to examine them. They proved to be harmless merchantmen, and Drake put about to resume his post, but on his way he fell in with the crippled *Nuestra Senora del Rosario*, which had fallen behind the Spanish fleet. Resistance being clearly useless – since he was alone amid the English fleet – Valdes surrendered. The *San Salvador* also was so damaged that the Spaniards abandoned her, and she was taken by Howard, who was close behind.

This was a bad beginning for the Spaniards. While Recalde repaired his damaged ship, Leyva took chief command of the rear, which was strengthened by three galleasses, three Portuguese galleons, and the Italian galleon *San Francesco de Florencia* from the van. On the night of the 22nd the fleets were becalmed off Portland. A group of English ships drifted apart from their main body, and in the bright moonlight the oared galleasses might have attacked them; but Captain General Moncada was sulking over a fancied slight, and would not move. At dawn a north-west breeze sprang up, and the Spaniards boldly bore down to the attack.

A tumultuous engagement followed, in which want of organization in the English fleet prevented it from gaining any real advantage. Drake succeeded in weathering the Spanish seaward wing; but on the other flank, Frobisher, the famous explorer, who commanded the *Triumph*, the largest galleon in either fleet, was cut off and fiercely attacked, and Howard and Drake had to come back to the rescue. Sidonia's flagship was badly mauled by Howard's flagship, the *Ark*, and no doubt the Spaniards suffered more than their adversaries; but on the whole the battle was drawn.

The English had learnt a lesson, and next day, as they awaited fresh supplies of ammunition, the fleet was organized into four squadrons, commanded respectively by Howard, Drake, Hawkins, and Frobisher. The latter owed his command to the courage which he had shown at Portland; but he was no tactician, and attributed Drake's scientific manoeuvres to cowardice.

The Spanish admirals knew well the weak point of Philip's design. Recalde had served under Menendez, and was especially urgent in pointing out that an English port must be seized as a base. It was eventually decided to occupy the Isle of Wight, and establish themselves there till a plan of concerted action could be managed with Parma. The English harassed the rearguard incessantly, and eventually it had to sail constantly in order of battle.

On the morning of the 25th the fleets lay be calmed to the south of the Isle of Wight. The Portuguese galleon *San Luis* had fallen behind the Armada, and Hawkins attacked her by towing up with his boats. The gallant Leyva came back to the rescue with three galleasses and some ships, whereupon Howard towed up to assist Hawkins. After a sharp encounter, Leyva rescued the *San Luis*, but the galleasses were very roughly handled.

A breeze now sprang up, and the English attacked. Frobisher, with bulldog courage, went at Recalde, and was again cut off. The Spaniards appeared to have the *Triumph* at their mercy, but her boats were lowered and took her in tow. The wind rose again; her sails filled, and she slipped away, leaving the pursuing Spaniards just as if they had been at anchor. So says Calderon, the Spanish Fleet Treasurer.

Howard apparently took little further part in the action, except to assist Frobisher and contain part of the Spanish fleet. But under cover of the banks of gun-fire smoke Drake and Hawkins carried out successfully a finely conceived and decisive stroke of tactics. Working well out to sea, they bore down irresistibly upon the Armada's weather wing, with the object of driving it upon the 'Owers,' the dangerous shoals which had had their place in Lord Lisle's plan of action against D'Annibault in 1545. The weather ships were forced helplessly to leeward. The attack on Frobisher and Howard died away, because Sidonia had to support Leyva's broken division; and to save themselves from being driven upon the Owers, the Spaniards were forced to retreat eastward. The triumph of the English tactics was complete. The Spaniards were prevented from occupying the island, and in despair sailed for Calais. They were badly demoralized by the English fighting and manoeuvring powers, and their losses had been heavy. Messages were sent on to Parma for ammunition and some vessels that might out sail the fast English ships. Meanwhile Howard could not find room for the soldiers who were streaming out from the coast to reinforce his crews.

Among the noble volunteers who hurried to join him were the Earl of Cumberland, soon to be a famous admiral, and Robert Carey (son of Lord Hunsdon), to whose Memoirs we owe an invaluable picture of Elizabethan times. Carey tells the story of their adventure. They 'took post-horse and rode straight to Portsmouth, where we found a frigate that carried us to sea; and having sought for the fleets a whole day, the night after we fell in among them: where it was our fortune to light first on the Spanish fleet; and finding ourselves in the wrong, we tacked about, and in short time got to our own fleet.' Evidently they had a narrow escape. They found Howard so well attended that he had no cabins to spare, and so boarded the *Bonaventure*, in which they took part in the Battle of Gravelines.

On the day after the battle Howard celebrated the victory by knighting some of his commanders, including Hawkins and Frobisher. All through the 26th and 27th the pursuit went on, until about four o'clock in the afternoon Sidonia anchored off Calais. Nothing had been heard from Parma, and the pilots said that they could answer for the safety of the fleet no farther, as they did not know the North Sea. The English anchored also, to windward of the Armada, and less than a mile away.

Meanwhile a pinnace had been sent to call in the Channel Squadron from the Downs. Seymour and Wynter had already made up their minds to join Howard wherever he might be, and wasted not a moment. They had only three days' provisions in hand, but none the less weighed and beat across to Calais. The disheartened Spaniards made no attempt to prevent the junction, and at nightfall the whole available naval forces of England were gathered within striking distance of the foe.

On Sunday morning a council of war assembled on the *Ark*, and it was decided to attempt to dislodge the Armada from its anchorage by drifting fire ships among its crowded ranks. Combustibles had already been collected at Dover, but lest valuable time should be lost it was decided to use vessels from the fleet. Drake and Hawkins immediately offered two of their own ships for the service. Eight in all were collected and hurriedly prepared. Guns and stores were left on board, for there was no time to remove them. Captains Yonge and Prouse were entrusted with the dangerous duty of directing them, and sometime after midnight they were fired and bore down with wind and tide upon the horror stricken Spaniards. Everyone thought of what Gianibelli's fire ships had done at Antwerp only a few years before. Sidonia, seeing no help for it, ordered or permitted cables to be cut, and there was a nerve breaking scene of disorder and panic. Ship collided with ship in the darkness, and there were many accidents. Moncada's flag ship, the *San Lorenzo*, lost her rudder; the *San Martin* herself was almost overtaken by a fire ship before she could work clear. Still, the material damage was small. Wind and tide carried the fleet clear, and the fire ships burnt out harmlessly. Sidonia, with the *San Marcos*, the *San Juan*, and one or two other ships, anchored as soon as they were clear, but the bulk of the fleet drifted away in a straggling line off Gravelines. The wind was about south-west, so that they could not easily close up on Sidonia. The latter therefore weighed to rejoin them.

At dawn the English admirals saw their foes scattered, but also perceived that Sidonia was endeavouring to reunite his fleet. At once they got under weigh and made sail, Drake leading the attack on the right, Hawkins to his left rear, then Howard, and then Frobisher, with Wynter and Seymour still farther back. All the accounts seem to show that the squadrons did not succeed in engaging simultaneously. The Channel Squadron came into action at least two hours after Drake.

It was now that the inexperienced Lord High Admiral committed a huge blunder. The *San Lorenzo* was seen on the right trying to get into Calais, and with a total lack of appreciation of his duties as Commander in Chief he turned off to seize her, followed by nearly all his squadron. He took and plundered the galleasse, and Moncada was killed; but for nearly four hours a fifth of the English fleet was absent from the critical point.

Sidonia's pilots were anxious. They assured him that if the fleet continued to run before the wind it must go ashore. It was a crushing announcement, but Sidonia, to his credit be it said, did not flinch. Courage Spaniards have never lacked. Pinnaces were sent to warn the fleet, and the devoted flagship and her consorts swung round to face the enemy. In front, and nearest to Sidonia, the ever famous *Revenge*, flying Drake's flag, was bearing down upon him, closely followed by three galleons of the Royal Navy, and for miles behind them the great English fleet was setting all sail and streaming to the attack. No time was to be lost. The Spanish captains knew the peril, and were coming back to the rescue of the Admiral. The English came on in stern silence, reserving their fire until the last moment, in order not to waste their already too scanty supply of ammunition. At sunrise Drake was within easy range of Sidonia's little group. The *Revenge* fired her bow battery into the *San Martin*, and then, hauling to the wind, sailed past her larboard broadside, letting fly with every gun that she could bring to bear. Behind her came the *Nonpareil* (Vice-Admiral Thomas Fenner) and so, one after another, all Drake's squadron filed past, cannonading furiously and holding on after their leader to beat off the main body of the Armada, which was standing out to the rescue of the admiral. Hawkins next came into action and fastened on Sidonia, but he does not seem to have supported Drake; and the result was that one by one about fifty of the best Spanish ships came into action about their Admiral. Frobisher apparently was in action soon after Hawkins, but the Channel Squadron did not come up till about 9 a.m.; and Howard, having wasted so much time, was not on the scene until past ten.

The Spaniards were never really able to form proper order, and as they struggled singly into action they were attacked by whole English squadrons and fearfully mangled. Recalde's division mostly found its way to Sidonia's right, or weather wing, and upon it the English concentrated their fiercest efforts. The English cannonade was overwhelming. The crowded Spanish ships were mere slaughter pens. Deserters declared that some of them were full of blood, but surrender was never heard of. They fought to the bitter end. The finest fighting was done by the Portuguese galleon *San Mateo*. She was full of veterans from the Tercio de Sicilia, and had on board its Colonel, Don Diego de Pimentel. She was surrounded by the whole Channel Squadron, and fought on, answering the storm of cannon balls with musketry, until Recalde rescued her. An English officer, filled with admiration, hailed her to surrender; but the desperate veterans shot him, and cursed the English cowards who would not close and fight like men. The *San Felipe*, under Don Francisco Alvarez de Toledo, a kinsman of the terrible Alva, vied with the *San Mateo* in the heroism of her resistance. In one of the shifts of the battle the *San Martin* was·out of action. She might have escaped, but Sidonia bravely went into the conflict again.

The English had to endure no such ordeal, but they fought with furious determination. The *Revenge* was severely battered. Wynter's *Vanguard* fired 500 30-, 18-, and 9-pounder shot – a remarkable achievement in those days. But so completely had the English the advantage that, according to Vice Admiral Fenner, they lost only sixty killed.

By three o' clock the battle was at an end. Nearly twenty Spanish ships were cut off (among them the *San Martin*, *San Mateo*, and *San Felipe*), all sadly shattered, full of dead and dying, and with not a shot left to reply to the merciless cannonade that was still pouring upon them. Nothing, it seemed, could save them, when suddenly a squall descended upon the struggling fleets. The English were forced to cease fighting to meet the danger. The crippled Spaniards, unable to manoeuvre, had to put before the wind, and the combatants were parted. The Spaniards had no power left to fight. All that night they fled blindly, followed by the English, while their shattered ships went down and drifted ashore. Several were lost in this way, including the *San Felipe* and the *San Mateo*, and with the wind as it was nothing could save them from all going ashore.

Sidonia, having confessed and prepared for death, turned to bay; but there was no heart left in the fleet to follow their Admiral's example, though Leyva and Oquendo, brave to the last, at once supported him. The English fleet was holding off to let the Zeeland sandbanks do their deadly work, and Leyva and Oquendo urged Sidonia to at least make a show of attacking. It could not be. Discipline was gone. They cursed him in their despair, and shouted to the crew to throw Diego Valdes overboard! Nearer and nearer to the banks drifted the miserable throng of shattered, blood-stained hulks that now represented the Fortunate and Invincible Armada, when suddenly the wind shifted. The English could not understand it. Twice God had intervened to save the foe! The Armada was able to bear out from the shoals and steer a course to the northward in deep water.

So ended the great struggle. On the surface the Armada had suffered little; its numbers were not greatly diminished. But in fact nearly all its fighting ships were so mangled that 'they could hardly hope to survive a severe gale'. They were mere floating dens of misery, full of men wounded, sick, and worn out. The loss of life at Gravelines can only be conjectured. The Spaniards admitted 1,400 killed and wounded. But it is known that the *San Mateo* and the *San Felipe* lost nearly all their companies, and the *Maria Juan* of Biscay over two-thirds of hers. Judging from such evidence as this, the total can hardly be estimated at less than 4,000.

Seymour, to his disgust, was left to watch Parma, while the English main fleet pursued the Armada until it was certain that it did not intend to put into the Forth. There was apparently some thought of fighting again. Howard's squadron still had a fair supply of ammunition on board, but the others had expended nearly all theirs; and on August 2 Drake flew a flag of council to discuss the matter. 'It was found,' says Carey, 'that in the whole fleet there was not munition sufficient to make half a fight.' Compelled to be content, the fleet ran for home. It was time, for already disease was beginning to rage in the insanitary ships, and many men died before the fleet could be paid off.

The story of how the beaten Armada made its retreat round Scotland and Ireland is better known than that of its engagements with the English fleet. There was little water, and rations were reduced to starvation limit. The shattered vessels could not fight the Atlantic gales, and sank in the raging seas, or went ashore on the ironbound shores of the Hebrides and Ireland. Such of the crews as succeeded in landing were massacred either by Irish kernes or English soldiers. Leyva perished near Dunluce. Some sixty ships only struggled through to the Biscayan ports. In some there was no water for fourteen days, and the wine was nearly out. The half-dead crews were often unable to work the ships, and they drifted helplessly into such harbours as lay in their aimless course. Recalde and Oquendo came home only to die exhausted and broken hearted, and the roll of death was swelled by thousands who had survived England's artillery and the Atlantic storms.

The popular impression of the catastrophe of the Armada still is that it was beaten by the English privateers. The Admirals did not think so. The pamphlet printed for general circulation, probably inspired by Drake, states that the work was done by the Royal Navy and a few merchants. Wynter said bluntly that the private ships were of hardly any use at all, and so another cherished idea fades into the limbo of ancient misconceptions. The real truth is set forth by the Italian writer Ubaldino, who points out that the English won because they had a properly organized Royal Navy, composed of excellent sailing ships, well-armed with artillery, not cumbered with useless soldiers, and directed not by medievally-minded soldiers, but by scientific seamen. In his summing up lies a lesson to be remembered by Englishmen for all time.

XIV

The Aftermath of the Armada

The defeat of the Armada of 1588 is commonly regarded as the end of any danger to England from Spain. This, however, is far from the truth. Had Elizabeth and her minister Burghley been less timid, it might have been. But they would not allow a great counter attack on Spain to be delivered by the whole strength of England; and the semi-private expedition of Drake and Sir John Norreys in 1589, though gallantly made, was hampered by injudicious instructions, and eventually failed. Worse still, Drake lost Elizabeth's confidence, and retired into private life. The English relapsed into mere aimless, commerce-destroying attempts, which had very little real success.

Philip, with a heroism which compels admiration, despite the misery which it entailed upon his people, set to work immediately after 1588 to build up a properly organized navy. His dogged determination never wavered. In his efforts he was splendidly assisted by Pero Menendez Marquez, son of Menendez de Aviles, who invented a new type of swift warship for treasure carrying service. Spain lacked good timber, and the supplies of it, brought from the Baltic, were often intercepted by English cruisers. Seamen also were lacking, and the old faulty threefold division of the crews was adhered to. Yet, in 1591, Don Alonso de Bazan, brother of Santa Cruz, was able to appear at the Azores with a fleet of sixty-three sail, and to drive away Lord Thomas Howard's squadron, with the loss of the far famed *Revenge*, the story of whose wonderful fight is enshrined in English poetry.

Meanwhile in France the Huguenot Henry of Navarre had become king. He was opposed by the Catholic League, which was energetically supported by Philip. Elizabeth sent troops to the support of Henry; but the Spaniards were able to seize ports in Brittany, and there establish a base of operations dangerously close to England, occupied not only by a strong force of troops, but by a squadron of galleys, available for brief raids in fine weather. The reports of the progress of the new Spanish Navy were more and more alarming. The English squadrons were kept off the trade routes by powerful Spanish fleets, and year after year the American bullion came safely home.

Elizabeth now did what she should have done before, and summoned Drake from Devon to take a fleet to America. The object was to attack Panama, and intercept Philip's treasure trains. But she made the mistake of associating with him his kinsman Hawkins, broken by age and ill health.

This was in the summer of 1595, and while Drake was organizing his squadron at Plymouth, four of the galleys in Brittany sailed, about July 15, from the Blavet River on a raid against the Channel Islands. They raided Penmarch, but found the wind foul for the Islands, and decided to make a descent on the Scillies instead. The galley was always useless for a voyage of any length, being unable to carry supplies sufficient for its crew of some 400 soldiers, slaves, and seamen. Water ran out, and the galleys put into Mount's Bay. On the 23rd they were before Mousehole. Six hundred soldiers were landed, and finding nothing to oppose them, they devastated the neighbourhood, burned Mousehole, Newlyn, St Paul, and the adjoining hamlets, and marched on Penzance. Sir Francis Godolphin hurriedly collected 200 peasants for its defence, but they dared not face the Spanish veterans, and dispersed. The Spaniards burned Penzance, and next day held a church parade on Western Hill, and vowed to found a monastery there when England was conquered. They might have done more mischief, but when they heard that the terrible Drake was at Plymouth, they withdrew forthwith. This petty operation, after years of patient toil, and though the war was to last for eight years longer, was the only Spanish landing on English soil.

Elizabeth's last West Indian expedition was a melancholy failure.

Hawkins died on the way out. The ports were now found fortified and garrisoned; Drake failed before Puerto Rico, and on January 27, 1596, the great seaman, baffled and broken hearted, died of dysentery off Puerto Bello, and was laid to rest in the waters whereon so many of his boldest deeds had been wrought.

His death was a national misfortune. In 1596 the Spaniards took Calais, and thus gained an outpost only twenty miles from England. Elizabeth retorted by a great expedition under the young Earl of Essex and Howard of Effingham. Cadiz was taken and destroyed, with twelve warships and a merchant fleet worth 8,000,000 ducats. The blow to Spanish industry was crushing, but, despite Essex's entreaty, Howard would not garrison the impregnable port. Had he done so, it might well have become to England what Gibraltar is now. As it was, Philip was goaded into a fresh attempt at invasion; but the ill-equipped fleet, largely composed of embargoed foreign craft filled with soldiers, which he hounded to sea in October, under the Conde de Santa Gadea, was so shattered by a storm, that little of it could ever be rallied again.

Philip was now bankrupt, but at the cost of misery, which left its mark on Spain for centuries, he prepared for yet one attempt more. In 1597 Essex sailed with a large fleet to the Azores on a nearly fruitless cruise against the Spanish treasure fleet. By amazing exertions a new Spanish fleet had been assembled in Ferrol, and while Essex was on his way home the last great Armada, 136 ships strong, reached the coast of Brittany. Another fleet was following from Lisbon, and in all there were some 18,000 troops on board. The plan of action was that which Menendez had laid down twenty years before. Essex, however, safely made Plymouth in a violent gale, which scattered the ill-found Spanish fleet, this time, happily, with little loss of life. It was Philip's last effort, and a year later he died.

After his death the war languished until 1601. The English Navy was only employed on abortive commerce-destroying expeditions, and was looked upon with contempt by the bold privateers who harried the Spanish Main. In 1602 Spain made a last effort, and, assisted by the slackness and want of foresight of Elizabeth's chief minister, Sir Robert Cecil, son of Burghley, succeeded in landing 4,000 troops in Ireland.

This woke up the drowsy government. The Spaniards were blockaded in Kinsale by the army of Lord Deputy Mountjoy and the fleet under Sir Richard Leveson. A reinforcing squadron was annihilated in Castlehaven, and Kinsale forced to surrender. In 1602 Leveson sailed to the Spanish coast and won a victory at Cezimbra, but in 1603 Elizabeth died. Her successor, James I, was only too ready to come to terms, and made peace forthwith, without settling the Indies trade question, over which so much blood was subsequently shed. It was the first ill-service done by the Stuarts to the country over which they had come to rule, and it was not to be the last.

The lessons to be drawn from the story of the first Anglo-Spanish War appear to be three:

1. So long as an island state hold the command of the sea, and it be exercised with reasonable skill and prudence, that state is practically invulnerable. Excepting Drake, no Englishman of the sixteenth century apparently understood how to utilize England's naval supremacy, hence the frequent approach to success of the Spaniards.
2. In a naval war the operations must be vigorous and drastic, and not wasted upon mere commerce destroying. All England's privateers and cruisers failed to take a single Spanish treasure fleet.
3. It is necessary to have (a) a regular military force strong enough to assist the fleet in its operations on an enemy's coast; (b) an organized defensive force to deal with isolated raids.

Portrait of Sir Francis Drake by Crispin de Passe.

A DUTCH TWO-DECKED BATTLESHIP.

With an armament of about 50 guns, the Dutch fleet which inflicted the great humiliation
on England in 1667 was largely composed of ships of this type.

(From a contemporary Dutch print.)

XV

De Ruijter and William of Orange

When the danger from Spain had passed away, it was not long before England and the Dutch Republic began to take up a position of rivalry. The two States had fought side by side against Spain, but they had had trade differences, which culminated in an abominable massacre by the Dutch East India Company of English merchants at Amboyna, in the Moluccas. This was in 1623, and the Governments of James I and Charles I had failed to obtain any success by diplomatic means. The Dutch were supreme in the world of sea commerce, and trade rivalry and political differences brought on the first Dutch War in 1652–53. The result was the victory of England, but it was by no means decisive or final, and twelve years later the two countries were again at war.

In the second Dutch War, twelve years later, there is little of which England can be proud. The Restoration Government's corruption and mismanagement had allowed the Navy to fall far below the high level of efficiency to which it had been raised by Oliver Cromwell. The ships were crowded with useless fine gentlemen from the Court. The seamen were so ill-provided that they deserted in numbers to escape the misery of life on shipboard. Scotland had no interest in England's wars, and many Scottish seamen preferred to serve under the Dutch flag rather than that of Great Britain. The result was several very bloody and indecisive battles, in which the Dutch, upon the whole, held their own. Finding that little advantage had been gained, Charles II was ready to come again to terms, and in May, 1667, Peace Commissioners met at Breda. In truth, there was hardly any other alternative. The Great Plague and the Great Fire of London had been stunning blows to the prosperity of England. Meanwhile, though Peace Commissioners were sitting, there was no armistice. Yet no attempt was made by the English Government to fit out for sea the Navy, which was lying dismantled in harbour after the late campaign. Only two commerce-destroying squadrons were sent out. At the same time measures were taken to fortify the coasts. In other words, the peace conference was considered as a sufficient protection, and the fleet was deliberately demobilized. Ineptitude could go no further. The Duke of York (afterwards James II), as High Admiral, approved – a fact which gives the measure of his essentially dull and stupid character. No one appears to have anticipated danger. The work of fortification went forward slowly or not at all. The Court was in the midst of its usual profligacies when, on June 7, the Dutch fleet was sighted off the North Foreland. While Charles was lounging among his courtiers at Whitehall, the Dutch, under the direction of the famous Grand Pensionary de Witt, were preparing to strike a blow. Late in May a squadron, under Admiral van Ghent, was despatched, presumably to distract English attention, to the Forth. Van Ghent failed to land anywhere, but he made havoc of the Scots' coasting trade, and then quietly withdrew to join the main fleet.

On June 1 seventy men-of-war left the ports of Holland, and, though scattered by a storm, reassembled off the North Foreland on the 7th. The Commander-in-Chief was Admiral Michiel Adriaanszoon de Ruijter, the hero of the war, and the greatest of all the great seaman whom his country has borne. His whole naval career is a splendid story of calm, dauntless courage, of unerring skill, of battle after battle gained, or maintained with honour against desperate odds.

At Whitehall all was confusion and dismay. Pepys has given a vivid description of the scene. He himself fully expected to be murdered in a burst of popular fury. The one man who could be trusted to do his duty – Monk, the Lord General – was sent to take command at Chatham. Train bands and militia were mobilized in frantic haste all too late.

On June 9 the advance squadron of the Dutch, under Admiral van Ghent, was off Gravesend, chasing merchantmen and naval light craft in panicterror up the Thames, while the boom of his guns could, it is said, be heard in London. There must have been few who on that day did not look back with regret to the victorious years of the Commonwealth. The Dutch fleet, however, carried no great landing force, and De

Ruijter, judging that London could not be safely attacked, decided to recall Van Ghent and turn against Chatham, the headquarters of the English Navy.

Monk reached Rochester on the 11th, but he could do little. His hard fate was to end his military career as a helpless spectator of the national disgrace. The available troops consisted of a weak Scottish regiment and some seamen at Sheerness, under Admiral Sir Edward Spragge. The fortifications were unfinished and unarmed. The ships were not manned, and, to complete the disgrace, the seamen refused point-blank to fight for the king who had starved and robbed them. There is an even darker side to the gloomy picture. The oncoming Dutch fleet was full of English and Scottish seamen, who preferred the good treatment and regular pay of the States to that of their discredited king. The dockyard hands – starving, unpaid, and mutinous – deserted en masse.

On June 10 De Ruijter entered the Medway. Sheerness fort was bombarded into ruins, though Spragge and his handful of English and Scots held their ground until an overwhelming force was landed for the storm. Fifteen guns and all the stores at Sheerness were taken, and the Dutch fleet worked on up the winding reaches of the Medway. On the 12th the leading squadron under Van Ghent, with the fireships commanded by Captain Brackel, arrived at Gillingham Reach, the usual harbourage of the naval ships. Two small and illarmed batteries guarded the entrance. Between them was stretched a heavy iron chain, and behind it were anchored three Dutch prizes and some smaller craft. Higher up Monk was striving desperately to save the ships. But the dockyard officials had all fled, and carried with them the ships' boats, so that the heavy vessels could not be towed away. Everywhere there was cowardice, selfishness, and confusion. Bracket drove straight for the chain on the flood-tide, and crashed through it, silencing the impotent forts, and burning all the ships at the barrier. A little farther up lay the *Royal Charles*, the finest ship in the British Navy. She had been the Naseby of the Commonwealth, and had carried Monk himself to victory. She was almost unarmed, and before Monk could fire her, the Dutch were at hand. Her crew fled to shore, and the exultant foe towed her triumphantly down the river to their fleet.

The tide was now turning, and Bracket retired some distance and anchored. Despairing of saving the Royal Oak, Great James, and Loyal London, which lay higher up, Monk scuttled them, and sank three ships in the fairway of the only channel by which, according to local information, the Dutch could approach. On the following day the Dutch came back with the tide and ran through another channel pointed out, no doubt, by their English comrades. Upnor Castle strove in vain to stop them. They passed its batteries in safety, and came on to the half-sunken ships which lay aground in the shallow stream. With hardly any resistance they fired and destroyed all three. Captain Douglas, of the Royal Oak, died on board his ship, and his gallant end was the one slight redeeming feature of the melancholy scene. Had they known the utter panic and lack of organized defence at Chatham, the Dutch might well have destroyed the dockyard. But they did not know; they had inflicted upon England the greatest humiliation that she has endured since the day of the Norse rovers, and so, well content, the small squadron that had done so much sailed triumphantly down the river, insulting their humbled enemies with thundering cheers and songs and victorious music.

For six weeks the victorious Dutch fleet dominated the English seas. So secure was De Ruijter that he left only Van Ghent's squadron to guard the Thames, and sailed down the Channel as a conqueror, sweeping up English trade, and terrorizing the coasts. What he might have done had his fleet carried troops may be judged from the pages of Pepys. Panic, confusion, and self-seeking reigned supreme at Court, and among the seamen discontent was rife. Sir Edward Spragge did at last succeed in forming a squadron sufficient to hold the Thames against Van Ghent, but this was all. When the Peace of Breda was signed in July De Ruijter still victoriously ranged the English seas.

So ten years after Oliver Cromwell had made Britain's name dreaded wherever her flag flew, Charles II, 'the Lord's anointed,' degraded her to the dust. He was to wage another war with the Dutch, and to see the heroic De Ruijter successfully withstand the combined strength of France and her jackal – England. He left his realm the vassal of France, the national escutcheon bearing a stain that has never been forgotten, and the once invincible navy reduced to a mass of rotting hulks that could not venture out of port.

When James II succeeded to the throne discontent was already rife among the people, and when his natural brother James, Duke of Monmouth, landed almost alone in Dorsetshire, the West country peasantry flocked to his standard. The hideous barbarity with which the premature and ill-conducted revolt was suppressed merely added fuel to the smouldering furnace. Had Monmouth been a stronger man, had he been better supplied with money, arms, and trained officers, matters might have been different. The navy could with difficulty mobilize a small squadron, which was at sea too late to prevent him from landing.

The fate of the Stuart dynasty was sealed when James alienated the sympathies of the hitherto thoroughly servile Anglican Church and the Court, or 'Tory' party, in Parliament. The result was a temporary, but for the time all-powerful, coalition against him. A nucleus of trained troops around which the discontented could rally was necessary; and the malcontents naturally turned to William, Prince of Orange, Stadtholder of the Dutch Republic, the husband of the King's daughter Mary. Every motive of statesmanship, interest, and personal inclination, combined to induce William to respond to the appeal. The great object of his life was to curtail the overshadowing power of Louis XIV. Without the assistance of England, this was all but an impossibility. It can hardly be doubted that William looked forward to his own ultimate election as King of England. That the men who invited him had no clear conception of this part of the political situation seems certain; but William, with his sagacity and experience, must have been perfectly aware of the only possible satisfactory solution.

By October, 1688, William had gathered a fleet of some 500 transports and store-ships, with an escort of over 50 men-of-war, at Helvoetsluys. The danger in his path was that of France, and had James II been less stupid and less proud at the wrong moment, there can be no doubt that William's plans would have been brought to an abrupt end by a French invasion. The great European alliance against France was already formed, and war was about to break out. The French armies were already collecting at the frontier. But James rudely repelled the offers of his ally and practical overlord, and Louis turned his arms against Germany. William was therefore left free to sail.

His expedition cannot be described in any sense as a hostile invasion. It is mentioned in this work in order to draw a comparison between the foreign attacks successfully repelled by England, and this officially hostile but actually friendly expedition which landed and did its work, because it was deliberately allowed to pass unopposed.

The fleet which James possessed was fully equal to crippling that of William, had it been directed with energy and fidelity. This was not the case. The ships had been for the most part reconstructed by James, and materially the navy was strong. The commander, Lord Dartmouth, was faithful. But the majority of the officers were disloyal, and they persuaded Dartmouth to take up a position from which it was impossible to work out of the Thames in time to stop any passing fleet. The army, though it was three times as strong as that of William, was rotten to the very core with discontent and treachery. Those of the superior officers who were faithful were often the least capable – notably the Commander-in-Chief, the Frenchman Louis Duras, Lord Feversham. The ablest of them all, General Churchill, was the worst traitor. It was practically certain that William would meet little effective resistance from the fleet and army which were nominally opposed to him. It must be admitted that England at this time presented to the world a very depressing spectacle. That the House of Stuart had proved poor and faithless guardians of the national honour was undoubted, and the Whigs, in endeavouring to oust them, could at least lay claim to political consistency. But the Church and the Tories were simply obeying the dictates of self-interest and injured pride. Open rebellion need not be dishonourable, but very many members, both of James's civil and defensive services, were traitors.

So far as its events are concerned, the story of the expedition may be told in a few sentences. William had at first intended to land in the North, where his adherents – the Whig Earl of Devonshire, and the Tory Lord Danby – were ready to receive him. He sailed on October 19, but was driven back, and unable to start again until November 1. The wind was favourable, and rapidly rose. The vast fleet went past the mouth of the Thames, and Lord Dartmouth, owing to the faulty dispositions into which he had been persuaded, could not come out in time to oppose it. William passed down the Channel unmolested, and landed, 'as every schoolboy knows,' at Brixham on November 5. Dartmouth was following down the Channel, but the wind again changed, and he put into Portsmouth. Had the fleets met, the result cannot be doubted. The Dutch fleet was commanded by the refugee English Admiral Herbert, and his ships were full of English seamen. The crews of James's fleet were thoroughly discontented, and half the ships would undoubtedly have been carried over by their captains. To discuss the events of 1688 as if they constituted a military campaign is a mistake. William's design rested upon the known fact that England as a whole was not merely passive, but actively friendly.

William, having landed, occupied Exeter with his army of 14,000, of whom over 3,000 were British infantry. For a week there was hesitation, for he had not been expected, and the memory of the Bloody Assize hung over the West. But soon the Western gentry, both Whigs and Tories, began pouring into Exeter, while all over England revolt blazed up. The royal officers deserted in a manner that can only be described as utterly shameless. William entered London on December 16 without any fighting on the route, except a skirmish at Wincanton, in which one of his Scottish battalions roughly handled Colonel Patrick Sarsfield's Irish regiment. James fled to France, and England was lost and won almost without a blow. Not only this, but Jacobitism was never again, except in one or two remote localities, a real militant force. From the military point of view, one may almost say that everything was pre arranged, and the main lesson to be learnt from the English Revolution is that, when public opinion is not dormant and the defensive services are amenable to its influence, it is impossible for the mere official administration to maintain itself.

XVI

The 'Fifteen' and the 'Forty-Five'

The efforts of the dispossessed Stuart dynasty to re-establish itself in the British Isles produced the last land invasions of England by way of Scotland. That of 1715 was insignificant. It cannot be said that either had the faintest chance of success unaided. Still, they were invasions in the true sense of the word and, as such, merit some notice.

Though the Stuart James II had been expelled in 1688, the dynasty continued in a sense to reign in the female branch until 1702, though with a gap caused by the death of Queen Mary II in 1695. But the male branch was now to all intents a foreign family with foreign ideas, and it was also Roman Catholic in its religion. It is unquestionable that the last Stuarts suffered for the misdeeds of their ancestors, but no one who studies impartially the record of the family as kings of Great Britain can well avoid the conclusion that the men who governed the country in 1714 were wise not to recall them.

It does not appear that there was any widespread Jacobite feeling in England. Certainly it assumed no practical form. That there was sympathy with the exiled family is probable, but it was largely the product of the chivalrous strain in the English national character which has so often impelled Englishmen to side with a losing cause.

In Scotland matters were somewhat different. There was a great deal of dislike to the Union of the two countries on the part of narrow Scottish patriots. At the same time the Presbyterian Lowlanders were thoroughly opposed to Stuart rule, and active Jacobite sympathy was practically confined to a few nobles and their tenants. That section of the Highlands which was at feud with the Campbells was the only part even of Scotland which sided with the exiled dynasty, and in this case self-interest had more to do with the action of the clans than loyalty.

On September 6, 1715, John Erskine, Earl of Mar, a shifty politician, nicknamed 'Bobbing John' by his contemporaries, raised the Stuart banner at Braemar. The 'Royalist' clans rose, and the Hanoverian general, John Campbell, Duke of Argyll, could only hold the line of the Forth and await reinforcements from England. The Hanoverian Government, ably directed by General Stanhope, was active to nip in the bud any Jacobite risings, and eventually the revolt broke out in the farthest corner of England.

It was not until October 6 that Mr. Thomas Forster, the son of a Cumberland landowner, rose in arms for the Stuart claimant, and was joined by Lords Derwentwater and Widdrington. They hoped to seize Newcastle and its coal-mines, but they were far too weak; and even when joined by the few Jacobite sympathizers in south-western Scotland, under Lords Kenmure, Nithsdale, Wintoun, and Carnwath, they mustered only 600 horsemen.

To assist this forlorn rising the Earl of Mar detached from the large force, now assembled at Perth, some 2,000 Highlanders under General Macintosh. Covered by a very feebly executed feint upon Stirling made by Mar, Macintosh crossed the Firth of Forth, cleverly evading the English cruisers which guarded the passage. He occupied Leith, and the terror in Edinburgh brought Argyll with a part of his scanty force back from Stirling, but in accordance with his orders Macintosh passed on southward to join the Border Jacobites. He found them at Rothbury in Northumberland, and the united force now amounted to 2,500 men.

From the first the seeds of disaster were present in the little army. The one commander of any capacity was Macintosh; but Forster, by virtue of a commission from James, was Commander-in-Chief. He had no military experience, and appears to have been hopelessly incapable. The Hanoverian commander in the north, General George Carpenter, had only four weak regiments of cavalry at his disposal; but he anticipated the Jacobites at Dumfries, which was found garrisoned.

Thereupon it was resolved to invade England. Lancashire was supposed to be strongly Jacobite. Widdrington believed that 20,000 Lancashire men would join if a Jacobite force appeared among them.

The resolution at once increased the dissension. Many Highlanders deserted. Nevertheless the march began. On November 1 the Border was crossed. Lord Lonsdale had collected a mass of totally undisciplined and half-armed peasantry, some 6,000 strong, at Penrith, to oppose the invaders; but they dispersed in terror of the wild Highlanders, and the Jacobites pushed on into Lancashire. The advance was slow. Desertions were frequent, and there were very few recruits. General Carpenter had been diverted by news of an attack on Newcastle, but was returning on his tracks; and General Willes was in front with the Government troops in Lancashire. Not until they neared Preston did they acquire a respectable reinforcement of some 200 well-armed men. But it was noted that they were all Roman Catholics – an ominous fact. At Preston itself a number of ill-armed men appear to have joined. By this time the Jacobites were also possessed of six or seven guns. It was decided to halt at Preston for a few days to rally the expected Lancashire recruits, but on the 12th, before there had been time to erect proper defences, the Government troops attacked them.

General Willes had collected six regiments of cavalry and a battalion of infantry – all very weak – perhaps 1,800 men in all. The Jacobites were certainly as numerous, and occupied a town which was easily defensible, and might have been made very strong. The bridge over the Ribble to the south of Preston was guarded by 300 men. At each of the four main entrances to the town barricades were in course of construction, and three were armed each with two guns. But the lack of resolute or skilful leading was apparent. The garrison at the bridge evacuated its post almost without resistance – at Forster's own order, so it was said. The Highlanders, however, fought gallantly, and repulsed several attacks made by dismounted cavalry. At nightfall the place was untaken; but early on the 13th Carpenter arrived on the north side of the town, and Forster tamely surrendered. He was indeed utterly unfit for his post. When accused of treachery by his associates he shed tears, and faltered out feeble excuses. But it cannot be said that he was much worse than the lords. Surely men of spirit and energy would have repudiated the cowardly surrender. Yet nothing was done. Even the Highlanders appear to have had enough of campaigning; probably they were too home-sick to care to fight when there was a chance of returning to their beloved hills.

The actual number of prisoners taken was 496, including six peers. The Government was guilty of outraging the most distinguished of the captives by parading them bound on horseback through the streets of London, but there was little bloodshed. The leaders, according to the ideas of the day, could hardly hope for mercy; but, as a matter of fact, only Lords Kenmure and Derwentwater suffered death. Lady Nithsdale heroically contrived her husband's rescue from the Tower, and Forster and Macintosh also escaped, Forster by the aid of his sister Dorothy. Certainly in this affair the female Jacobites showed to better advantage than their men. Of the other prisoners, 26 were executed, and some hundreds transported – a contrast to the awful butchery which had followed Sedgemoor only thirty years before.

Meanwhile the Jacobite rising in Scotland had come to an ignominious end. Though the claimant himself had appeared among his followers, the army, demoralized by dissension and poor leading, was melting fast away, and James soon left for the Continent. He was himself apparently the most estimable of the Stuarts – brave, regular in his life, and not devoid of ability, but he was not a man to inspire devotion. His son, Charles Edward, was of a different type, and, besides considerable capacity, possessed all the fascination of his ancestress, Mary. The influence which the memory of 'Bonnie Prince Charlie' exercised over the susceptible Highlanders is remarkable, and is, indeed, hardly extinct at the present day. In 1745 England was at war with France in the cause of the Empress Maria Theresia, and was faring badly. Prince Charles saw his chance. His father had no confidence of success, and his son's action was taken against his wish; but the Prince raised a small sum of money, and with this and a slender supply of arms and ammunition landed on the west coast of Scotland in August, 1745.

The story of the brilliant campaign that followed lies without the bounds of this book. The success of the Highlanders was rapid and complete. Yet, in the midst of victory, the shadow of disaster lay upon the Jacobites.

It was but too obvious that nearly half the Highlands were hostile, and that clans which had once been Jacobite now held aloof. Charles's noblest supporter, the chivalrous Cameron of Lochiel, had little hope of victory. There were differences in the Prince's suite. His best, perhaps it should be said his only, general, Lord George Murray, was at variance with the Franco-Scottish nobles and gentlemen of the Prince's entourage. Money and supplies were scanty, and not easily collected. Assistance was promised by France, but, such as it was, it was difficult to send it in face of the English fleet, and, even so, it probably did harm by giving a dynastic war the appearance of a foreign invasion. In England and the Scottish Lowlands a prosperous peace of thirty years had almost obliterated the memory of the Stuarts, and in neither country had educated men any reason to look back upon it with pride. The Hanoverians were not popular, but Jacobitism was already tending to recede into the region of dreams.

By the end of October Prince Charles had collected near Edinburgh some 7,000 men. They were nearly all Highland infantry; there were only four weak squadrons of cavalry and thirteen small field pieces, with very few trained gunners. Against this small force the English Government had in the field three armies, each some 10,000 strong. The first lay at Newcastle under the now aged and worn-out Marshal Wade, the constructor of the famous military roads of the Highlands. The second was in Staffordshire. It was commanded in succession by General Ligonier and the young Duke of Cumberland. The third force – royal guards, and London militia and volunteers – was at Finchley, under the personal command of George II, now advanced in years. London itself formed several volunteer corps, one composed entirely of lawyers and law-students. The military value of these corps does not affect the issue – the point is, that public sentiment was strongly anti-Jacobite. The Prince's enterprise, in fact, was regarded as a foreign invasion.

Prince Charles and his advisers had resolved to enter England by way of Carlisle, thus avoiding Wade, who lay about Newcastle. On November 16 the Jacobite army reached Carlisle, which was practically defenceless, and on the next day it surrendered. A small garrison was left there, and the advance continued. The forlornness of the enterprise is to be gauged from the fact that already the Highlanders were deserting by hundreds. When, on the 28th, Charles entered Manchester, he probably had not more than 5,000 foot and 250 horse. Manchester welcomed him with an illumination, but the material results of the march through Lancashire were only 200 recruits and £2,000 in cash. The only favourable circumstances were that Wade was far in the rear, and that Cumberland, anxious that Charles should not enter Wales, where Jacobitism still retained some vitality, was moving north-westward by Stone, thus leaving the main road to London uncovered. Charles broke up from Manchester, slipped over the Peak, and came down the dales to Derby, which he entered on December 4. Cumberland was already falling back towards Coventry to regain the main road, but Charles had fairly outmanreuvred him. He was rather less than 130 miles from London by road, and might perhaps have covered the distance in a week had he continued his advance. But the heart was beaten out of his staff, and they would go no farther. They saw the hopelessly meagre results of the daring march, and they insisted upon a retreat. There were reinforcements awaiting them in Scotland which would double their strength; substantial aid might be obtained from France, and the line of the Forth defended against the Hanoverians. As is well known, even this modest programme could not be carried out. Indeed, Edinburgh and most of the Lowlands had returned to their allegiance as soon as the Jacobite army marched southward. The hostility of Scotland, except the Central Highlands, to the Stuart cause was apparent.

Would Charles have succeeded had he pressed on? It is more than doubtful. The fact that there was considerable panic in London on December 6, and a run upon the Bank of England, proves nothing. Englishmen have a most remarkable capacity for such panics, and also for seeing their enemies double on every possible occasion. King George had at Finchley some 4,000 highly trained and mainly veteran troops, a powerful artillery, and at least 5,000 militia and volunteers, who were hardly likely to be entirely useless, especially in street fighting. They show a somewhat robust faith who believe that Charles's 5,000 men or less, almost destitute of cavalry and artillery, would have gained the day, and have been able to capture London before the arrival of Cumberland. From the military point of view, Murray and the staff were perfectly right in advising retreat. Politically, perhaps Charles was correct in his contention that he must push on, but it was a gambler's chance. If one thing is more certain than another, it is that Jacobitism, everywhere in Great Britain except part of Scotland, was already moribund.

The Jacobite army evacuated Derby on the night of December 6. Its retreat was disorderly. The hopes which had buoyed up the chiefs were dying away, and they had to face a gloomy prospect of overthrow and ruin. The men, too, could not fail to see the depression of their leaders, and drifted out of hand. Straggling and pillage became general. The villagers began to cut off those who strayed from the line of march. The people of Manchester, friendly on the advance, now broke into rioting, and were mulcted in a fine of £5,000. At Wigan an attempt was made to shoot the Prince. He was disheartened and depressed, and made little attempt to restrain his men, who streamed along the road with scarcely any discipline. Only the rearguard under Murray still closed the march in good order, and brought along with it the artillery and baggage which would otherwise have been abandoned.

Cumberland was near Coventry when he heard of Charles's retreat. He at once began to pursue with his cavalry, while the country gentry supplied 1,000 horses to mount part of his infantry. He hurried northward through Cheshire and Lancashire, but the Highlanders had a long start, and were well in advance. At Preston General Oglethorpe joined with some of Wade's cavalry. That weak old commander was still drifting 'in the air,' and Cumberland acted wisely in superseding him, though his own choice, Sir John Hawley, was hardly a success. On December 18 Charles was at Penrith, while Murray with the rearguard was strongly posted in enclosures at Clifton, two miles to the south. Here he was overtaken by Cumberland's mounted infantry, and a brisk skirmish ensued. The fire of the infantry made little impression upon the well-posted Highlanders, and Murray, making a fine charge with the MacPhersons, drove them back with the loss of 100 men. By the morning Cumberland had his whole mounted force in hand, but Murray had already retired, and on the 20th joined the Prince at Carlisle. There the English sympathizers were left as a garrison, to surrender, as was inevitable, a few days later. Charles crossed the Border on the 20th, and continued his march to Glasgow, which he reoccupied on the 26th.

So ended the bold adventure. The small Jacobite army, partly by good fortune, partly by skilful strategy, had penetrated to within a week's march of London, and had returned to its advanced base in safety indeed, but without success, and with scarce an English recruit to swell its ranks. General Hawley's stupidity was to give it one more victory, and then Jacobitism as a political factor was to be trampled out of existence on the bleak moor of Culloden.

XVII

French Raids
1690–1797
Teignmouth and Fishguard

Aristophanes, in 'The Acharnians', puts into the mouth of Dicreopolis some sarcastic observations as to what the Athenians would do if the Spartans manned a skiff and stole a pug-puppy from one of the islands. The poet's imagined invasion of the Athenian Empire is very much on a par with the two French landings which have taken place in England since the year 1689.

The Revolution left England under the rule of a monarch of her own choosing, but torn with faction, and committed of necessity to a war with France. At this time the French Navy was more powerful than it has ever been; but it was hampered by the inexperience and timidity of its officers, and did far less than might otherwise have been accomplished. On June 30 the famous French Admiral, Anne Hilarion de Costentin, Comte de Tourville, gained a complete victory over the allied English and Dutch under Herbert, now Earl of Torrington, off Beachy Head, and for some weeks was master of the Channel. On July 27 he put into Torbay, while the galleys which accompanied the heavy ships rowed a few miles northwards, and landed about a thousand men, who burned the fishing village of Teignmouth. The inhabitants escaped. Some fishing-boats were also burned, but after remaining on shore for awhile the landing party re-embarked. Tourville had with him several galleys fit for inshore work, but this insignificant operation was all that Louis XIV's seamen were capable of effecting after a great victory. Its effect was to rouse the somewhat dormant national spirit. The militia of Devon assembled with enthusiasm and marched down to the coast, burning with desire to meet the invaders.

For over a century no French force landed on the shores of England, though they were successful in effecting various landings in Ireland, chiefly during the early years of William III. The centre of British naval defence was always the mouth of the Channel, and it was comparatively easy to slip past the defending fleets to Ireland. It was this design which the great French general Hoche took up in 1796, and which brought about the last landing of French troops in England.

Lazare Hoche was, perhaps, the greatest of the warriors produced by the Revolution, with the exception of Napoleon. He had made his mark by a victorious defence of the eastern frontier against the Austrians in 1793, being then only twenty-five years of age. His next service – the greatest that he ever rendered to his country – was to end the terrible civil war in the west. It was in the course of this that he came into communication with the Irish leaders who were busily engaged in rousing their countrymen to rise against the harsh English rule.

Hoche's sympathies were naturally with the Irish, and his hatred of England, as evidenced by his letters, amounted to passionate folly. La Vendee was at last tranquil, and Hoche proposed to employ part of his great army of 100,000 men in an invasion of Ireland. On December 16 a fleet of seventeen battleships, twenty frigates and brigs, and seven transports, under Vice-Admiral Morard de Galles, sailed from Brest with Hoche and some 16,000 troops. The expedition was a failure, though not owing to active British naval operations. Hoche and the Admiral lost touch with their fleet. Ships were wrecked, and the armament was scattered, but Rear-Admiral Bouvet actually reached Bantry Bay with a number of ships and 7,000 troops. But the weather was bad, and though urged to disembark the soldiers by General Grouchy, the senior military officer, he eventually put back to Brest. Hoche arrived in Bantry Bay to find his fleet already gone, and could only follow it. Had he actually landed; even with only 7,000 men, in smouldering Ireland, there is no predicting where his victorious career would have ended. The Protestant militia of Ireland were utterly worthless against the fine French troops, as was proved a year later.

One of Hoche's subordinate designs in this great expedition was to land subsidiary and distracting detachments in England itself. Unhappily for his fame, he allowed himself to be led by his bitter hatred of England into very discreditable methods. He proposed to form columns of military delinquents and released convicts which should lay waste and terrorize the enemy's country. Such a scheme had been devised by the Committee of Public Safety; but it is a blot upon the fair fame both of Carnot, over whose signature the plan appears, and of Hoche.

Two regiments were eventually formed out of these disreputable elements. They were called the 1st and 2nd Legions of Franks; but the criminal regiment was called, if not named, the 'Black Legion.' The whole design was distinctly foolish, despite its specious air of cunning. The men of whom the legions were composed were scarcely likely to risk hardships and death for the sake of the Government that had imprisoned them, and it is tolerably clear that their capacity for mischief must have been greatly lessened by their ignorance of the English language. Open brigandage they might commit, but it could only be in large bodies which could easily be hunted down. In fact, if there were not evidence to the contrary, one might conclude that the French Government only wished to be rid of these criminal elements.

On February 22, 1797, three frigates and a lugger, under Commodore Castagnier, appeared near Fishguard Bay in Pembrokeshire, and landed some 1,400 of 'the legions.' The Commander was an Irish-American adventurer named Tate. The intention had been to put them ashore in Somerset in order to burn Bristol. The actual landing was made at Llanwnda, about two miles from Goodwick, in an inlet called Careg Gwasted Bay. One life was lost, but otherwise by the 23rd the force was landed in safety, with its ammunition, and bivouacked on the heights above the inlet.

Now, however, the weak point in the nefarious design showed itself. Owing to a recent wreck there were great quantities of wine and spirits available in the surrounding cottages. The men, devoid of any sense of duty or discipline, and only too ready to forget the misery of their life in prison, seized upon liquor with avidity, and before long General Tate's force was either helplessly intoxicated or completely out of hand, engaged in reckless pillage. Castagnier, having accomplished the landing, set sail and stood out to sea. It certainly seems as if he had had orders to abandon the 'legionaries' to their fate. No attempt could be made to capture Fishguard itself, and Tate and his staff seem to have been powerless among their ruffianly followers. There is evidence that they endeavoured to suppress the excesses that were going on around them, but the men refused to obey orders. Brutal violence there was none; the invaders only seized all the food that they could find. Tate even endeavoured to return his property to a bold Welshman who remonstrated with him.

Meanwhile the men of the countryside were assembling *en masse*. Near Fishguard there were but 300 militiamen, seamen, and gunners, but before evening on the 23rd they were joined by Lord Cawdor with 60 yeomanry and 320 of the Pembrokeshire and Cardiganshire Militia. By this time there were collected on Goodwick Sands, headed by all the gentry of the neighbourhood who had been able to join, 2,000 furious Welshmen, armed with every sort of weapon – scythes, hayforks, picks, mattocks, and reaping-hooks – everything, in short, that had an edge or a point. Of properly armed men, including the militia, there were probably less than 1,000. There was a lack of ammunition, and lead from the roof of St David's Cathedral was used for moulding bullets. The women of the counties streamed after their men, and it is quite likely that, as has been said, their high black hats and red cloaks were mistaken by the befuddled 'legionaries' for regular uniforms. Tate saw the seemingly formidable force collecting in his front; he knew that his own men were helpless, and would in any case probably refuse to fight. He sent a letter to Cawdor offering to surrender on terms. Cawdor replied that, in view of his own great and increasing superiority of strength, he could only insist upon unconditional surrender! So next day the episode ended. The number of prisoners is given as 'near 1,400'. A light is thrown upon the real intentions of the French Government by what subsequently happened. They refused to exchange the prisoners. The British Government thereupon threatened to land them in Brittany to do their worst. This brought the Directory to their senses, and the exchange was effected. France received back her criminals; Britain regained an equal number of good fighting men, and thus, in circumstances not far removed from the proceedings of comic opera, ended the famous episode of Fishguard.

The fact that Hoche's large expedition did actually, in part at least, reach the shores of Ireland was due largely to the slackness of Lord Bridport, the commander of the Channel Squadron. The British admirals had not yet adopted the plan of close and relentless blockade, which was soon afterwards initiated by Jarvis. The French were further assisted by the violent gales which, while they scattered their own fleet, also forced the British to run to port for shelter. The Fishguard raid, like that of General Humbert in Ireland shortly afterwards, is of value as demonstrating the impossibility, even to a great naval power, of preventing the landing of small invading forces. A close blockade might, in the days of sailing ships, be broken by exceptionally bad weather; but since the introduction of steam, blockades are more effective, and naval movements generally are carried out with infinitely greater precision.

XVIII

The Napoleonic Design 1804

No work dealing with the invasions of England would be complete without some notice of the attempts, or supposed attempts, of Napoleon to invade this island. To discuss them in detail here is unnecessary, especially in view of the fact that more than one excellent work has been produced on the subject in recent years. In any case Napoleon did not approach success so nearly as Philip II of Spain, since he never brought his fleet to the vital point. He was never able, even in the height of his power, to land a single company on the shores of England. Taking this into consideration, it is only proposed here to very briefly discuss the extent and scope of Napoleon's preparations, and to give a summary of expert opinion upon them.

The naval position in 1804, when France and Spain were united against Britain, was as follows: The British Navy was nearly twice as strong in numbers as those of the allies together, and enormously superior in quality. The allied force was, furthermore, scattered in fragments in a dozen ports from Toulon to the Texel, and closely blockaded by superior British squadrons. Here and there, by taking advantage of favourable circumstances, French squadrons did escape from their harbours; but a general concentration in the face of the British fleet was always impossible, and without the command of the sea invasion was hopeless.

Napoleon, it must be remembered, was regardless of veracity, and, except when his statements are confirmed by independent testimony, they can rarely be accepted. His bulletins are masterpieces of mendacity, and his correspondence, though much of it was suppressed by admiring editors, shows how prone he was to paint rose-coloured pictures for the benefit of his subjects, if not to deceive himself. Moreover, as is well known, he was so surrounded by treachery that he often literally dared not speak his inmost thoughts, and coined fables for the misleading of his betrayers.

Finally, there is one fact that cannot be overlooked. Napoleon was no seaman. He was a great soldier – in his prime probably the greatest of modern times – but in naval matters he was an amateur. His admirals knew it only too well. His able Minister of Marine, Decres, was always warning him that the concentration and manoeuvring of sailing squadrons was a very different operation to that of the massing of troops on land. Others said the same. No doubt the timidity which has always characterized the French at sea had much to do with their caution and nervousness. But they were certainly right in the main. The French Navy was bad in quality; the Spanish Navy worse. Both together were inferior in numbers to that of Britain, and in quality there was no comparison. Numbers alone are no test of efficiency, and had Napoleon succeeded in concentrating 60 French and Spanish battleships in the Channel, the fleet would have been unable to meet with success a British force of 40, even discounting the great strength of the latter in three-decked vessels. Mr. Julian Corbett, who has discussed the question exhaustively in 'The Campaign of Trafalgar', is of opinion (1) that Napoleon was only saved from disaster up to Trafalgar by the crafty French admirals whom he despised so much; (2) that had the Franco-Spanish fleet really appeared in the Channel, the result would have been its utter destruction.

Colonel Desbriere, who has discussed the problem from the French side, and has collected almost all the evidence available, sums up Napoleon's plans for gaining the command of the Channel in a scathing paragraph:

> Two escapes from ports blockaded by a superior force; two blockades to be broken at Cadiz and Ferrol; a junction at Martinique, already indicated to the English by the despatch of Missiessy – such was the programme, if we confine ourselves to the letter of the instructions. It is useless for historians to admire it.

And when Desbriere examines it further in order to find the Napoleonic touch, he practically comes to the conclusion that the Emperor was ready to stake all on a mere gambler's throw with all the chances against him. If he won, it was well. If he lost, he sacrificed only his weak and inefficient navy. In fact, whether he won or lost, his reputation was safe; and how nervously tender he was of his untarnished renown it is easy to see in the multitudinous letters in which he tries to explain away his failures.

So much for the naval situation. Considering next the army of invasion and its means of transport, the position was briefly as follows:

There were in the harbours of Boulogne, Etaples, Wimereux, and Ambleteuse, some 2,000 flat-bottomed craft of all kinds, mostly armed with guns, and capable of carrying 131,000 men and 6,000 horses. In appearance the armament was a formidable one. But, in the first place, the vessels themselves, armed though they were, could not move without an overwhelming naval escort. Hastily built, useless in rough water, almost entirely without trained crews, one British 'seventy-four' was a match for scores of them. This Napoleon knew as well as anyone, and though sections of the great flotilla crept at times along the coast from harbour to harbour, they never ventured a couple of miles from land. The vast swarm of vessels was more than the harbours could contain. Enormous sums were spent on clearing and deepening them; but as fast as they were cleared they silted up again, and the task had to be begun anew. So packed were the harbours that not half the vessels could be floated out on one tide, even if the troops could have been embarked in time to take advantage of it.

This, however, might have been expected. It is true that very different and highly-coloured accounts were spread abroad in Great Britain, and produced that extraordinary combination of panic and preparation which seems to be the normal condition of the British people in the face of a remote possibility of invasion. But the strangest circumstance to all who have been accustomed to believe in Napoleon's overwhelming military superiority, is that while his transport was sufficient for 130,000 men, he had only 90,000, with less than 3,000 horses within reach at the critical moment. More than half his cavalry were without horses. Had he landed in England he would have been opposed by a regular force almost as large as his own, with 12,000 excellent cavalry against his 3,000, besides the local forces, some 400,000 strong. Many of these volunteers had been in training for nearly two years.

Such, in short, is a summary of the situation which caused the British public so much uneasiness, if not fright. One can but observe once more that a tendency to panic before an undefined danger seems inherent in the English national character. Had Napoleon landed, his chances of success were remote. In quality the British Regular Army was at least as good as the Grande Armée. The Egyptian campaign of 1801 had proved it; the victory of Maida was soon to drive the lesson home. Whatever disaster our generals might expose themselves to, their men might fairly be trusted to pull them out of it. Wellington, later, calmly counted upon this as a factor in warfare. On the whole, it is probable that Napoleon's career would have ended in 1805 instead of 1815, and in Kent or Sussex instead of at Waterloo. But the chances of his landing were of the faintest, and the British admirals knew it very well. It is customary to believe that Napoleon deceived them. In reality, as Mr. Julian Corbett grimly remarks, they were playing the strategic game in assured mastery high over his head.

The Site of the Battle of Aclea

Aclea was formerly generally supposed to be Ockley in Surrey, near Horsham, but Mr. C. Cooksey (Proceedings of the Hampshire Field Club) gives good reasons for believing it to be Church Oakley, near Basingstoke, close to the London–Winchester road. The Northmen had just sacked London, and one hardly sees why they should plunge into the Andredsweald when the capital of Wessex offered a fair prospect of booty. In Domesday Book also Oakley is called Aclei while Ockley is Hoclie. It is not true, as Professor Oman says, that Ockley is far from any road; it is, of course, on the Roman road (Stane Street) to Regnum (Chichester); but it is certainly a somewhat unaccountable place in which to find the Viking horde. Oakley is, at any rate, almost on the direct route from London to Winchester, and is decidedly the more probable site of the two.

The English and Spanish Fleets in 1588

It is difficult to estimate the numbers of the fleets at any definite date. The lists collected by Captain Fernandez Duro in his work 'La Armada Invencible' differ widely. The tables of the Spanish fleet are based upon a careful study and comparison of these lists, especially Nos. 145, 150, and 180. It is worthy of note that the approximate total arrived at is that given by Admiral Pedro de Valdes to Drake as the strength of the Armada.

As regards tonnage, that of the English ships is, with few exceptions, calculated on the contemporary Burden Rule (length of keel, multiplied by the beam and the draft of water, and the product divided by 100), with 25 per cent added. The amount added for 'ton and tonnage' varied from 25 to 33 ⅛ per cent.

The tonnage of the Spanish ships is taken from the official figures. Mr. Julian Corbett thinks that the Spanish system of measurement gave results much higher than those of the English, but after studying and applying the English and Spanish rules to the same ship-dimensions, the authors have come to the conclusion that the discrepancy in this respect was non-existent. The English measurement was 441 tons burden; by Spanish rules, apparently, 430. The main deduction, therefore, to be made from the Spanish figures is in respect of the difference between the Seville tonelada (53'44 cubic feet) and the English ton (60 cubic feet). But even here it cannot be said that this can be applied to any but the Andalucian ships. On the whole, if a fair comparison be needed, perhaps about 10 per cent should be deducted from the official Spanish figures; but nothing definite can be said.

The English and Spanish Fleets in 1588

Of these, some 35 were detached or paid off on account of sickness, 145 were present at Calais, 8 were burnt as fireships, leaving 137 in action at Gravelines.

Total crews	... ...	about 14,000 men.
Commander-in-Chief	...	Lord Howard of Effingham (Lord High Admiral of England).
Vice-Admiral ...	...	Sir Francis Drake.
Rear-Admiral ...	...	Mr.(afterwards Sir John) Hawkins.
2nd Rear-Admiral	...	Mr. (afterwards Sir Martin) Frobisher.
Admiral of Channel Guard		Lord Henry Seymour.

THE SPANISH FLEET

Type of Ship.	Name of Ship.	Official Tonnage.	Guns.
Royal galleons (18)	San Juan	1,050	50
	San Martin	1,000	48
	San Luis	830	38
	San Felipe	800	40
	San Marcos	790	38
	San Mateo...	750	34
	San Juan Bautista ...	750	34
	San Christobal (Castille)...	700	36
	San Juan el Menor ...	530	24
	Sant' Jage el Mayor ...	530	24
	La Asuncion	530	24
	San Medel y Celedon ...	530	24
	San Felipe y Sant' Jago ...	530	24
	San Pedro	530	24
	Sant' Jago el Menor ...	520	24
	San Christobal (Portugal)	350	24
	San Bernado	350	24
	Santa Aña	250	24
Italian galleon (1)	San Francesco de Florencia	960	52
Galleasses (4)	San Lorenzo	1,000	50
	Napolitana	1,000	50
	Girona	1,000	50
	Zuñiga ., ...	1,000	50

Appendix B

Type of Ship.		Official Tonnage.	Guns.
Armed private	1	1,250	—
galleons and	1	1,200	—
great ships	2	1,150	—
(41)	1	1,100	—
	4	over 900	—
	8	over 800	—
	7	over 700	—
	6	over 600	—
	5	over 500	—
	2	over 400	—
	4	over 300	—
Armed *urcas*	27	150–900	—
Large *zabras* (barks)	4	150–160	—
Pinnaces and small armed craft of all kinds	30 approx.	40–100	—
Water caravels	9 approx.	—	—
Feluccas	7 approx.	—	—

Total vessels   ...   141

Of these, apparently 3 large ships and 14 small craft parted company or were captured in the Channel, so that at Calais the total number was 124.

Total of seamen ...	...	...	about 7,500
Total of soldiers ...	...	...	about 17,000
Total of volunteers, gentlemen, etc.			about 1,000
Total of galley slaves	...	...	about 1,000

Grand total   26,500

Commander-in-Chief   ...   Alonso Perez de Guzman, Duque de Medina Sidonia.

Chief of Staff and virtual
  Commander   ...   ...   Don Diego Flores de Valdes.
Lieutenant-General   ...   Don Alonso Martinez de Leyva.
Vice-Admiral   ...   ...   Don Juan Martinez de Recalde.

The English and Spanish Fleets in 1588

Brigaded Troops on Board the Armada.

Brigade (Tercio).		*Maestro de Campo.*
Tercio de Sicilia ...	...	Don Diego de Pimentel.
Tercio de Napoles	...	Don Alonso de Luzon.
Tercio de Entre Douro y Minho	...	Don Francisco Alvarez de Toledo.
Tercio de Isla ...	...	Don Nicolas de Isla.
Tercio de Mexìa ...	...	Don Agostin de Mexìa.

MARTELLO TOWERS ON THE SUSSEX COAST ERECTED DURING THE PERIOD OF NAPOLEON'S PROJECTED INVASION.

An old map of the British Isles.

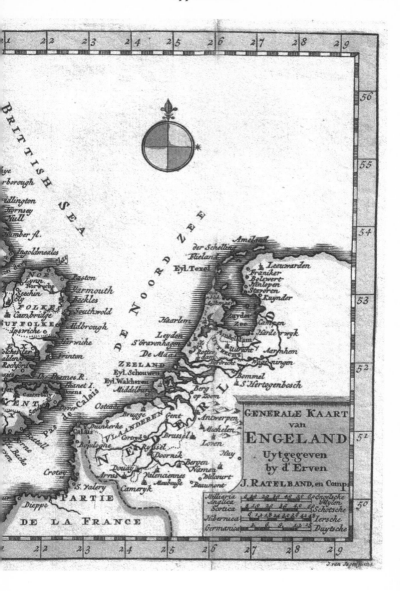

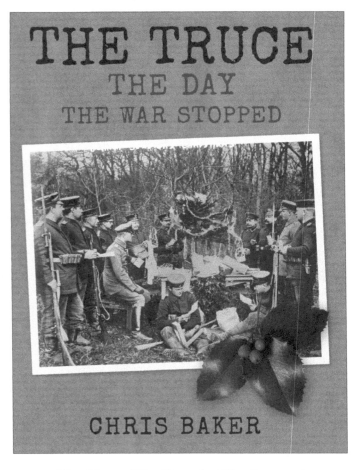

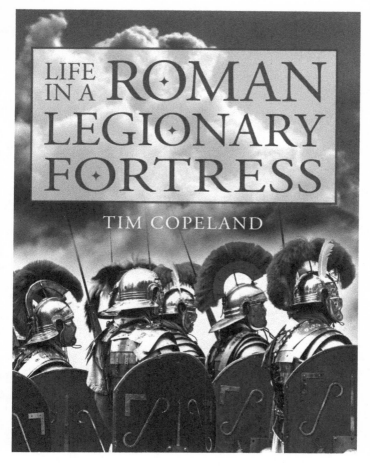

Life in a Legionary Fortress
Tim Copeland

Tim Copeland reconstructs the complex workings of Roman camps and
provides readers with an insight into the life of the soldier behind the
high walls.

978 1 4456 4358 8
96 pages, full colour

Available from all good bookshops or order direct
from our website www.amberleybooks.com

THE WAR OFFICE

THE BRITISH ARMY COOK BOOK

1914

The British Army Cook Book

Anon

Drawn from original sources, this book gives an intriguing insight into life in the trenches and the meals that the average Tommy subsisted on, from Maconochie stew, pea soup, brown stew and meat pie.

978 1 4456 4342 7

160 pages

Available from all good bookshops or order direct from our website www.amberleybooks.com